Walt Disney World
for
Couples

Rick and Gayle Perlmutter

PRIMA PUBLISHING

PRIMA PUBLISHING and its colophon are registered trademarks of Prima Communications, Inc.

ISBN 07615-0940-2
ISSN 1091-5850

97 98 99 00 01 HH 10 9 8 7 6 5 4 3 2 1

Printed in the United States of America

Maps by Shane Acker and Rick Perlmutter

The prices herein reflect 1997 figures. Rates for resorts, prices for meals, and ticket costs are all subject to change by Walt Disney World.

This book is not affiliated with, sponsored, or licensed by Walt Disney World.

How to Order
Single copies may be ordered from Prima Publishing, P.O. Box 1260, Rocklin, CA 95677; telephone (916) 632-4400. Quantity discounts are also available. On your letterhead, include information concerning the intended use of the books and the number of books you wish to purchase.

To our mothers,
who taught us how to enjoy life.
And to our children,
who we hope learned it from us.

Contents

PART I

What You Can Do Before You Leave Home

PART 2

What to Do Once You Get There

PART 3

The Ultimate Romance at Walt Disney World

$\mathscr{I}$ntroduction

Just what makes this the guidebook for you?

There are Walt Disney World guidebooks for children, for families, and for the budget-minded. This book has a different slant. We have written it especially for couples wishing to spend a romantic and special vacation at Walt Disney World.

Whether you are a couple going to Disney World to celebrate your honeymoon, your anniversary, or simply to celebrate being in love, this is the guidebook for you. If you are a "couple with children" and are looking for a relaxing Disney vacation that will include romantic time together, then this is the *only* guidebook for you. And if you have never imagined that Walt Disney World is romantic at all, then we have a surprise for you. "Hidden" inside the Disney World that everyone else visits is an unforgettable place where you can be pampered at a luxurious resort, enjoy the finest of dining and nightlife, and still delight in all the excitement and magic of the most fun place on earth. This hidden Disney is the perfect destination for lovers of any kind. This is the Walt Disney World that *we* know, one where we go to relax, delight in each other's company, and to have fun together.

The Romance of Walt Disney World

"What's the most romantic thing about Walt Disney World?"

This is the question that we are asked most often. We used to reply by describing one of our favorite romantic adventures: a private fireworks cruise, a stroll on the beach at sunset, an intimate dinner on our balcony, a midnight soak in a hot tub, or an afternoon at the spa. There were other adventures too, but we never quite felt that any one of them captured what was so romantic about a Disney World holiday.

Like all great vacations, the romance really begins with *where* we are staying, and it is this that makes the Disney experience so sublime. Not merely "places to stay," the luxurious Walt Disney World resorts are concoctions designed to transport you to a fantasy world. Each resort tells a story, and a stay there will immerse you in that tale. There is the turn-of-the-century opulence of the Grand Floridian, the South Seas adventure of the Polynesian, the Beach Club's early American holiday at the shore, the romance of Old New Orleans, or the high-timber quest of the Wilderness Lodge. There are others, too, and their experiences are unique, interesting, and fun. Our answer to the above question is now simple and sure: What's the most romantic thing about Walt Disney World? It's the resorts.

But there's more to Walt Disney World than just the resorts. Much more. For us, a trip to Disney means live jazz after a fine dinner, a boat ride at sunset, a stroll along the World Showcase, a picnic lunch in a wildlife sanctuary, all the excitement of a parade, the enchantment of the Studios Animation Tour, and the thrills of Splash Mountain. For incurable romantics such as ourselves, Disney is the perfect place to make an exit from the real world and its demands.

Disney World is over 42 square miles large. Tennis, boating, five championship golf courses, horseback riding, swimming, spas, an island of nightclubs, and nearly 200 dining opportunities make it the most unique vacation place on planet Earth. Throw in Epcot, Disney–MGM Studios, the Magic Kingdom, the Animal Kingdom, and a host of other attractions such as Blizzard Beach, Downtown Disney, and Discovery Island, and you'll quickly see why Walt Disney World calls itself "The Vacation Capital of the World." It is the last word in resorts and, for couples, a real land of enchantment.

The "World" is so big that going there without some kind of plan is like going to Europe without any plan beyond a pair of air tickets to Paris. You need a strategy, which this guidebook will provide.

This book will help you with virtually every phase of your Disney vacation. Since where you will be staying will be one of the most important elements of your time together, we have created the most complete guide to the Walt Disney World resorts ever written. We will help you select the resort that best suits your needs and guide you through every phase of planning your special time at Disney, to make your vacation an easy one. (If you had wanted difficult, you'd be camping out in the jungles of Panama.) We'll tell you how to find the level of comfort, convenience, and luxury that suits you both.

And since you have neither an oil well nor a gold mine in your backyard, we'll show you how to get as much for your money as possible. If by chance you do have a gold mine in your backyard or if you are planning that once-in-a-lifetime event, we will give you the whole lowdown on the very best Disney has to offer. And how suite it can get! We will show you how to plan the ultimate Disney experience. For the last word on anniversaries, weddings, or honeymoons, Disney is *the* place. In our guide to Disney's Fairy Tale Weddings, we'll show you the options available for a unique, unforgettable Disney wedding. We will also describe some of the weddings that have been staged at Disney, from the small and intimate to the lavish and extravagant.

Wondering if you should opt for a package or make all of your own plans? We'll provide you with more than enough information to make this decision with confidence. Traveling with the kids? No problem. You can still have a wonderfully romantic time. We will tell you everything you need to know about doing things as a family and how to get away on your own for those special times together.

And once you have arrived, we will help you avoid the pitfalls common to Disney visitors. We will help you find your own special rhythm that will keep the two of you feeling comfortable, pampered, and relaxed: three of the ingredients essential to romance.

For your dining adventures, we have gone beyond anything done before. We will provide you with first-hand information about the World's many wonderful dining establishments. We have seen, done, and eaten it all, and if you are looking for the rarest of steaks, the freshest of fish, or simply the best cup of coffee, we'll let you in on all of our secrets.

For your Disney adventures, you'll get some real insider information, the kind of stuff that you can get only by spending a lot of time looking for it, which is exactly what we have done. From Adventureland to parasailing, from Star Tours to Wine Flights, from high tea to fireworks, we promise not to leave a Disney stone unturned. Looking for that something special? An exotic dinner, a stroll along a quiet beach at sunset, or a quiet cafe for lunch? If you expect Walt Disney World to be more than just some great rides, then take a good look at what we have written here.

If you are lovers of any age, looking for the time of your lives, then this guidebook is for you. Take the "road less traveled," the path to a magical and romantic adventure. Let us show you the Walt Disney World for lovers.

It's a Matter of Attitude

We didn't always think of Disney World as a romantic place. There was a time when going to Disney meant thrill-packed days of running from attraction to attraction, spending hours waiting in long lines, gulping down counter food, and exhausting ourselves trying to do and to see everything. Our days were filled with fun, but we found ourselves stumbling back to our hotel room at night with just enough energy left to ask, "What will we be able to fit in tomorrow?" It was fun, but it wasn't romance. Then we learned how to do it right.

We discovered that our days at Disney could become opportunities to enjoy the tranquil luxury of a top resort that just happens to be located in this incredible vacation place. We have managed this transition by not only learning *what* to do at Disney World and when to do it, but also by changing our *attitudes*. In short, we have learned how to find and to sustain a relaxed and romantic mood while visiting Disney.

Finding Romance at Walt Disney World

Daylight was fading as we made our way across the deserted beach. The blazing reds and brilliant ochers of the fleeting sun ignited the fiery clouds and spilled onto the lagoon, setting it afire with shimmering lights. The sand beneath our bare feet still held the warmth of the day. Hand in hand, we passed empty cabanas to a large swing, where we sat together, savoring those final moments of daylight.

Dinner at a nearby restaurant had been elegant and intimate. We had decided to kick off our shoes and find some place to enjoy the sights and sounds of the evening when we discovered the secluded swing. We watched the boats make their way across the lagoon. We could hear the people aboard them, laughing and talking. Their voices and the thrumming of engines faded as the boats disappeared in the distance. There was something special about being here, away from everything. It seemed dreamy and blissful.

We sat silently, swinging slowly. There was nothing to say after what had seemed to be yet another perfect day. This was a contentment so powerful that we simply shared it in a knowing silence. Just when we were sure that it couldn't possibly get better, fireworks began to flash in the sky across the water. We could hear the dull thuds of rockets as they exploded over Cinderella Castle, igniting the sky with clouds of gold and showers of red. Huge and brilliant flowers of sparks blossomed in the darkening sky only to be carried gently away in the breeze. We watched in awe as we realized that the entire display was being mirrored on the surface of the lagoon before us. We squeezed each other's hand just a bit harder.

It *was* a special moment for us. Relaxing, romantic, *magical*. It was that kind of moment that we take vacations hoping to find. If we were going to rate it as a romantic experience, we would consider it special and sublimely romantic.

Romance is a personal thing, and we do not pretend to know what will make everyone experience it. We do feel that there are ingredients conducive to romance, as well as elements that are incompatible with it. Things romantic involve an enhanced chemistry of togetherness. This kind of intimacy can occur when you are alone on a beach at sunset, or it can happen in a crowded theater. It is a special feeling of closeness that transports you together to a place away from the everyday. It is something special and out of the ordinary, that seems to occur just for the two of you.

As you read through this guidebook, look for heart symbols (♥). The more ♥ you see, the more likely we think you will be able to ignite this chemistry. We have tried to savor a place for its ability to enhance our own feelings of togetherness, for its potential to elevate us above the everyday and to let us know that this special thing is happening just for us. Not surprisingly, Disney has a real knack for creating these moments. Sometimes romance just happens, and sometimes we can help it happen.

♥	**A hint of romance**
♥♥	**An air of romance**
♥♥♥	**Intimate and enchanting**
♥♥♥♥	**Unforgettable, sublimely romantic**

PART I

What You Can Do Before You Leave Home

CHAPTER I

Making the Decisions

In this chapter, we will cover a host of topics on making your special vacation together easier and more relaxed and, we hope, setting the stage for some real romance. We will help you make the big decisions regarding your upcoming Disney romance vacation: when to go and where to stay. If you are making your romantic holiday a family affair, we'll give you lots of information about the special accommodations for families and how the two of you can get off by yourselves for some special time together. We will also describe the many tickets and passes, the variety of discounts available, and how to fit everything neatly into your budget. In short, we'll help you to prepare for your special Disney World vacation.

The Ever-Changing Walt Disney World

If you think it's the same old Disney World year in and year out, you should try writing a guidebook. New attractions, new resorts, new restaurants, and even a new theme park are just some of the new things happening. Walt Disney World is much more a process than a place. Some of what's new this year include *The Hunchback of Notre Dame: A Musical Adventure, Mickey's Toontown Fair, Backstage Pass, Test Track,* and *Ellen's Energy Adventure.* This year will also be the year for Downtown Disney, Disney's Coronado Springs Resort, the Grand Floridian Spa, the World of Disney store, and new and exciting menus across the spectrum of Disney restaurants.

Even if you visited a few short months ago, we can promise that this year's Walt Disney World will have much more that's new. In fact, so much is new, we may have missed a thing or two. Don't worry, though, because we'll tell you how to keep abreast of all that's changing. Remember, all of the prices in this guidebook reflect 1997 prices.

Rates for resorts, prices for meals, and ticket costs are all sure to rise slightly over time. What we have given you here will provide a clear idea of the relative expense of Walt Disney World.

When to Go

When the two of you head off to Disney, you will discover more seasons there than the old and familiar summer, fall, winter, and spring. These seasons describe the weather, but the Disney seasons take into account other important considerations such as crowds, holidays, and special events.

The Disney folks speak in terms of regular season, value season, and holiday season. Regular season refers to those times of year that the park is operating at full tilt. Schools are out of session, and the parks, resorts, and other Disney attractions are at their busiest. Holiday season refers to the two weeks around Christmas and the two weeks around Easter. During the two brief holiday seasons, resort rates are higher than at any other time of year.

Value Season is what remains of the year. During these off-season times, Disney World is less crowded. Many resorts offer discounted rates and attractive vacation packages. Here's how the three seasons run:

Regular Season and Holiday Season

- More people, bigger crowds, longer lines
- Few, if any, discounts
- Holiday season means even higher resort rates and larger crowds
- Parks open early and stay open later
- Numerous special events, such as fireworks and parades

FOR VALUE AND MODERATE RESORTS

- Regular season: end of first week of February to third week of March; early April to the third week of August
- Holiday season: two weeks around Easter; December 18 to 31

FOR DELUXE AND HOME AWAY FROM HOME RESORTS

- Regular season: end of first week of February to third week of March; early April to end of first week of July
- Holiday season: two weeks around Easter; December 18 to 31

Value Season

- Fewer people; every place is less crowded
- Numerous special rates, offers, and discounts
- Parks open later in the day and close earlier
- Fewer special events such as fireworks and parades

ℱOR VALUE AND MODERATE RESORTS

- January 1 to end of first week of February
- August 24 to December 17

ℱOR DELUXE AND HOME AWAY FROM HOME RESORTS

- January 1 to end of first week of February
- End of first week of July to December 17

Good Times to Visit

During the course of the year, there are many special and seasonal events. Whether it's the Fourth of July or Chinese New Year, the folks at Disney love a party. Most of these events are memorable. Besides the usual holidays are celebrations of Mother's Day, Mardi Gras, a spring garden festival, a summer swing music celebration, and even a winter kite festival. For more information and dates of special events, call Disney Information at (407) 824-4321. If you are planning to visit Disney World on a big holiday, such as Independence Day, be fore-warned: park attendance hits record highs on these days.

Our favorite time of year has always been during the three weeks after Thanksgiving and before Christmas. At least several of the premium Disney resorts offer greatly reduced rates, and the World is dressed in its finest holiday attire. There are special events, such as the Jolly Holidays Dinner Show, nightly tree-lighting ceremonies, wandering carolers and musicians, and the Very Merry Christmas Party. It is beautiful, festive, and fun. During these weeks, you may enjoy all the benefits of the holiday season without the crowds.

Other times of year attract fewer people as well. The week following Labor Day is the slowest of the Disney year. January to early-February are nice months and the weather is generally quite nice. The final week of August, though hot, is not usually crowded. The entire fall, except for Thanksgiving weekend, is a wonderful time for a Disney visit.

Walt Disney World 25th Anniversary Celebration

"Remember the Magic" is the theme for this year-long gala in 1997. Just for openers, the Magic Kingdom will feature both Fantasy in the Sky fireworks and the SpectroMagic Light Parade every night and the new anniversary-theme parade each day. Cinderella Castle, too, has been transformed for the occasion into a giant birthday cake, complete with 26 towering candles. Main Street's 25th Anniversary Welcome Station will greet guests as well as display memorabilia and a film about the past and future of the Walt Disney World Resort. Drop in here for a free lithograph and Guest of Honor badge. There's more excitement, including a special 25th Anniversary IllumiNations at Epcot. This year promises to be one of the most exciting and busiest years ever for you to visit Walt Disney World.

OUR RECOMMENDATIONS

- If possible, go during value season.
- Take advantage of numerous resort discounts, fewer crowds, and discount vacation packages.
- Even though 1997 will likely be the busiest year in Disney history, we think it is a good year to visit. Considering all of the extra festivities and attractions, it should be well worth the larger crowds.

Weather

Weather-wise, central Florida is a mixed bag, encompassing all of the four seasons without the severity of, say, New England. Winters are usually cool and balmy with occasional cold snaps. If you are coming from colder climes, you will likely find the winter weather at Disney World to be most agreeable. Summers in Florida range from hot to HOT. Spring and fall land somewhere in between with a mix of warmer and cooler days, a sort of leftovers time.

OUR SUMMER RECOMMENDATIONS

- Prepare for heat: brings lots of light, loose clothing, hats, and bathing suits.
- Make full use of Disney pools and water attractions.
- Be ready for brief afternoon thundershowers.

OUR WINTER RECOMMENDATIONS

- Expect any kind of weather except very hot; be prepared clothing-wise; try layering clothes.
- Don't forget your bathing suits: most pools and water attractions are heated, and there are always the hot tubs.
- Avoid holidays or college break periods, to keep crowds low.

OUR SPRING AND FALL RECOMMENDATIONS

- Pack for almost any weather except very cold or very hot.

Here's a month-by-month look at weather and crowds:

January

Weather: Be prepared: expect occasional cold spells, with cool nights and balmy days. Average high: 70°. Average low: 50°.

World Conditions: After January 1, everything slows down beautifully. An excellent time for a romantic visit.

February

Weather: A very likely month for wintery cold snaps. Still, February can be a nice month for weather. Expect more balmy days and cool evenings. Average high: 72°. Average low: 51°.

World Conditions: Attendance is low through the first week and average for the remainder of the month. Things begin to pick up a bit in the last few days of February. Value season lasts until about the sixth of this month. After this, the regular season begins and runs until a week before Easter. Parks are open late for the busy President's Day week.

March

Weather: March can be a blustery month with a mix of weather. It's usually one of the wetter winter months. Rarely will March be very cold. Average high: 76°. Average low: 56°.

World Conditions: Attendance begins to pick up, getting busy during the spring break season. This month is all regular season.

April

Weather: This is a nice month! The climate is usually breezy, with warm days and balmy nights. Average high: 82°. Average low: 60°.

World Conditions: The two weeks around Easter are now considered the holiday season. The remainder of the month is regular season.

May

Weather: Another month of splendid weather. The days become a bit warmer than April but only occasionally does it get hot. This is spring in central Florida. Average high: 88°. Average low: 66°.

World Conditions: Fewer crowds and wonderful spring weather make this a great time for your romantic Disney getaway. Just watch out for the busy Memorial Day weekend and you'll have it made.

June

Weather: Summer begins to arrive and with it . . . HEAT. Evenings are still fairly pleasant. Average high: 90°. Average low: 71°.

World Conditions: The first week is not too crowded, but after that, watch out. School gets out, the summer season begins full-tilt, and the hoards arrive. It is still regular season all month.

July

Weather: This is summer—expect it to be HOT. Afternoon thundershowers are fairly common. Average high: 92°. Average low: 73°.

World Conditions: Summer is in full swing now, and Disney World is about as crowded as it gets. The weekend of the fourth is the busiest of the year. If there is one month to avoid, this is it. Regular season all month in moderate and value resorts; the value season for deluxe and home away from home resorts begins after the first week.

August

Weather: This is definitely a hot month: hot days, hot nights. A good chance of afternoon thundershowers, too. Average high: 92°. Average low: 76°.

World Conditions: The first two weeks are very busy and then the crowds begin to leave. By the last week of the month, things are starting to get pretty nice. Regular season lasts until about the third week for moderate and value resorts; value season all month for the other resorts. It's still hot but getting to be a good time to visit, due to fewer people.

September

Weather: Don't forget, it's still summer here in Florida, which means more hot days and hot nights. Also, the rainy season begins. This mostly means afternoon thundershowers, nothing like the monsoons of India. Average high: 89°. Average low: 72°.

World Conditions: The week after Labor Day is the slowest week of the year at Walt Disney World. The rest of the month is also slow: few crowds, short lines. Value season all month long.

October

Weather: Still warm, but the real heat of the summer has passed. Nights are beginning to get balmy. Average high: 82°. Average low: 68°.

World Conditions: A nice month for a visit. The weather is pleasant and the crowds are still elsewhere. Another month of discounts: it's value season.

November

Weather: The weather is really starting to get nice now. Days are balmy and evenings are cool. Don't forget your bathing suit. Average high: 76°. Average low: 57°.

World Conditions: This is a nice month to visit, with few crowds until Thanksgiving week (a good week to stay home). After this: our favorite time of year. Value season all month.

December

Weather: This is usually a very nice month but occasionally cold. Average high: 72°. Average low: 52°.

World Conditions: It's value season for about the first three weeks. Crowds are less than normal until about December 18, when the official holiday season begins. After this, the World is very crowded. Swimming suits are still useful, especially in a hot tub.

Deciding Where to Stay

Yes, this is the big decision. Selecting where to stay will set the backdrop and mood of your entire visit. Convenience, luxury, and even romantic atmosphere are all very much related to your resort.

Basically, you have two choices if you are visiting Walt Disney World: you can stay inside the World or you can stay outside. Inside, known to cast members (the Disney Folks) as "on-property," means staying in one of the many and varied Disney resorts. Staying outside, or "off-property," means staying in one of the many hotels or motels located in the surrounding areas, such as Kissimmee, Lake Buena Vista, or Orlando.

There are, indisputably, many fine hotels and even a few resorts in the areas surrounding Walt Disney World. Many of them may be cheaper than staying inside Disney, but they all share one thing in common: they are *not* in Disney World.

Outside, you will be staying at least several miles from the fun. Even though an off-property motel may advertise that it is "five minutes from Disney," this doesn't mean that it will take you only five minutes to make the trip. The motel may actually be a five-minute drive from Disney's front gate, but by the time you add parking, walking, traffic, and a host of other impediments, we seriously doubt that you will be able to leave your off-property room in the morning and get to the park of your choice in less than 45 minutes.

If you stay off-property, you'll quickly discover that all of this going back and forth eats up valuable vacation time. And staying outside usually means that it isn't very practical to drop back to your hotel room for an hour's rest or an afternoon together. If you are driving, the dense crowds at the gates in the morning and at closing time spell H-A-S-S-L-E.

If this doesn't sound so discouraging, consider what it is like to stay inside Disney. Every bed on property is located in what Disney calls a "themed resort." At a Disney resort, you will find yourselves the pampered guests at accommodations that have been carefully themed to enfold you in the very Disney magic that you have come looking for. Each Disney resort has its own specially designed atmosphere. Everything at Dixie Landings, for example, reflects the Mississippi River theme of the resort. The look of the resort, the Bayou cuisine of its restaurants, the dress of the cast members, the room furnishings— everything down to the smallest detail enriches that theme. Each resort is designed to enhance your Disney visit, to make it easier and more fun. Once you have left the theme parks and returned to your resort, you will not feel as though you have left Disney World. It will mean exciting days and luxurious and intimate nights.

And this is really just the beginning. Disney resort guests get special benefits such as early admission into the theme parks, special passes, and full use of Disney transportation.

But, you are thinking, it costs a fortune to stay at a Disney resort. Not true. There are now Disney resorts for virtually every budget, with prices beginning at $69 per night. If you take a close look into the off-property "bargains," you will find that regular season prices in basic motels will be this much, frequently more. Even the most basic Disney resort compares favorably to most of the more expensive off-property lodgings.

So, are we trying to talk you into staying in a Walt Disney World resort? You bet we are! We want you to have to best possible vacation, and staying on property is the way. We feel sure that there is a Disney resort for you and staying in it will make your romance vacation what it should be: fun, easy, and relaxing.

How Much Will It Cost?

There is a place to stay at Walt Disney World to satisfy virtually any desire. From the basic All-Star Resorts to the Victorian elegance of the Grand Floridian, the folks at Disney have it all covered. There are campsites, trailers, suites, multiroom villas, treehouses, vacation homes, and much more. There is a tremendous offering of truly luxurious places in a range from $69 to $250 per night, and up to $1,500 for the Roosevelt Suite at the Grand Floridian (yes, that's per night!).

Types of Disney Resorts

There are five types of Disney accommodations: deluxe, moderate, value, home away from home, and campground (see Fort Wilderness, page 145). Each has unique offerings and each has its own price range.

As you would expect, the rooms are larger and have more lavish furnishings in the deluxe, full-amenities resorts. "Amenities" mean services, and here at Walt Disney World, you will get what you pay for. The grounds and lobbies of the deluxe resorts are the most lavish and elaborately styled. The choice of dining and recreational activities is always greater at the deluxe resorts. These accommodations offer room service as well as bell service, and many provide a nightly turndown as well. Some even feature luxurious bathrobes for guests.

While the moderate accommodations do not enjoy quite this level of luxury, rooms are comfortable, well appointed, and, though not as large as rooms at the deluxe resorts, lodgings are still fairly spacious. Theming here is always enchanting. Dining options at each moderate resort include one table-service restaurant and a food court. Recreational offerings, while not as extensive as the deluxe resorts, are usually quite good.

The value resorts, while offering smaller rooms and simpler furnishings, still manage to be themed and quite "Disney." Resort grounds and pool areas are all exciting but, besides swimming, recreational offerings are minimal. Value resorts offer only food courts.

While many of the home away from home accommodations are not new, this category is. Simply, these all offer some type of kitchen. Most include accommodations for a family, and a host of these "rooms" even feature everything, including a complete kitchen, washer and dryer, and entertainment center.

There is, we feel, one important advantage to rooms in the deluxe resorts. Here, the entrance to each room is through a hallway *inside* the resort. This makes for large windows that look onto landscaped grounds, often onto a lagoon, a forest, or even a castle; most include a balcony or patio. The moderate and value resorts, on the other hand, have *outside* walkways. Windows look onto these and, with curtains open, the result is a loss of privacy. Neither the moderate nor value accommodations feature balconies or patios.

⑦ELUXE RESORTS

Prices begin at $165 per night.

- The Contemporary
- The Polynesian
- The Grand Floridian
- The Yacht and Beach Clubs
- The Wilderness Lodge
- The Swan and the Dolphin
- BoardWalk Inn

MODERATE RESORTS

Prices range from $114 to $149 per night.

- Port Orleans
- Dixie Landings
- Caribbean Beach
- Coronado Springs (opening August 1997)

VALUE RESORTS

Prices range from $69 to $89 per night.

- All-Star Music
- All-Star Sports

HOME AWAY FROM HOME

Prices begin at $185.

- Old Key West Villas
- The Villas at the Institute
- Fort Wilderness Homes
- BoardWalk Villas

The Disney World of Discounts

If the Disney resort that sounds best to you seems out of reach, you'll be happy to know that list prices at Disney are like list prices everywhere else. Disney offers a large variety of discounts for both resorts and vacation packages. Experience has shown us, however, that these discounts must be pursued. They are usually not widely advertised or generally known. With a bit of research, though, you should be able to find something that suits your needs.

To begin with, discounts are affected most by the season. Of course, we are talking about value season. During the regular and holiday seasons, discounts become hard to come by and, if you are able to get one, it will not be as large as during value season. So, if you are looking for a deeply discounted resort or package rate, begin by planning an off-season visit.

The following sections describe sources of Disney discounts.

Disney Central Reservations Office (CRO)

Yes, discounts are available through the regular reservation process. Simply ask the reservationist about specials or special deals for the dates that you have selected. Remember that most discounts are scheduled for value season. Try a variety of dates to see what you can get. Call Disney Central Reservations at (407) W-DISNEY (934-7639).

The Magic Kingdom (MK) Club

Membership to the Magic Kingdom Club is available to state employees (usually any state), employees of hospitals, large corporations, or businesses, and often university employees.

If you are not eligible, you may purchase a Magic Kingdom Club Gold Card for $65. Persons over 55 and Walt Disney Company stockholders may purchase the Gold Card for $50. The Gold Card offers the same discount as the Magic Kingdom Club, with a few extras. Gold Card membership is good for two years.

The Magic Kingdom Club is the most widely-used discount. Check with your employer's human resources or personnel department to see if one is available for you. Using it can mean big savings. Even if you have to pay the $65 for a Gold Card, you will likely discover that the card will pay for itself in a single visit, especially during value season. Call or write:

Magic Kingdom Gold Card
P.O. Box 3850
Anaheim, CA 92803
(800) 893-4763

DISCOUNTS AND PRIVILEGES

- Disney resort discounts up to 10% or 20% on select resorts for select dates and for select vacation packages.
- Other discounts include admission tickets and passes, golf, dinner shows, select theme park restaurants, merchandise at Disney stores nationwide and shops at Downtown Disney, and Disney Cruise Lines.
- Gold Card membership includes a two-year subscription to *Disney Magazine*, a tote bag, luggage tag, and newsletter.

American Express

The official credit card of Walt Disney World, American Express offers an ever-changing assortment of promotional packages, each aimed at encouraging you to use your card to pay for your Disney vacation. These packages seem to vary throughout the year. Some are bargains, some are not. Simply checking-in with your American Express card will get you a free fanny pack. Call American Express Disney Reservations at (407) 827-7200.

*D*ISCOUNTS AND PRIVILEGES

- 10% discount on boating activities and select dinner shows
- 20% discount on select Disney tours and programs
- An assortment of promotional add-ons and packages

Walt Disney World Annual Passport

The Annual Passport is available to anyone willing to spend $285 for it (about $245 for children). Besides providing an entire year's worth of admission to the three theme parks—Magic Kingdom, Epcot, and Disney–MGM Studios—it can be a source of outstanding resort discounts, both during the regular and value seasons.

Only one of you needs a passport to get the resort discount, and you may book your discounted room before you even buy it. Just be prepared to present either your pass or its voucher at check-in. There is even a discount on the Annual Passport for both Magic Kingdom Club members and Florida residents. To obtain information and book reservations for Annual Passport discounts, call Disney Central Reservations and tell them you are a passholder. Discounts during value season are always greater than those offered during regular season. Call Disney Central Reservations at (407) W-DISNEY (934-7639).

*D*ISCOUNTS AND PRIVILEGES

- A hodgepodge of resort discounts, some very good. Some resort discounts may be as much as 50% off of regular resort rates.
- Bearer gets unlimited admission to the three theme parks for one full year.

American Automobile Association (AAA)

Because this organization functions as a travel agency, it offers a variety of resort and package discounts to its members. Some are quite good. These are worth looking into.

*D*ISCOUNTS AND PRIVILEGES

• Resort rate and vacation package discounts (available to AAA members only)

Delta Airline Dream Vacations

Delta is the official airline of Walt Disney World and offers its own assortment of Disney vacation packages. Some are on property, and others are not. These are sold in conjunction with airline tickets, usually to Orlando. Because Delta's packages and promotionals change throughout the year, we suggest that you call for their current offerings. Call Delta Airlines Dream Vacations at (800) 872-7786.

*D*ISCOUNTS AND PRIVILEGES

• A variety of vacation packages that include airfare with Delta

Your Local Travel Agent

Several years ago, Disney began discounting vacation packages to travel agents. This has enabled travel agents everywhere to be competitive in a previously closed market.

Florida Resident Discounts

Mickey loves Floridians. After all, he lives in Florida, doesn't he? A number of benefits are afforded to Florida residents. Usually offered during value season, discounts include resort rates, packages, and admission tickets. If you are Florida residents planning a visit, you will certainly wish to take advantage of one. Simply call Disney Central Reservations at (407) 934-7639 and ask when Florida residents' specials are being offered.

Discounts are available to anyone with a Florida driver's license or other proof of residency, such as a rent receipt or a utility bill.

The Disney Dining Experience   This little-known organization is for Florida residents only. Membership, which costs around $40, provides a 20% discount in a large selection of Disney restaurants and half-price admission to Pleasure Island. This includes both food and alcoholic beverages and is good for the cardholder's entire party. If you are a Florida resident and enjoy dining at Walt Disney World, this card will pay for itself in short order. Call (407) 828-5792 for information.

$\mathcal{D}$ISNEY DISCOUNT TIPS

- Be comparative shoppers. Look around for the best deal. Check out every source possible.
- Don't pass up a good deal waiting for a great one. You can make a reservation and cancel it later when a better deal arrives.
- When talking with a CRO reservationist, be sure to ask a lot of questions. Carefully explain what you are looking for. These people know a lot, but they also seem trained to not offer the cheapest alternative unless you ask for it.
- For best-room availability, try calling Central Reservations around 10 A.M., eastern time. This really works.

Doing It All on Your Budget

We are sure that you, like most couples, are planning your Disney vacation to fit a budget. It is important that you know ahead of time how much your Disney vacation is going to cost so that you will be able to enjoy yourselves without worry. Nothing can ruin a vacation like the nagging concern that you are overspending. If you have elected to purchase one of the all-inclusive packages, then you will be enjoying one of its greatest advantages: you will already have a very good picture of what your Disney vacation will cost.

If you are making your own plans, you will have to do some figuring to know what your Disney adventure is going to cost.

The Major Expenses

After the expense of getting to Walt Disney World, the major expenses fall into three categories: resort expenses, admission ticket costs, and food expenses.

Resort Expenses   Resort and admission expenses are the expenditures easiest to factor. Take a look at our guide to the Disney resorts in Chapter 2 and see which resort looks good to you. Modest price increases are yearly events at Disney, so you might want to check with Central Reservations to make sure that you have the most current rates. Don't forget to add a combined Florida state sales and resort tax of 11% to your room.

Admission Ticket Costs   Admission tickets will also be a simple matter to calculate (See "Admission Options" later in this chapter). Once you have made your admission choice, you should have a clear figure to deal with.

Food Expenses   Figuring your food expenses will be a bit more complicated. Whatever your tastes and habits may be, you should know that dining out, three meals a day, at Disney World will constitute a significant part of your vacation budget. Just how big a part will depend on you.

It is *possible* for a couple to eat at Walt Disney World for $70 per day. However, it will have to be done very carefully. A $70 per day food allowance will require dining largely at the more inexpensive, counter-service restaurants with one moderately priced meal per day. Dining exclusively in the fast-food eateries is not our idea of a romantic vacation.

For a more realistic figure for a couple's food expenses, we suggest planning on $120 per day. Allowing for this amount, you will be fairly free to eat in all of the moderately priced restaurants and even include one or two expensive restaurants during your vacation. Needless to say, a larger budget will mean more lavish meals in fancier restaurants. Please note that this $120 does not include alcoholic beverages in significant amounts. For tips on where to dine, how to eat at the finer restaurants without spending a fortune, bargain meals, and a host of other information, see what we have to say about the Disney dining experience and the Disney restaurants in Chapter 6. Remember, of the big three expenses, food is really the only one that can be difficult to predict.

Putting It All Together: What Will It Cost?

Now that you have some idea of what the major costs will be, all that remains is to add them up and to see what you can get. To give you a good idea of the scope of possibilities, we have constructed a sample budget. (Note that the value season version of the sample budget includes a 30% room discount with Annual Passport.) Remember that it does not include anything extra that you elect to spend on memorabilia or alcoholic beverages. Other extras such as dinner shows should also be taken into consideration. For the most part, we have elected to use Length of Stay Passes to provide admission to the Disney attractions. We have also included taxes and tips.

A Four-Night Stay for Two at the Beach Club

Garden view room	$1,244
Meals	480
Length of Stay Passes	406
TOTAL	$2,130

Value Season Version of Beach Club Four-Night Stay

Garden view room	$660
Meals	480
Annual Passport for one (includes all add-ons)	349
Length of Stay Pass for one	203
TOTAL (saves nearly $450)	$1,692

☉IPS FOR DOING IT BEST ON A BUDGET:

- Take advantage of off-season specials and lower rates to get the most for your money. Plan ahead.
- Try a variety of resorts and admission ticket combinations before making your final decision.

Admission Options: Which Ticket Is for You?

While it is not necessary to purchase your admission passes before you arrive, it is wise to know which will be the best choice. Disney offers a confusing assortment of tickets and passes. If you are opting for a vacation package that includes admission to the Disney attractions, then you will not have to choose among these. For descriptions, comparisons, and recommendations to help you select what is best for you, see the table on pages 20–21. All prices include taxes and were correct at press time. Prices are subject to change.

Getting Your Tickets, Passes, or Passports

If you elect to get either an Annual Passport or a Florida Resident's Seasonal Passport, you would be wise to do it before you arrive at Walt Disney World. All of the other passes and tickets are easily available at your resort's Guest Services.

For either of the two passports, you can go to any of the 200 Disney stores across the United States. There, you may purchase a voucher that can be converted into the actual pass once you arrive at Walt Disney World. This process can only be done at one of the Guest Services at a front gate of one of the three theme parks. It is very simple, especially if you arrive 30 minutes before the park opens. Passport vouchers can also be purchased by telephone with a credit card, by calling (407) W-DISNEY, or from many travel agents.

Vacation Packages: Are They for You?

Like the Disney characters, Walt Disney World vacation packages come in many shapes and sizes. Typically, they include at least room accommodations and admission tickets. Many include much more. Some offer airfare to Orlando and others offer meals as well as unlimited recreation. There are even plans that include virtually everything that you might want to do at Walt Disney World, from golf and boating to a champagne breakfast in bed. There are family packages, holiday packages, golf and sports packages, honeymoon and wedding plans, and the ultimate in vacation experiences, Disney's Grand Plan. This assortment of packages is priced for either value season or regular season.

There are basically two sources for packages to Walt Disney World: the first is independent agents and tour guides, and the second is Disney. Independent packages usually provide accommodations in off-property locations. Many also include air or bus transportation. Most provide Disney admission tickets and frequently little else. This is the type of package deal that you are likely to find in your local newspaper. If you are considering one of them, we can only warn you to be very careful. Off-property accommodations are often not what they're described to be or what they look like in photos. And once you get to

Ticket	Price	Cost/Day	Features	Drawbacks	Recommendations
One-Day/ One-Park A = adult C = child	A $42 C $34	$42 $34	One-day admission to one of the Disney theme parks	No park hopping Limited use of WDW transportation	Good for short visit or if you are on a tight budget Use to fill in extra days with other passes
Four-Day Value Pass	A $142 C $113	$36 $29	Admission to one theme park per day Unused days do not expire	No park hopping Admission to other attractions requires additional tickets	For $17 more, get Four-Day Park Hopper and park hop to several theme parks in one day
Four-Day Park Hopper Pass	A $159 C $127	$40 $32	Unused days do not expire	Admission extra to: Blizzard/Typhoon $26 Pleasure Island $19 River Country $17 Discovery Island $13	A good value Stay five days with this pass and spend one day at a water park, only $26
Five-Day World Hopper Pass	A $217 C $174	Calculated for 5-day usage	Five days of admission to theme parks PLUS seven days of admission to other Disney attractions: Admission to additional attractions good for seven days after first use of pass Park hopping allowed Unused admissions to theme parks that do not expire	If you are staying on-property, this pass is more expensive than the equivalent Length of Stay Pass	A good value only if you use admission to other attractions To use for longer than five days, spend first few days at "other" attractions, then five days at the theme parks

Pass	Price (A / C)	Break-even	Features	Restrictions	Value Notes
Annual Passport	A $285 / C $217	Break-even on day seven of stay	Unlimited admission to theme parks for one year; Resort discounts to 30%; Park hopping allowed; Unlimited use of WDW transportation	No admission to other attractions: Premium Pass $380/353 provides admission to other attractions; Other attractions by daily admission rate also	Great value for visits of seven days or longer; Outstanding bargain when used with resort discount during value season
Florida Resident's Seasonal Passport	A $158 / C $135	Break-even on day four of stay	Unlimited admission to theme parks for 282 select days of the year; Seasonal resort discounts up to 30%; Park hopping allowed; Unlimited use of WDW transportation	Florida residency required; Not valid on holidays or during busier seasons	The best value for Floridians; Get this pass, get a resort discount, and SAVE!
Length of Stay Pass *(see below)*	A / C		Admission to all WDW attractions for any length of stay or any number of days during your stay; Park hopping allowed; Valid until midnight of the last day of your stay	Available only to Disney resort guests; This pass is not available to guests of the Swan, the Dolphin, or Hotel Plaza Hotels	Cost-effective only if you use admission to additional attractions; Get this pass and do everything!

Length of Stay Pass	A / C	
1-night/2-day	$100/80	$50/40
2-night/3-day	143/116	$48/39
3-night/4-day	184/147	$46/37
4-night/5-day	214/172	$43/34
5-night/6-day	242/194	$40/32
6-night/7-day	267/214	$36/30
7-night/8-day	290/232	$36/29

Walt Disney World, you may be amazed at what these "all-inclusive" package deals don't include.

Vacation plans created by Team Disney will be our focus. With these, you will be able to stay in one of the many themed Walt Disney World resorts or, if you prefer, in a good-quality non-Disney hotel.

The Nuts and Bolts of Packages

Disney vacation plans are figured on a per person, per day cost. Youngsters are accounted for at either of two cost levels: juniors (10 to 17 years old) or children (3 to 9 years old). Children under 3 years of age are free. Different packages and prices are available for the entire spectrum of Disney resorts. If you opt for a vacation package, you should know that after your initial deposit, the balance of your package cost is due no later than 21 days before the first day of your vacation.

The first step in the quest for your vacation package should be to call the Walt Disney World Travel Company. Request their catalogue of vacation packages. This booklet will give you all of the basic package combinations and their list prices. To get your booklet, call the Walt Disney World Travel Company at (800) 828-0228.

Walt Disney World Travel Company is not the only source of vacation packages. A growing number of companies deal in Disney vacation packages. What they offer and how much they charge vary greatly. Armed with the Walt Disney World Travel Company basic price booklet, you will be ready to shop around and select a package that is priced right.

ꙅOURCES FOR DISNEY VACATION PACKAGES

- WDW Central Reservations Office (CRO): (407) W-DISNEY (934-7639)
- Walt Disney World Travel Company: (800) 828-0228
- The Magic Kingdom Club: (407) 824-2600
- American Automobile Association: call your local AAA travel agent
- Delta Airlines Dream Vacations: (800) 872-7786
- American Express: (407) 827-7200
- Your local travel agent

Three Types of Package Vacations

There are three basic types of resort packages: the Classic Plan, the Deluxe Magic, and the Grand Plan. The Classic Plan (also known as the Resort Magic) is the most basic and offers room accommodations, passes to all Disney attractions, limited use of recreation such as canoes and bicycles, and a choice from a variety of activities or gifts such as a character breakfast, a commemorative book, a tour of Epcot's gardens, or a Mickey 'n You photo session. A five-night Classic Plan for two at the Yacht or Beach Clubs costs $1,872.

To the features of the Classic Plan, both the Deluxe Magic and Grand Plan add such a host of amenities that further expenses may simply not be necessary. The Deluxe Magic ♥♥♥ includes accommodations for three or more nights, passes to all Disney attractions, three meals daily in any of more than 70 Disney restaurants (including nearly *all* of our favorites), use of all Disney World recreational facilities (including unlimited tennis and golf), and a Mickey 'n You photo session. Also part of this plan is free use of the Wonders of Walt Disney World educational program for juniors (ages 10 to 15 years).

A five-night Deluxe Magic package at the Yacht or Beach Clubs costs around $3,034 for two. The same package at the Wilderness Lodge is $2,784.

The Grand Plan ♥♥♥♥ provides an even greater level of luxury and even more features. For about $150 per couple per night above the cost of the Deluxe Magic, this package adds personalized itinerary planning, in-room dining, private tennis or golf lessons, health club use, a video camera, baby-sitting services, and special room amenities. It also adds the incomparable Victoria and Albert's to the already impressive list of restaurants.

Either the Deluxe Magic or the Grand Plan packages will give you a sublime Disney experience, during which you would both feel privileged and pampered. Expensive, yes. But, if you can afford it, the experience will be unforgettable.

Specialty and Seasonal Packages

Besides the three basic vacation packages, Disney also offers a variety of packages designed both for special interests and for special events. The Golf Getaway features accommodations and one round of golf daily with transportation to any of Disney's five courses. There are packages for the Disney Institute, the Indy 200 auto race, the Night of Joy Christian music celebration, and a host of other events. From the Epcot Garden Show to the Disneyana Convention, the possibilities are numerous. For details and dates, call Disney Central Reservations at (407) 934-7639.

There are also packages for the many seasonal events at Walt Disney World, including the Fall Fantasy package and the Winter Sunshine Getaway. One of our favorites is the Magical Holidays package. Often an outstanding bargain, this package includes accommodations and a choice of one of the World's marvelous holiday events. Choose from Mickey's Very Merry Christmas Party with a dinner at a select restaurant, the Jolly Holidays Dinner Show, or Epcot's Candlelight Processional with dinner at an Epcot restaurant. We have always enjoyed the Jolly Holidays Dinner Show, a real extravaganza and turkey dinner with all of the fixings. The Magical Holidays package usually runs from late November to several days before Christmas.

In addition, here are some possibilities to further customize your vacation package:

ADD THE FOOD 'N FUN PLAN

This plan seems to change every year. For 1997, it will cost $50 per adult and $22 per child, per day, and it will provide a daily $55 credit for food ($25 for children) that may be used in nearly every Disney restaurant. This credit is cumulative, which means you can "save" up from one day to the next to dine somewhere a bit fancier. Unused credit at vacation's end is not refundable. To this is added unlimited use of select recreation, which includes sailboats, water sprites, horseback riding, tennis, and more. Even without use of the recreational activities, this package provides a 10% discount on food. If you make good use of recreation (and we suggest you do), the 1997 Food 'n Fun Plan looks like an attractive option.

Upgrade Your Package to a Suite or Concierge Service   We have been told countless times by Central reservationists that a package cannot be applied to a suite or to a concierge room. Like other things in life, it depends on who you talk to. To begin with, a package can only be upgraded to a suite by the "suite people," and they will not speak to you. Simply call Central Reservations and request that they arrange it with the suite people.

Are Packages a Bargain?

The first question to ask yourselves about vacation packages is: "Can we do better by ourselves?" This can usually be answered by adding up the features of a package plan and comparing the total to what you are able to get on your own. Generally, most Classic Plan packages seem to save a small amount of money over the same features purchased separately. If you have managed a particularly good deal on a resort room, however, you may find that no package can compete with it.

The all-inclusive packages are, most certainly, expensive. They do, however, provide a special and lavish way to experience the magic of Walt Disney World. Either the Grand Plan or the Deluxe Magic package would be just the thing for a special romantic getaway or anniversary. One of the less-tangible pluses of an all-inclusive package is the carefree and relaxed feeling it provides.

What makes a package worthwhile economically is making use of all it has to offer. The more you use the recreational features of the Classic Plan package, the more worthwhile it becomes. The same can be said for either the Deluxe Magic or Grand Plan packages or any of the specialty packages. None of these packages are economical unless you make good use of all their features.

The Romantic Family Trip

If having children meant the end to romance for married couples, then everyone would be an only child. We hope that if you have children, romance is alive and well in your lives. If it isn't, may this be your wake-up call. With a bit of planning, you will be able to visit Walt Disney World as a family and still have romantic moments for just the two of you.

Making a family trip to Disney World is a large undertaking, one that will take even more planning than a visit for two. It will be more expensive, and there will be a greater number of logistical concerns, especially if you are traveling with very young children or an infant. Consider, though, that it's a free ride for kids under 3 years of age at Disney World. No admission tickets are necessary, they do not count as people in resort rooms, and they eat for free at buffet meals.

Walt Disney World has been imagineered with families in mind. When it comes to meeting the needs of a family, the facilities are nearly limitless.

Making Plans: When to Go

The best time to visit Walt Disney World is during the off season. Unfortunately, this means while schools are in session. Yes, we are suggesting that you take the kids out of school for your Disney vacation.

Fall is the perfect time for Walt Disney World. It is still early in the school year and it should be an easy time to arrange a short absence. Off season is also the value season. Hotel rates, packages, and admission tickets are all available at discounted rates. While people are still at the parks, they will be significantly fewer in number. You will see much more, do much more, have a more relaxed time of it, and spend less money. Need we say more?

Accommodations: An Even Bigger Decision for a Family

For us, staying off property with children is even less appealing than doing it by ourselves. There's a lot of travel, a host of logistics, and a lot of lost time. It's a lot easier to get the kids back to a Disney resort for an afternoon of rest than it is to get them back to a motel on Highway 192.

Along with the choice of off property or on, you will be faced with the decision of how to accommodate all of you. There are more options than you think.

One Family, One Room   Sharing a room with your family will not make having a romantic time impossible, it simply makes things more of a challenge. Getting a room in a Disney resort is expensive enough. Getting two may be a fatal blow to an already stretched budget. While we cannot speak for accommodations outside of Disney World, we can tell you that children younger than 17 stay for free at all Disney resorts. Standard resort rooms feature two large beds, and cribs are available at every Disney resort at no extra cost.

Most Disney resorts permit a maximum of four people in each room. The Wilderness Lodge, besides its standard room with two queens, has a number of rooms with one queen bed and a set of bunk beds, which is a more interesting option for a family of four. Many of the premium resorts allow five. This is usually managed with two queen beds and a daybed/sofa. One moderate resort features accommodations for five. A trundle bed comes standard at Dixie Landings, but only in the non-king rooms of Alligator Bayou. If you have a family larger than five, you'll have to do something besides share a standard resort room.

One Family, Two Rooms   Two rooms is another way to go. All Disney resorts offer connecting rooms, and some feature a room with two beds connected to a room with one king-size bed. This sounds to us like the perfect layout for a small family. If you are considering sharing a room at one of the premium resorts, we would suggest that, for about the same expense, you get two rooms at one of the more moderately priced resorts, such as Port Orleans or the Caribbean Beach.

A Suite for a Family   Suites offer yet another route to accommodate a family. Virtually all of the premium resorts offer a selection of suites, some with as many connecting rooms as you might care to add. While these can be the perfect place for a family, they can be very expensive.

Family-Sized Accommodations   These are Disney's home away from home accommodations, and each features a kitchen, providing an economical alternative to restaurant dining. For about the cost of a single room at the Yacht or the Beach Clubs, you can get a luxurious one-bedroom villa at either Old Key West or the BoardWalk. Here you can enjoy a washer and dryer, a living room with fold-out queen bed, and your own king-size bedroom. Add to this a balcony and an oversized Jacuzzi tub, and your romance family vacation begins to take shape.

The Villas at the Institute offer another variety of family accommodations. The Treehouse or Fairway Villas can each sleep six in luxurious and woodsy surroundings for under $400 nightly. Deep discounts are often available off-season, some reducing the prices to that of a single deluxe resort room. On the budget end of the spectrum are the Fort Wilderness Homes. Here you can enjoy a double bed in your own room and bunks for the kids.

All of the home away from home accommodations feature maid service, which includes washing your dishes. Now that's a vacation!

Family Necessities

If you have an infant, bring all the baby supplies that you might need. Though widely available at Disney, choices are limited and prices are high. We would also suggest bringing snacks and drinks for the kids. Boxed juice drinks and refillable plastic drink cups with straws will come in handy too. And, if you are able, bring your own folding stroller. While these are easily and inexpensively rentable at the theme parks, you will frequently find yourselves standing in line to get one. Besides, a stroller will come in handy at your resort and while shopping at the Village Marketplace. Be sure to mark it with your name and your resort.

Preparing the Kids

When our kids were young, we took them to Walt Disney World as a surprise. "Let's go out for donuts," we told them as we dragged them out of bed at 6 A.M. All the way to the front gate (it was 120 miles), we pretended that we had no intention of actually going in. We just want to *look* at it, we told them. Meanwhile the kids whined and cried. By the time that we'd gotten our tickets, they were beginning to smell a rat. Or at least, a Mouse.

This was certainly a memorable adventure but, in reality, none of us were prepared for our visit, and pandemonium reigned supreme. We suggest that you do a few simple things to prepare your children for the kind of visit to Walt Disney World that you wish to make. Get them set to enjoy spending some leisure time at the resort and, if you plan to take advantage of the many and varied children's activities, you might prime them for these. We are sure that you know just how to do it.

You might also ask Central Reservations what attractions will be closed (in rehab, as insiders say) during your visit. Better to head off expectations now than later.

Setting Your Pace

Let your family know that this visit will not include spending every waking moment trying to cram in one more attraction. You'll spend plenty of time in the theme parks but you'll also take time to relax around the pool and to explore other areas of Walt Disney World. Take them for a boat ride or explore Discovery Island. Try to keep to your child's regular schedule. If naps are the rule at home, then they should be at Disney too. Try to eat and snack at the normal times also.

Logistical Concerns

If you have children, you know what an art it is to travel with them. We always enjoyed finding ways to make travel with our kids easier and more fun. When our children were younger, we traveled so much that they were in correspondence school, but that's another story.

Disney World is built to accommodate families, so you should find facilities for almost every situation. Each of the three theme parks has a baby-care center where you will find facilities for heating formula, rocking chairs for breast feeding, and a large assortment of expensive baby supplies. Diaper-changing stations are available in both men's and women's restrooms throughout Walt Disney World.

Getting Some Time Alone Together

Being here in "The Happiest Place on Earth" will be paradise for you and your family. There are lots of things to do here together, and there should be no shortage of time to enjoy each others' company. We have always found that being here with our kids somehow made us feel even more like a family. Having this kind of fun together is something that none of you will ever forget. A Disney vacation will bring you nearer to your children and it will make you, as a couple, feel closer. If this isn't romance, we don't know what is.

Still, having time alone together is both natural and healthy for a couple in love. You may wish to spend an evening together, perhaps have a romantic dinner and go out for some grown-up entertainment. No problem. Depending on the age of your children, there are a number of alternatives.

If you are traveling with an infant or very young children, KinderCare, Disney's sitting-service, will be your best alternative for an afternoon or evening out. With older children, the options increase to include activities ranging from Disney activity centers to educational programs.

KinderCare   This service provides in-room baby-sitting. These trained sitters will show up with toys and games to entertain your kids. Since this is done in your resort room, your children will feel more "at home." While these sitters are not permitted to take your kids on any Disney transportation, they are allowed to walk them around your resort or to a nearby restaurant.

Reservations should be made at least 24 hours in advance. Cost is $11 per hour for one to three children, with a four-hour minimum. Charges for four or more children will be dependent on their ages. If you have a sitter for eight hours or more, you will be required to provide a meal.

For information or to make arrangements ahead of time, call KinderCare at (407) 827-5444.

Disney Children's Activities Centers   If your child is at least 3 years old and potty-trained, then one of these "clubs" will be your best bet. Each will provide your child with a memorable evening of entertainment and his or her very own Disney experience. There are six such centers for the children of Disney resort guests. We have heard many wonderful things about these centers and can tell you, first hand, that children love them—ours did, during our visit to the Polynesian years ago. For more information or to make reservations at the Disney clubs, call (407) WDW-DINE (939-3463).

The Neverland Club   The Neverland Club at the Polynesian is open nightly from 5 P.M. to midnight and features a dinner buffet from 6 to 8 P.M. Foods usually include chicken strips, pizza, hot dogs, and ice cream. Activities include a live animal show from Discovery Island, video games, films, and a picture with Goofy. $8 per hour per child with a four-hour minimum. This imaginative Peter Pan experience begins with a trip through an open window out of Wendy's bedroom and into Neverland—fun and memorable.

The Cub's Den   The Cub's Den at the Wilderness Lodge also offers a buffet dinner. The cost here, though, is only $7 per child per hour and includes a Discovery Island animal show, video, games, and movies. The menu usually includes hamburgers, hot dogs, pizza, macaroni and cheese, corn on the cob, and peanut-butter-and-jelly sandwiches. Hours are 5 P.M. to midnight, with dinner from 5:30 to 7:30 P.M. Open to guests of all Disney resorts, this western-themed adventure is great for boys and girls.

The Sandcastle Club   This children's center is located at the Beach Club and is available to guests at the Yacht and the Beach Clubs; it is also free to anyone dining at Ariel's. While the Sandcastle Club does not include a buffet, it has plenty for kids to do. Computers, video games, a large library, and arts and crafts are a few of the offerings here. Hours are 4:30 P.M. to midnight and cost is $4.50 per hour per child. Meal arrangements must be made through room service if your child is visiting during mealtime or for more than four hours.

The Mouseketeer Clubhouses   There are two Mouseketeer Clubhouses: one at the Contemporary and the other at the Grand Floridian. At $4.50 per child per hour, these activity centers do not offer as much as either the Cub's Den or the Neverland Club and have facilities for far fewer children. While the clubhouse at the Contemporary is open to all Disney resort guests, the one at the Grand Floridian is available only to its guests. Reservations are strongly suggested and may be arranged through the Mouseketeer Clubhouses at (407) 934-6290. Dinner is available for an additional charge.

Camp Dolphin and Camp Swan   Both hotels offer evening programs for children that include arts and crafts, movies, music and books, and other supervised activities. Camp Dolphin's dinner club runs from 6 P.M. to 11 P.M.; the cost is $45 for one child and a bit less for each additional youngster. Extended hours are available. The evening program at Camp Swan costs $5 per hour, per child ($3 per hour for each additional child) and runs from 4 P.M. to midnight.

Lil' Toots Harbor Club   Located at the BoardWalk, this children's activities center features both day and evening programs. Evening programs are for ages 4 to 12, run from 4 P.M. to midnight, and cost $4 hourly per child. Activities include board and video games, Disney movies, supervised arts and crafts, and snack time. Dinner can be arranged at 6 or 7 P.M. for additional cost.

Special Activities for Children

The Chip and Dale Rescue Rangers Discovery Island Kidventure Available Wednesdays for kids 8 to 14 years of age. This four-hour exploration of Discovery Island includes lunch, arts and crafts materials, and a souvenir photo. Cost is $32 per child or $25 for children of Disney resort guests. For information and reservations, call (407) 824-3784.

Disney University Programs   These programs offer hands-on, behind-the-scenes learning activities. Structured and supervised, the programs should be reserved in advance. For information and reservations, call (407) 939-8687. Discounts are available for American Express cardholders.

Disney Day Camp   This camp takes 7- to 11-year-old youngsters on exciting, hands-on adventures each day, from 8:30 A.M. to noon and from 1:30 to 5 P.M. Expeditions are to destinations such as Epcot, Discovery Island, and Disney Studios. Take one or both adventures for $79. Box lunches are available for an additional charge.

Wonders of Walt Disney World   These are six-hour, behind-the-scenes programs, such as "Wildlife Adventure" and "Art Magic," and they are designed to spark creativity in youngsters as only Disney can do. From animation to costuming, children get an inside look and hands-on-the-magic approach. Cost is $79 per child (11 to 15 years old) and includes lunch and certificate of completion.

Disney Discoveries   This is another behind-the-scenes Disney activity, but it's for teenagers 16 years or older and adults. With varied programs, such as "Inside Animation," "The Gardens of the World," and "Epcot Divequest," prices range from $25 to $140 per person.

OUR RECOMMENDATIONS FOR ROMANCING WITH KIDS

- Take your vacation during the off season. It will be cheaper and more relaxing.
- Thoroughly explore the possibilities of getting your own room or your own bedroom. It will make a big difference.
- Keep your pace a relaxed one. Don't wear yourselves out. Spend time at your resort. The kids will play happily in the pool and not get cranky and overtired. Same for you.
- It is important that both of you share the chores involved in taking care of your children. It's no fun for one person to be stuck with all of the work while everyone else is vacationing.
- Make use of Disney's children's activity centers to take an evening off for yourselves. Wine, dine, and enjoy yourselves while the kids are having their own Disney adventure.
- Try a family activity such as bike riding or boating. Do something special together.

Making Your Resort Reservations

There are over 700 cast members at the Disney Central Reservations Office (CRO) taking an incredible 20,000 reservations daily. The special rates and least-expensive rooms are the first to go, so we suggest that you have plan A, plan B, and even a plan C in the event that your choice is not available. Here are the numbers to call:

Disney Central Reservations Office (CRO) (407) W-DISNEY (934-7639)

Magic Kingdom Club (407) 824-2600

Magic Kingdom Gold Card (800) 446-5365
- Open 8 A.M. to 10 P.M. (Monday through Friday); 9 A.M. to 8 P.M.(weekends and holidays)
- Reservations for all resorts and Disney vacation packages

Walt Disney World Travel Company (407) 828-3232

- Open 8:30 A.M. to 8 P.M.(Monday through Friday); 8:30 A.M. to 5 P.M. (Saturday)
- Reservations for Disney vacation packages only

Before you make your call, here are some things to think about beforehand:

- Views: A variety of views are available in all of the Disney resorts. Selecting one of these will be part of making your reservations.
- Types of beds: Most resort rooms come with two queen beds or two doubles, but as we have mentioned earlier, there are a number of king-size beds available at most of the Disney resorts. This is the time to reserve one of these if that is your choice. Making a king-size bed reservation usually means that the view cannot be guaranteed. However, you can still request a view and, when you check in, request it again.
- Room location: In our guide to the Disney resorts in Chapter 2, we describe the various choices of room locations. If you have a preference for a certain location, you should make this request when you reserve your resort room. Although no guarantee can be made, a mention of this will be attached to your reservation.
- Smoking or nonsmoking room: Be sure to mention your preference when making your call.
- Connecting rooms: If you are bringing your children along, consider a room that connects to your own. Disney reservations can guarantee connecting rooms.
- Discounts or specials: Always ask about specials or promotions when you make your reservations.
- Dinner show reservations: If you're planning on a dinner show, you should make reservations at this time.
- Special comments: If this is your honeymoon or anniversary, be sure to tell your reservationist. This will come up when you check in, and most Disney resorts will do something—usually a card, a rose, and a small gift.

Making Reservations

You will probably want to begin your reservation odyssey by simply gathering the most current information. Once you get a Disney reservationist on the telephone, you will immediately discover that the system is designed to make reservations, not to dispense information. The very first thing that you will be asked for is a date. If you are simply shopping for prices and have no date, pick any date during value season to get those prices or any date during regular season to compare prices.

$\mathcal{R}$ESERVATION TIPS

- Make your reservations in the morning, around 10 A.M. For some reason, resort availability seems best at this time.
- Keep trying if at first you are unable to get what you really want. There are plenty of cancellations that produce more available rooms.
- A CRO reservationist can act as your intermediary in reserving a suite. Simply call and spell out what you want. There will be some communicating back and forth, but eventually you'll get what you want. Suite availability is limited.
- Reservations that begin with a value season rate maintain that rate for the entire visit. The lower rate remains good as long as you wish to stay, up to the maximum reservation limit of 30 days. Since some value season discounts can be as much as 50%, simply arriving a day earlier can pay for several nights of your holiday visit.

What to Bring with You

Don't forget a liberal amount of sun screen with a minimum SPF of 15 or higher for the summer. The Florida sun can burn you even on an overcast day. We recommend that you not only bring sunscreen but that you *use* it, too.

Be sure that you have a handful of dollar bills for tipping, especially if you are staying in one of the premium resorts.

You can always bring your own snacks, liquor, or wine. Ice machines are convenient to all rooms, and an ice bucket and glasses are standard furnishings.

If you are interested in having some of your favorite music in your room, you might want to bring a small portable stereo. It might be just the thing for creating that special mood.

Available Items in Disney Resorts

Housekeeping will be happy to provide you with an assortment of items. Available at every resort, for no charge, will be extra pillows, blankets, iron and ironing board, and hair dryer.

If you need a refrigerator in your room, whether for pleasure or medical reasons, you should know that some resorts charge $5 per day for them and some do not. A limited number of microwave ovens are available at the Grand Floridian. Coffeemakers are standard at the Caribbean Beach and Coronado Springs and come with some of the rooms and suites at the Dolphin and most concierge rooms elsewhere.

Some of the premium resort rooms have minibutlers. These small refrigerators are stocked with wines, liquors, soft drinks, candy, and snacks. The selection is impressive. So are the prices.

Each Disney resort has a "general store" section in one of its shops. In this area, you will find sunblock, magazines and newspapers, film, insect repellent, Band-Aids, and a whole gamut of items dealing with everything from a headache to the munchies.

Your First Day at Walt Disney World

On your first day, you'll need to make arrangements to get to your resort. If you are arriving by automobile, you will be delighted to know that the roadways are well marked. Once on property, you will find that Walt Disney World has its own system of road signs. They are large and easy to read.

If you are staying in a Disney resort, all that you really need to know is which resort area your resort belongs to. Simply follow the Florida highway signs to the exit for that area and then follow the red and purple Disney signs to your resort.

If you are flying or taking the train into Orlando, you may be surprised to learn that Disney World is not there. It is 20 miles south, near Lake Buena Vista. Fear not. An entire industry has evolved solely to transport guests from the airport or train station to Disney. You will find a variety of cabs, limousines, and van services that will take you directly to your resort (or not so directly, if that is your wish). Several transportation options are available.

Florida Town Cars is a service that has many repeat users. With a fleet of Lincoln town cars, this company provides a personalized option for getting to the Disney resorts from either the Orlando airport or the Amtrak station. All you have to do is to make arrangements via a toll-free number, and you will be met at the gate by a friendly driver holding a sign with your name on it (we've always wanted to do that). Round-trip fare for five persons or less is $70. You are promised the same driver on both ends of your vacation. We have heard glowing reports of this

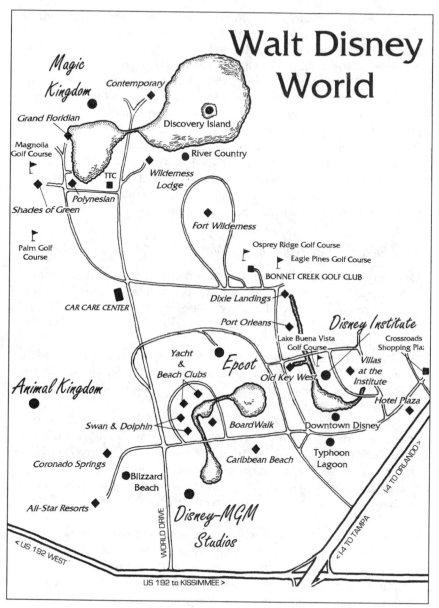

Walt Disney World Overview

company. Arrangements and inquiries should be directed to Florida Town Cars at (800) 525-7246. Town car service seems particularly personal and even a bit romantic.

Mears is the other company providing a similar service and offers both van and town car service. Van service (round-trip) is $25 for each adult and $17 for each child. Arrangements should be made in advance with Mears at (800) 759-5219. A Mears booth can be found at the Orlando International Airport on the second level. Passengers may make arrangements upon arrival at this kiosk. Because this service is used by the Walt Disney World Travel Company for its packages, lines here can get long.

Cab fare from either the Orlando train station or airport to a Disney resort is $40 each way, making the round-trip fare no bargain.

Getting Your Own Wheels

A rental car is yet another option for transportation between airport and resort. Of course, you will be paying for the car every day that you keep it. Rental car rates vary greatly during the course of the year, from company to company, and with special deals and packages. A midsized car for one week at $120 may be twice that at another time of year.

So, is having a car while you are at Walt Disney World a good idea? This is a tough question to answer simply. If you are able to find your way around easily, then it might be a convenience to drive from your resort to other resorts, to play golf, or to go to the Village Marketplace—which are all easily reachable via Disney transportation.

Arriving at Your Disney Resort

If you are staying in a Disney resort, check-in time is 3 P.M. If you are arriving earlier than this, you will be entitled to preregister, which means that you will be able to check into your resort but you will not get your room until it is ready, sometime later in the day. During the slower times of year, we have frequently found that we could arrive early in the morning and move right into our room. This, of course, is subject to chance availability. Preregistration, however, can be done as early as 8 A.M.

As part of preregistration, you will be able to check your baggage for storage. You will also receive your resort ID cards, which will immediately enable you to charge things to your room.

If you are staying in one of the hotels or resorts outside of Disney World, what happens to you when you arrive is bound to vary considerably. Check-in times differ from one hotel or motel to the next, so be sure that you have worked out, in advance, all of the details.

Special Requests and Last-Minute Changes

If you were unable to reserve the room that you had wanted, this may be a good time to remedy that situation. When you check in, remember to ask for what might not have been available earlier. While there is no guarantee, cancellations and last-minute changes may pay off.

Your Last Day at Walt Disney World

It seems cruel to have to think about this before you even arrive at Disney, but your last day, like your first, demands a few considerations. Check-out time at Disney resorts is 11 A.M. If you plan to leave Disney World before that time, no problem. Simply get packed up and depart. Give yourselves an hour to get to the airport from your room (add a little longer during a holiday). If you are returning to the train station or to the airport, the process is pretty much the same as arriving.

If you are departing later in the day, early check-out will mean that you will have to vacate your room no later than 11 A.M. Again, you will be able to place your luggage in storage until you actually leave. Your resort ID cards and Length of Stay Passes will be good until midnight of your last day, so you will be able to carry on with your Disney adventures.

Late Check-Out

Disney resorts are usually able to grant a 1 P.M. check-out each day for a limited number of rooms. These two extra hours can make a big difference. If you want late check-out, call the front desk at your resort on your last night to see what that resort's policy is.

Some Things You Might Need to Know

A Few Tips on Gratuities

For some reason, tipping situations tend to make both tipper and tippee uncomfortable. However, knowing when to tip and what amount is appropriate should alleviate the awkwardness.

- Cab, limo, town car drivers: 15%
- Valet parking: $1 to $2
- Bellpersons: $.50 to $1 per bag
- Housekeeping, maid service: $1 to $2 per day
- Room service: 15% included in bill, add more as desired
- Housekeeping, delivery: $1
- Table-service restaurants: 15%–20%
- Cocktail service: 15%–20%

Banking Around Walt Disney World

Running out of cash at Walt Disney World should pose no problem (as long as you are still solvent). Banking facilities and automated tellers are convenient and numerous.

ATMs are located:

- In the lobbies of all Disney Resorts
- Near City Hall, Main Street USA, Magic Kingdom
- At entrance to Disney–MGM Studios
- At main entrance to Epcot
- Outside Guest Services at the Village Marketplace
- Outside the Rock 'n Roll Beach Club, Pleasure Island
- At Gooding's Market, Crossroads Plaza (near Hotel Plaza)

Banking facilities can be found at several locations:

- Full-service Sun Bank on Main Street USA, the Magic Kingdom, and on Buena Vista Boulevard, directly opposite the Village Marketplace
- Foreign currency is exchanged at the Guest Services of all three theme parks, at City Hall in the Magic Kingdom, and at Earth Station in Epcot. Also at the Sun Bank on Main Street and the Marketplace and at all Disney resort front desks.
- Disney resort front desks will happily cash personal checks for all resort guests.

Food Shopping

If you are staying in one of the many Disney resorts that offers a kitchen or even if you are simply looking for a place to buy beverages and snacks, you'll probably need a supermarket. While the gourmet Pantry at the Village Marketplace is certainly handy for limited groceries, lots of baked goods, and an outstanding selection of wines, it is expensive. An alternative is not far away: Gooding's Market is a large and modern supermarket located at the Crossroads Shopping Plaza at the end of Hotel Plaza Boulevard. To find it, drive a bit past the Village Marketplace until you come to Hotel Plaza Boulevard. Turn onto it and continue through the intersection at Route 535 and into the shopping plaza. By the way, you're still on Disney property.

CHAPTER 2

Our Guide to Walt Disney World Resorts

We are always surprised how little we are able to learn about a Disney resort before seeing it for ourselves. For example, learning just how convenient the resort really is to the parks and attractions, the atmosphere of its guest rooms, and where in the resort we should have booked our room are things we would love to know ahead of time. Once we had spent time at a particular resort, the answers to these and other questions became apparent. We learned quickly what is meant by "insider information."

This chapter is an insider's look at the resorts of Walt Disney World, written by a couple who has stayed everywhere seeking out that something special for a memorable and romantic experience.

Services Available to Disney Resort Guests

Certain services are provided by all of the Disney resorts. Note that although they are on Disney property, the Dolphin, the Swan, and all of the hotels at Hotel Plaza are not Walt Disney resorts. Therefore, the following discussion of available services will not apply to these establishments, although they may offer such services. See the following descriptions of each for a list of available services.

Resort ID Cards

When you check into your Disney resort, you will each receive a resort ID card. These cards will be your tickets to unlimited use of the Walt Disney World transportation system and free parking at any of the attractions, and, if guaranteed with a credit card, they will be your Disney credit cards. Your resort cards will allow you to cover your Disney expenses virtually everywhere simply by charging everything right to your room account.

On the morning of your departure, a fully detailed bill can be prepared to give you a complete picture of what you have spent. These cards are valid from check-in or preregistration to midnight on the day of your departure. Everything charged to them after your check-out will appear on a final bill that you will receive in the mail.

The Length of Stay Pass

For Disney resort guests only, this pass provides unlimited admission to all Disney attractions for the exact length of your Disney vacation.

Surprise Mornings

The Surprise Mornings program is a powerful perk that will admit you both to a different theme park each day, 1 1/2 hours before the general public.

Guest Services

This essential service, usually located in the lobby or main building of each resort, will be invaluable in planning and executing your stay at Walt Disney World. You can go to Guest Services to buy tickets or to make your reservations for dinner, tennis, golf, or for entertainment. Guest Services will also be your source of Disney information. Brochures, menus, and schedules for virtually everything are available here. Whether you want to know the time for a parade or ignition time for a fireworks show, your Guest Services should have it all.

Resort Newspaper

Each resort has its own little themed information newspaper that you'll receive at check-in. The Polynesian's paper is the *Island Palm Press* and Dixie Landings' newspaper is called *The Sassagoula Times*. Each paper will give you lots of information about your resort, its restaurants and shops, and its services.

Refillable Resort Cups

Some Disney resorts offer their own thermal logo cup. It's a quality and useful souvenir, and with it you will get unlimited refills at your resort's fast food outlet. The mug costs around $8—with soft drinks, coffee, and tea around $1, it will not take long for the mug to pay for itself.

First Aid

Emergency service and in-room health care are available on a 24-hour basis. Guests are responsible for any charges.

Wake-up Service

If you need to be up early, simply press the appropriate button on your room telephone to arrange a wake-up call. You won't believe who is going to make the call.

Additional Services

- Guest messaging system
- Pager rental
- Walt Disney World Foreign Language Center
- Same-day dining reservations by telephone
- Four full-service barber and beauty shops
- Luggage assistance
- Overnight use of Walt Disney World Kennels is available only to Disney resort guests. For information, call (407) 824-6568.
- Package delivery to your resort room from any Disney shop
- Sunday church services held at Luau Cove at the Polynesian
- Children's activities centers and in-room baby-sitting
- Coin-operated laundry and laundry service
- Quality two-hour film developing
- Walt Disney World Florist is available to deliver a variety of floral arrangements, food baskets, and wine or champagne to any Disney resort room, including your own; call (407) 827-3505. Send someone you love a rose.

The Resorts by Area

There are six resort areas at Walt Disney World. Each occupies its own little piece of Disney turf, and each has a unique offering of resorts.

THE MAGIC KINGDOM RESORTS

- The Polynesian
- The Contemporary
- The Grand Floridian

- The Wilderness Lodge
- Shades of Green

It should come as no surprise that all of the Magic Kingdom resorts are near the Magic Kingdom. If you want to be as close as possible to Cinderella Castle, than take a careful look at this group. The Grand Floridian, the Polynesian, and the Contemporary are all right on the famous monorail loop that runs around the Seven Seas Lagoon. Although they're nearby, neither the Wilderness Lodge nor Shades of Green enjoys a location on the Seven Seas Lagoon. Shades is located over on the golf courses near the Polynesian, and the Wilderness Lodge can be found on Bay Lake, not far from the Contemporary.

THE EPCOT RESORTS

- The Yacht and the Beach Clubs
- The Caribbean Beach
- The Swan and the Dolphin
- Disney's BoardWalk Inn and the BoardWalk Villas

Except for the Caribbean Beach, the Epcot resorts are all premium resorts, and all are adjacent to Epcot and Disney–MGM. Convenience to all other Disney destinations from these resorts is about as good as it gets.

The Caribbean Beach is a charming, moderately priced resort. Neither the Swan nor the Dolphin are Disney hotels. The Swan is managed by Westin Hotels and the Dolphin is managed by Sheraton.

THE DISNEY VILLAGE RESORTS

- Port Orleans and Dixie Landings
- Old Key West Resort
- The Villas at the Disney Institute

The Village resorts are all located on the east side of Walt Disney World, scattered along the man-made Sassagoula River. They are all convenient to the two new Disney golf courses as well as to Pleasure Island and the Village Marketplace.

The Villas at the Disney Institute (once known as the Disney Village Resort) boast an assortment of home away from home lodgings. From the one-bedroom bungalows to the luxurious Grand Vista Homes, this area includes some of Disney's most unique accommodations.

THE STUDIO RESORTS

- Coronado Springs (opening August 1997)
- All-Star Sports
- All-Star Music

This area, located in Disney's southwestern area, is near both Disney–MGM Studios and Blizzard Beach. The All-Star Resorts are Disney's entry into the budget market.

THE FORT WILDERNESS CAMPGROUND RESORT

- Fort Wilderness Homes
- Fort Wilderness Campsites

Not to be confused with the Wilderness Lodge, this area is a world of its own. Fort Wilderness has its own beach and a water park called River Country. There are restaurants and even a popular dinner show "out there."

THE HOTEL PLAZA RESORTS

- The Grosvenor Resort
- Buena Vista Palace Resort and Spa
- The Hilton
- The Hotel Royal Plaza
- Travelodge Hotel
- DoubleTree Guest Suites Resort
- The Marriot Courtyard

These are not Disney resorts. They are, however, well located compared to off-property accommodations, and prices at some of them can be attractive, especially off season.

The Magic Kingdom Resorts

Disney's Polynesian Resort

This lovely "South Seas" resort was our first experience staying at Walt Disney World. Located along a white sand beach, directly across

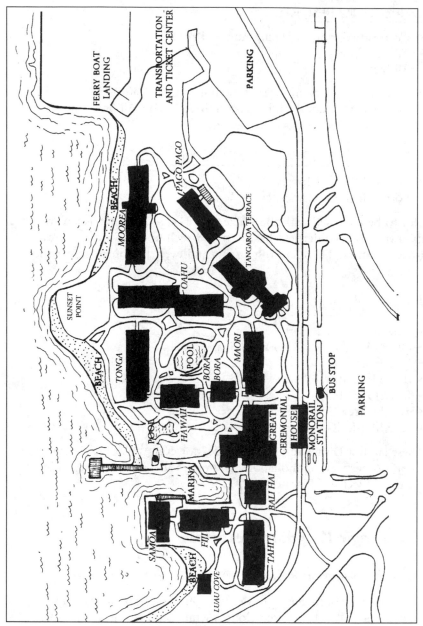

The Polynesian Resort

the lagoon from Cinderella Castle, "The Poly" enjoys one of the most spectacular views in all of Disney World.

The atmosphere here has been meticulously imagineered to re-create the magic of Polynesia, Disney-style. The lush grounds are dense with tropical foliage, and the lilting serenades of the South Seas are heard everywhere through a hidden sound system. Coconut palms, banana trees, gardenias, and orchids are but a few of the more than 75 species of tropical plants that make the resort grounds a veritable garden. A stroll at night here will work its powerful and romantic charm on any couple. The flickering light of torches, the lagoon's balmy breezes, and the scents of the flowering foliage all combine to create this potent piece of Polynesia.

The Great Ceremonial House lies at the center of life in Disney's South Seas. It is surrounded by a profusion of exotic plants and fish ponds. Native statues stand sentry at the entrance. Inside, the mingling of Hawaiian music and rushing water set the stage for your Polynesian adventure. Mammoth hewn beams and woven bamboo are the makings of this place, all trimmed carefully with hanging baskets of brightly col-ored orchids and birds of paradise.

The centerpiece of the Great Ceremonial House is its towering gar-den of palms, volcanic rock, and splashing water. It reaches to the domed glass ceiling three stories above. The gurgling waterfalls, brilliant blos-soms, and verdant foliage produce a sensation that is both cool and soothing. Large wooden ceiling fans spin slowly, and several brightly col-ored macaws squawk in the branches of a tree.

The Great Ceremonial House is home for this resort's front desk, Guest Services, shops, and several of its restaurants and lounges. "Aloha" is the usual greeting here at the Polynesian, where there is a Hawaiian word for nearly everything. The real theme of this tropical paradise may be best expressed by "Ho'Onanea," which means the passing of time in ease, pleasure, and peace.

The Polynesian's guest rooms are located in the "longhouses" that surround the Great Ceremonial House. With names such as Tonga, Moorea, Tahiti, and Bora Bora, the longhouses offer not only a variety of locations but also an assortment of accommodations. Some of the buildings are near the Great Ceremonial House, others surround the pools, and still others can be found along the white sand beach of the la-goon. The Bali Hai houses the Polynesian's suites, while Tonga is home to the Royal Polynesian concierge service. Given the lay of the land and the size of this resort, you will find that certain longhouses are closer to some things and farther away from others. But nothing is very far, and walking around the Polynesian is a pleasure.

There are two pools, one standard and one themed. The quiet pool is located in a lovely garden area in the center of the resort complex. The themed swimming area is located along the Polynesian's beautiful beach. Nestled amidst dense tropical foliage and bordered by huge rocks and waterfalls, it is lavish and tropical. There is one small water slide, intended for children. This is a fairly small pool, considering both the size of this resort and the fact that most guests come here to swim and play. It and the rooms that surround it get pretty noisy, especially in the evening hours of summer. This pool also features an underwater sound system and a poolside bar.

Rooms at the Polynesian

After the Great Ceremonial House, the lovely guest rooms at the Polynesian should come as no surprise. Each is spacious (409 square feet) and splendidly themed. Fabrics feature traditional Polynesian designs of browns and greens. Furnishings are tropical creations of wicker and bamboo. A room at the Poly does not provide a mere hint of tropical paradise but will immerse you in the romance of Polynesia.

Guest rooms each have two queen-size canopy beds and a daybed. None of the standard rooms feature king beds. Each room also has a small table and several handsome wicker chairs. A large tropical armoire hides the television and, along with the closet, provides room enough even for travelers like ourselves, who can never seem to decide what not to bring. Large marble baths feature counters of green and black with a spacious vanity and shower-tub combination.

There are 11 three-story longhouses. First-floor rooms have patios, third-floor rooms have balconies, and second-floor rooms simply have sliding glass doors that open against wooden railings. Requests for your selection should be made when you reserve your room. Reminding the front desk at check-in should ensure your choice.

Polynesian rooms feature garden, marina-pool, or lagoon views. Naturally, the most expensive overlook the lagoon, its white, sandy beach, and Cinderella Castle. If you can afford the difference, you will find the view memorable and romantic. At night, the lights of the monorail make their way around the lagoon and fireworks sparkle above Cinderella Castle. Garden rooms are beautiful as well; at night, the torchlit footpaths and dense greenery will transport you.

1997 Room Rates for the Polynesian

Accommodation	Regular Season	Value Season	Holiday Season
Garden View	$264	$249	$279
Pool/Marina View	$285	$270	$299
Lagoon View	$320	$305	$335
Concierge Garden	$325	$305	$340
Concierge Lagoon	$395	$380	$410

Royal Polynesian Concierge Service

The Tonga longhouse is home to the Polynesian's concierge service. It is located right on the lagoon, and rooms on that side of the building boast exceptional views. Determined to get a first-hand experience of everything, we happily stayed here in the tropical lap of Polynesian luxury. Royal Polynesian concierge service provided additional room amenities such as bathrobes, a coffeemaker, a full array of toiletries, and a lovely decorative gift box of Polynesian stationery.

As concierge guests, we relished the use of Tonga's lounge. Amidst the plush Polynesian furnishings, we savored a day-long offering of foods, snacks, beverages, and desserts. Each evening found us sipping cordials, nibbling desserts, and watching the fireworks over the lagoon. Like passengers on a small cruise ship, we were able to chat with other guests, some of whom we had seen at breakfast.

A small but dedicated staff was ready to spring into action for reservations, transportation, and any of our other concerns. We found the Polynesian's concierge service to be romantic and unforgettable—the perfect choice for us or for any other couple in love.

Suites at the Polynesian

The Bali Hai longhouse, located next door to the Great Ceremonial House, accommodates the Polynesian's suites. The Bali Hai is much smaller and more intimate than the other longhouses. It has only two stories and a dozen or so suites.

While all of the suites and rooms at the Bali Hai include concierge service, the concierge lounge is far enough away to make it less than convenient. To accommodate guests of the suites, a continental breakfast from room service is standard. The concierge staff is available, and use of the Tonga's concierge lounge is encouraged.

The smallest and least expensive suite here is not really a suite at all; it is a single oversized room. While considerably larger than the regular resort room, this luxurious accommodation is grand enough to accommodate a comfortable sitting area, a small desk and chair, and a dining table. The bathroom is large and offers a shower-tub and bidet. With either a single king bed or twin queens, this room comes as a garden-view room only. Marina-view versions are available on the lagoon side of the building, but they offer only dual queen-size beds. Garden kings or queens cost around $375 per night. These rooms are exceptionally nice and are on our small list of favorite Disney accommodations. The marina queen version is about $25 more per night and features a waterfront panorama.

The King Kamehameha suite is one of the most lavish in Walt Disney World. This two-level set of rooms commands a panoramic view of the marina area and lagoon. At over $1,000 per night, it is the stuff that dreams are made of. It has a large living room downstairs with a wet bar and enough space for a small wedding reception or party. The upstairs king bedroom is luxurious and perfectly themed. The bathroom features an oversized Jacuzzi tub. By adding adjoining rooms both upstairs and downstairs, this suite could accommodate the largest of families.

Transportation and Convenience

The Polynesian is right on the main monorail loop that runs around the lagoon. The monorail station at the Poly is located on the second floor of the Great Ceremonial House. It is a relatively short walk from most of the longhouses, giving this resort a real convenience to the Magic Kingdom and the other resorts around the lagoon. A boat also runs from the Magic Kingdom to the Grand Floridian and then to the Polynesian and back to the Magic Kingdom. From the longhouses along the lagoon, getting to the Magic Kingdom by boat is especially pleasant and convenient.

If you are guests at either Moorea or Pago Pago (pronounced Pongo-Pongo), you might find that the short walk from your longhouse to the ferryboat landing or monorail station at the Ticket and Transportation Center (TTC) may provide more convenient travel to the Magic Kingdom. Other Disney destinations are reachable by bus from a bus stop near the main entrance of the Great Ceremonial House. We found bus service to be quite good.

- To the Magic Kingdom: monorail, boat from dock, or ferry from TTC
- To Epcot: monorail with transfer at TTC to Epcot monorail
- To Discovery Island, River Country: boat from the Magic Kingdom
- To Disney–MGM Studios, Blizzard Beach: direct bus
- To Village Marketplace, Pleasure Island, Typhoon Lagoon: 8 A.M. to 4 P.M., by bus to TTC and transfer; after 4 P.M., by direct bus

Dining at the Polynesian

With five restaurants in the Polynesian and the many others at nearby resorts along the monorail, your dining options are considerable. Guests enjoy three table-service eateries and two snack bars. There's even a dinner show, called the Polynesian Luau. 'Ohana at Papeete Bay offers a character breakfast and Disney-style Polynesian dinner show and buffet. The Polynesian has an all-purpose restaurant, the Coral Isle Cafe. Serving three meals daily, its menu has a definite Polynesian accent. For in-room dining, 24-hour room service is available. No resort would be complete without some sort of fast-food offering, and at the Poly it's Captain Cook's Snack Isle. It's open 24 hours.

For reviews and more information about the table-service restaurants and dinner shows at the Polynesian Resort, see Chapter 6.

Lounges at the Polynesian

There are two tropical lounges at the Polynesian: the Tambu Lounge and the Barefoot Bar. Both offer a tantalizing selection of specialty drinks. The Tambu Lounge, which adjoins 'Ohana, has been recently redesigned. Appetizers are from the firepit of 'Ohana. The Barefoot Bar is the Polynesian's poolside bar.

Shops at the Polynesian

Trader Jack's is located on the second floor of the Great Ceremonial House. It offers character merchandise, toys, gifts, films, postcards, and Polynesian logo items, and an assortment of beers, wines, liquors, sundries, and snacks. There is an excellent selection of clothing shops on the ground floor of the central building. Whether you are looking for something special for yourselves or for a gift to bring home, these places definitely have nice stuff. Kanaka Kids, Robinson Crusoe, Esq., and the Polynesian Princess all make for interesting browsing.

Recreational Activities at the Polynesian

- Two heated swimming pools
- Watercraft rentals
- Evening fireworks cruise
- Moana Mickey's Video Arcade
- The Neverland Club children's activity center and dinner club
- 1.5-mile jogging and walking path

OUR IMPRESSIONS OF THE POLYNESIAN

- A beautifully themed resort, with rooms that are some of the best in Disney World. This is a first-class place to stay. We found it romantic and memorable. The Polynesian's motto is "Aita Peatea": there will be another day tomorrow just like today.
- All in all, convenience to the Magic Kingdom is good to very good; convenience to other Disney destinations is average. Consider using the boat to travel to the Magic Kingdom, especially if you are staying in one of the longhouses near the dock.
- The main pool is small. There is no hot tub at the Poly, which is a real shortcoming for us. The quiet pool seems a sensible alternative to the noisy central area. A major rehab planned for both pools will include several hot tubs. The timetable for this is, as yet, uncertain.
- The Polynesian is currently undergoing a refurbishing. It is evolving into a resort that more reflects the *real* Polynesia rather than an idealized misrepresentation. This year, guest rooms are enjoying a complete face-lift. Many are already complete. This will be done one building at a time and should continue throughout the year. We would expect no disruption for guests. The Coral Isle Cafe is also slated for improvement.

RECOMMENDATIONS FOR RESERVATIONS

- Pool-view rooms are considerably noisier than other rooms. Try a quiet pool-view room, if you must.

ROMANCE AT THE POLYNESIAN

- The rooms at the Polynesian: ♥♥♥
- Royal Polynesian concierge service or garden king room at the Bali: ♥♥♥♥

- Breakfast in bed: ♥♥♥♥
- Breakfast on your balcony or patio: ♥♥♥
- Dining by a window at 'Ohana at Papeete Bay: ♥♥
- Strolling around the grounds after dark; exploring; sitting in the comfortable two-person swings along the beach: ♥♥♥
- Viewing the Electric Water Pageant or fireworks from Sunset Point, a small grassy area along the beach near the Oahu longhouse: ♥♥♥
- Fireworks cruise for two, available at the marina: ♥♥♥
- Renting a boat and taking a cruise: ♥♥

The Contemporary Resort

The Contemporary was one of Disney World's first resorts. It is an impressive display of the imagination and vision of the Man himself, Walt Disney. There's more than just a little excitement to this place. The monorails streak back and forth through the colossal lobby. Each train is filled with awed visitors, whose faces are pressed to the windows as the train glides through. The Contemporary is a marvel of steel, glass, and concrete. It is itself a Disney icon.

This may be one of Disney's oldest resorts, but it is no dowager. Seeming as new as the day it was created, this resort keeps a firm grip on its first-rate status. The Contemporary offers a variety of spacious rooms and suites and a complete package of resort amenities. These, and its unequaled proximity to the happiest place on planet Earth, are what this exciting place is all about.

The resort's main building is the Tower. Adjacent to it are two newer additions called the Garden Wings. Each wing lies along the north and south sides of the Tower building. The ambience at the Contemporary is definitely modern. It is fast-paced and high-energy. In the 1970s, the Contemporary was the forefront of architectural innovation. Twenty years later, it has lost only some of its distinction, as the rest of the architectural world has been playing catch-up. The Contemporary is still an impressive site on the Disney horizon.

The Tower building is an enormous 15-story, A-frame structure. Its atrium-style lobby is the Grand Canyon Concourse. Tiers of guest rooms hang suspended from its sides. The ends of the building are large, open expanses of glass. Within them is an entire world of restaurants, shops, and lounges. A dazzling mosaic leaps hundreds of feet from floor to ceiling.

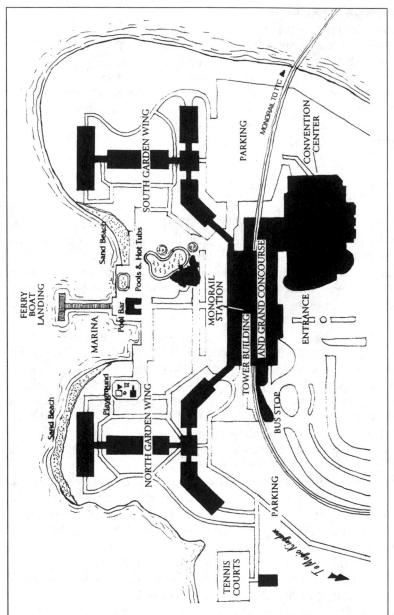

The Contemporary Resort

Rooms at the Contemporary

The rooms at the Contemporary, at 422 square feet, are some of the largest standard rooms at Disney. Compare them to the All-Star's 260 square feet. Each room is light, airy, and spacious. The decor is modern with a color scheme of beige trimmed with black. The bedspreads are light, with a splash of brightly colored, confetti-like patterns. There is a large, Danish modern armoire with plenty of drawer space and a television. The vanity area is large and has a single sink. The bathroom features the usual shower-tub. While well appointed and comfortable, the rooms lack the charm and fantasy that are so present at other Disney resorts.

All of the rooms in the Tower have balconies; none of the standard rooms in the Garden Wings do. Rooms in the Tower building face either the Magic Kingdom or Bay Lake with views that range from very good to astounding. Furnished with several chairs and a small table, balconies in the Tower are large and comfortable. Our room was located on the twelfth floor overlooking the Magic Kingdom. After dark, the view was spectacular. Tower rooms with panoramas of the Magic Kingdom are the most requested at the Contemporary. So, if this is your wish, reserve early.

Rooms of the Garden Wings overlook the parking area or landscaped gardens and Bay Lake. With only three floors here, views are pleasant but not panoramic. The larger Garden Deluxe rooms feature a small foyer and spacious bath with either a single king bed or one queen with fold-out sleeper/sofa. Views from these rooms are particularly pleasant. Not as convenient to the services of the Tower building, these rooms do offer a certain tranquillity and sense of seclusion not found in the Grand Canyon Concourse.

Most rooms at the Contemporary offer the usual two queen beds and a daybed/sofa. There are only 33 rooms with king beds, counting both the Tower and Garden Wings, and many of these are suites. The rooms at the Contemporary do not have minibutlers.

1997 Room Rates for Disney's Contemporary

Accommodation	Regular Season	Value Season	Holiday Season
Garden Wing, standard	$219	$199	$234
Garden Wing, garden	$250	$230	$265
Garden Wing, deluxe	$280	$260	$295
Tower room	$299	$280	$315
Tower concierge	$379	$350	$395

Concierge Service and Suites at the Contemporary

Concierge service here begins weeks before you arrive. Over the phone, you'll be asked about what most interests you at Walt Disney World. You'll be mailed information about these interests, then a month prior to your arrival you'll receive another call to make your reservations. Once you arrive, you'll be greeted downstairs and whisked up to the concierge floor for check-in. Other privileges include private check-out, nightly turndown, use of the resort's health club, VCRs and complimentary movies, and access to the concierge lounge, located on the exclusive fourteenth floor. Offerings there include continental breakfast, midday snacks, afternoon hors d'oeuvres and champagne, and evening cordials and desserts. And, of course, the concierge staff is on hand to help with all your requests.

Two floors of this resort are reserved for concierge guests. The twelfth floor features upgraded Tower rooms, each with coffee-maker and refrigerator. The fourteenth floor offers an assortment of suites, the simplest beginning around $850 per night. There are two Presidential suites, and each offers a spacious king bedroom with Jacuzzi tub (these are the Contemporary's only rooms with Jacuzzis). With wet bar, dining area, large parlor room with sofa and chairs, and two oversized balconies, this suite runs $1,000 nightly. More than once, an Arab prince and his entourage have occupied the entire floor. There are suites in the Garden Wings too, but they do not include concierge service. With 1,313 square feet, you will certainly not feel cramped in these luxurious rooms. Each provides a large bedroom with adjoining parlor and sico bed and, depending on view and season, cost from $655 to $750 nightly. This is plenty of room for a family, but at these prices you could get two rooms in the Tower.

Transportation and Convenience

With the Contemporary right on the monorail loop, travel to and from the Magic Kingdom is both easy and exciting. Arrivals and departures are from the monorail station on the Tower's fourth floor. Be advised that during peak hours the trip to the Magic Kingdom can take upwards of 20 minutes. There is also a short walking path to the Magic Kingdom. This is a pleasant stroll past some amusing topiary. The walk is especially convenient from the north Garden Wing.

Except for the pleasant monorail ride to Epcot, travel to other Disney destinations is not quite so much fun. It is relatively easy, though. Several areas require transferring buses at the Ticket and Transportation Center (TTC), which can be reached easily from the Contemporary by either monorail or by direct bus.

- To the Magic Kingdom: monorail or a short, pleasant walk
- To Epcot: monorail with transfer at TTC to Epcot monorail
- To Discovery Island, River Country: boat from the dock at the lakeside of resort
- To Disney–MGM Studios, Blizzard Beach: direct bus
- To Village Marketplace, Typhoon Lagoon, Pleasure Island: 8 A.M. to 4 P.M., by bus to TTC transfer; after 4 P.M., by direct bus

Dining at the Contemporary

Dining here is outstanding. Along with the Contemporary's three full-service restaurants, room service, and fast-food eatery, you will find many fine choices at the other resorts around the Lagoon. Atop the Contemporary is the California Grill, one of Walt Disney World's finest and most exciting dining destinations. The Concourse Steakhouse is yet another good dining choice, with a variety of well-prepared breakfasts and lunches. Evenings here feature fine dining with seafood and cuts of beef. Chef Mickey's is the Contemporary's place for Disney character meals with both breakfast and dinner buffets. For more information and our reviews of these table-service restaurants, see Chapter 6.

The Food 'n Fun Center is located on the ground floor, adjacent to the video arcade. A bit noisy, the Food 'n Fun Center offers a selection of Disney fast foods and is open from 6 A.M. to 1 A.M.

Lounges at the Contemporary

The California Grill Bar is located right inside the restaurant and shares the Top of the World view. Besides an extensive wine list and a full complement of liquors, it offers a menu of appetizers, sushi, taster plates, and pizzas from the Grill. The Grill Bar is open from 5 P.M. to 1 A.M. and offers wine tasting "classes" on Fridays at 6 P.M.

The Outer Rim Cocktail Lounge is on the fourth floor of the Tower building, overlooking Bay Lake and Discovery Island. Open from 12 P.M. to 11 P.M., this lounge offers an assortment of cocktails and appetizers. It is often crowded with guests waiting to get into Chef Mickey's, however, and it is also noisy, due largely to its location in the Grand Canyon Concourse.

The Sand Bar is located in the marina complex near the pool, on the lakeside of the resort. This lounge operates seasonally.

Shops at the Contemporary

Except for the Bay and Beach and the Racquet Club, all of the Contemporary's shops can be found on the fourth floor in the Grand Canyon Concourse.

Concourse Sundries and Spirits should pretty much take care of any loose ends. Whether you are in search of souvenirs, snacks, newspapers or magazines, film or tobacco products, or nonprescription medicines, here is where you will go. Concourse Sundries has a large offering of beers, wines, and liquors. Bayview Gifts is the perfect place to stop for that little something special. Fresh flowers and unique gifts are the specialty here, so you can surprise someone you love. Other shops offer character merchandise, jewelry, and men's and women's sportswear.

Recreational Activities at the Contemporary

- Two heated swimming pools
- Two hot tubs
- Kiddie pool and play fountain
- The Olympiad Health Club
- Marina Pavilion with watercraft rentals
- Waterskiing, parasailing
- Six lighted tennis courts, backboards, ball machine
- Volleyball and shuffleboard
- Lakefront beach area
- Children's playground and spray fountain
- Food 'n Fun Center video arcade
- Free Disney movie every night in the theater at the Food 'n Fun Center
- Fireworks cruises, summer only

OUR IMPRESSIONS OF THE CONTEMPORARY

- While this resort may not offer the same sense of storytelling as other resorts and is not romantic in the same sense as the Grand Floridian, it is nonetheless a very exciting place to stay.
- This resort is very convenient to the Magic Kingdom.

RECOMMENDATIONS FOR RESERVATIONS

- Neither Garden Wing is convenient to the Tower building or the monorail. The north wing is, however, convenient to the tennis courts and the footpath to the Magic Kingdom.
- Garden Deluxe rooms in the Garden Wing are quiet and beautiful. Add-ons to the suite at the end of the wing, these rooms enjoy king beds and upgraded amenities.

ROMANCE AT THE CONTEMPORARY

- Resort theme: ♥
- Breakfast in bed: ♥♥♥♥
- Breakfast on your balcony overlooking Disney World or Bay Lake: ♥♥♥
- Having a drink at the California Grill Bar during the evening fireworks show: ♥♥♥
- The fifteenth-floor observation deck at night, especially during the fireworks shows at any of the parks: ♥♥
- King bed Garden Deluxe Room: ♥♥
- A stroll on the beach behind the north Garden Wing, then watching the Electric Water Pageant: ♥♥♥♥

The Grand Floridian

Even from a distance, there is something very romantic about this place. Its red-shingled roofs, ornate turrets, and intricate latticework all seem to belong to a time long past. We confess gladly to a little thrill each time we are near it. In our hearts, this lovely resort represents an unhurried age when the quality of life was held dear and when time was something to be savored. Here amidst the stately palms and gas lamps and among the verandas and the rose gardens, old-world craftsmanship has been brought to life.

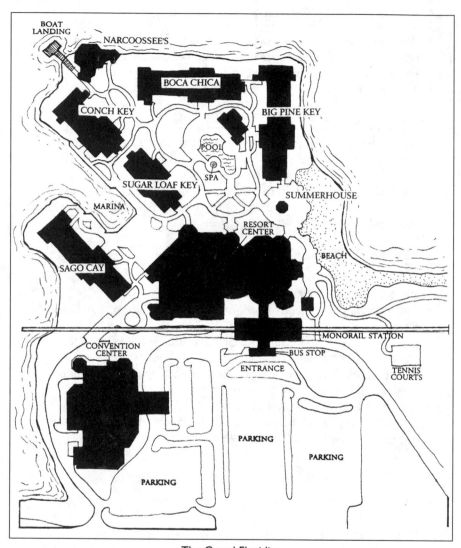

The Grand Floridian

This is the Grand Floridian, and it is the jewel in the Disney crown. A stay here will immerse you in a richness and elegance that will be the stuff of your romantic dreams. Details are everything at the Grand. From flawless service to sumptuous bathrobes, the luxurious and the lavish come standard.

Arriving at the Grand Floridian is definitely exciting, and it is likely something that you will never forget. The tree-lined drive leads through manicured gardens and up to an entrance where a dozen costumed valets and bellpersons scurry about. Knickers, knee socks, and pastel jackets are the uniforms of the day. Once inside the huge lobby, you begin to understand why this place is called Grand. Level upon level of formal balconies surround this cavernous space, they lead the eye upward towards the domed ceiling high above. Rows of turned white posts are capped with rails of gleaming mahogany. Sunlight filters through stained-glass skylights onto sparkling chandeliers.

Fabrics, decor, and design are all in perfect harmony. Details attract your eye: A topiary Cinderella Castle occupies one space, while above it an old-fashioned cage elevator ascends slowly. This striking Grand lobby is an awesome and even a dizzying sight. Everything about the Grand Floridian appears to be first-class, and everything most certainly *is* first-class. A stay here will be, for both of you, a celebration of everything that is special and memorable.

Set perfectly along a combed, white sand beach on the Seven Seas Lagoon, the Grand Floridian is but a stone's throw from Cinderella's front door. The monorail slips quietly from the station and whisks guests away to Disney adventures.

The Grand's five lodge buildings are neatly arranged around a large pool area. Connected by garden walkways, these buildings reflect the Victorian charm of the lavish Grand lobby and house the resort's luxurious guest rooms. Each building is named for a Florida key: Sago, Boca Chica, Conch, Big Pine, and Sugar Loaf.

Rooms at the Grand Floridian

Each charming and luxurious room in this resort is decorated much as it might have been a century ago, with marble-topped sink, ceiling fan, and antiqued armoire. Each marvelous remembrance is made complete with plush carpets, pastel floral fabrics, and lightly colored woodwork. Large glass doors open onto a spacious balcony that looks onto the lovely garden grounds. Costumed housekeepers arrive daily carrying wicker baskets of fresh linens.

Rooms here are large (400 square feet) and comfortable. They are the perfect marriage of the elegance of yesterday and of the creature comforts of today. Each has two queen-size beds, several chairs, and a small table. A daybed/sofa lends the perfect place to lounge. Every guest room features twin marble vanities in a spacious and well-lit area adjacent to the bathroom.

Because of the unusual shapes of the lodge buildings, standard room sizes and shapes vary slightly within each building. Top-floor attic rooms, while a bit smaller, feature quaint dormer balconies and vaulted ceilings. Lodge Tower rooms are a bit more expensive and are a little larger than the standard rooms; a comfortable sitting area substitutes for the balcony or patio.

Rooms at the Grand enjoy two different views, of either the garden or lagoon. Each has its charm. Many of the rooms overlooking the lagoon feature an impressive panorama of Cinderella Castle. The sparkling water, fireworks, and the Electric Water Pageant all make evenings here magically romantic. Whatever your choice, the Grand Floridian is a luxurious place to celebrate your honeymoon, anniversary, or romantic Disney vacation.

1997 Room Rates for the Grand Floridian

Accommodation	Regular Season	Value Season	Holiday Season
Garden view	$309	$284	$324
Lagoon view	$360	$335	$375
Lodge Tower	$375	$350	$390
Concierge	$495	$475	$510
Concierge Deluxe	$515	$495	$530
Honeymoon, Clarendon	$515	$495	$530
Honeymoon, Turret	$515	$495	$530

Concierge Service and Suites at the Grand Floridian

Your Grand concierge experience will begin weeks before you arrive, when you receive your Personal Vacation Itinerary. The staff here is dedicated to making your concierge visit unforgettable, and this questionnaire will tell them what they wish to know: your arrival time, special arrangements, favorite characters, desired dinner reservations, and more. Once you get to the Grand Floridian, you will have *arrived*. You will be greeted at the entrance and escorted to your room. The dedicated and friendly staff will try to anticipate your every need.

The luxurious concierge rooms at the Grand are located on the private, upper floors of the main lobby building. All rooms include plush bathrobes, slippers, VCRs, and complimentary movies. This is the life! The beautiful and comfortable concierge lounge is located on the fourth floor, and here you will enjoy a sumptuous offering of treats served throughout the day: continental breakfast, midday re-freshments, afternoon tea, and hors d'oeuvres and wine before din-ner. Drop by in the evening, sip cordials, and share a dessert while you listen to the music of the Grand's orchestra waft up from the landing below. Once you have been a guest here, you will understand why so many who have visited before will not even consider a stay elsewhere.

There are a variety of rooms here in concierge that range from a standard resort room to the elegantly modern Roosevelt Suite (where Princess Di and the boys stayed during their Disney holiday). There's a Deluxe Concierge room too, and it's larger than the standard. The Grand Floridian also features two types of exceptionally romantic concierge rooms, and our favorite is the Turret Honeymoon Suite. Six of these octagonal rooms are located in the two towers of the main building. Each features a large bathroom, walk-in closet, and a bedroom with a spectacular panorama. Several command views of Cinderella Castle right from the four-poster king bed. From our own experience, we can tell you that, for sheer magic, one of these suites has no equal here at Walt Disney World. The other honeymoon rooms are on the secluded Clarendon Concierge level. Room ameni-ties here include a Jacuzzi tub and love seat. These too are enchanting and romantic.

There are other suites as well, but none so perfect a place for a couple in love. With names such as the Biscayne, the Cypress, and the Sanibel, they offer a variety of bedrooms and parlors each with enough space for a family. Prices begin around $900 nightly. A handful of one- and two-bedroom suites are also located on the top floors of the lodge buildings. These are simply attic rooms with adjoining parlors. Each parlor features a pull-out queen, sitting area, and bathroom. A second bedroom can be added. Prices begin around $700 per night and concierge service is not included.

Transportation and Convenience

Guests at the Grand Floridian enjoy the same monorail and bus transportation as the Contemporary and the Polynesian. The motor launch that makes the trip from the Polynesian stops at the dock near Narcoossee's (a restaurant) on its way back from the Magic Kingdom. We suggest that you monorail to that park and return by boat.

- To the Magic Kingdom: monorail or water taxi
- To Epcot: monorail with transfer at TTC to Epcot monorail
- To Discovery Island, Fort Wilderness, River Country: monorail or boat to Magic Kingdom, then boat
- To Disney–MGM Studios, Blizzard Beach: direct bus
- To Village Marketplace, Pleasure Island, Typhoon Lagoon: 8 A.M. to 4 P.M., by bus to TTC and transfer; after 4 P.M., by direct bus

Dining at the Grand Floridian

Some of Walt Disney World's finest eateries are located here. Victoria and Albert's ♥♥♥♥, a gourmet dining experience, is considered by many to be one of Florida's best places to eat. There is also Narcoossee's, specializing in seafood, as well as the elegant Flagler's ♥♥♥ and the wonderful Grand Floridian Cafe. These places all rate high and are among our very favorite spots in all of Walt Disney World.

As if these weren't enough, 1900 Park Fare is a delightful breakfast and dinner buffet-style restaurant. It features Disney characters galore at both meals. For snacks and fast food 24 hours a day, visit the Gasparilla Grill, which serves a large variety of counter foods that are a notch or two above the standard Disney fare. To complete the largest selection of restaurant offerings in any Disney resort, an elegant afternoon high tea ♥♥♥ is served at 3 P.M. in the Garden View Lounge. The Grand also offers round-the-clock room service. For more details regarding these and other Disney dining spots, see Chapter 6.

Yet another dining option available to guests of the Grand Floridian is the Romance Dinner. This special service provides an unforgettable private dining experience delivered to the Grand Floridian location of your choice. Enjoy it in your room, on your balcony, on the beach, in the garden, or even out on the lagoon in one of the resort's Flote boats. Just about any location is possible. There are no set menus, but sample meals such as the Italian Romance Dinner or the Romance from the Sea hint at what is possible. Needless to say, such a dinner would be simply enchanting and, of course, expensive. The suggested menus are all around $200 for a five-course dinner for two (tax and gratuity included). For a bottle of wine, add another $30. A Flote boat would be an additional $75. This unforgettable experience, served white-glove with crisp linens and candlelit table setting, is included with the Grand Plan vacation package. For information, call room service.

Lounges at the Grand Floridian

The Grand Floridian is home to three quite different lounges. The charming Garden View Lounge is on the ground floor of the lobby building. It features not only the lavish afternoon high tea but also a full service bar from 11 A.M. to 11 P.M.

Mizner's is located on the second floor of the main building. Specialties here include ales, ports, and select brandies. Each evening, a small orchestra plays on the landing right next to this handsome and comfortable lounge.

Summerhouse is the Grand's pool and lakeside lounge and snack bar. Beer, wine, specialty drinks, and a small assortment of sandwiches are available in a Victorian beach setting.

Shops at the Grand Floridian

A good selection of shops can be found at the Grand Floridian, all of which are located in the lobby building. As you might expect, though, the emphasis is on classy and expensive. Still, you will find a good selection of Disney character merchandise, in addition to some rather fancy clothing and accessories for both men and women. Sandy Cove is the resort's gift and sundries shop, where you will find film, sunblock, and other such items. There's also a hair salon, and new here at the Grand is Bally's, offering some of the world's finest leather goods.

Grand Floridian Spa ♥♥♥♥ and Health Club

Get yourselves in the perfect mood for your romantic holiday with pampering treatments at this luxurious spa. From a sensual variety of massages to mineral soaks, facials, wraps, and aromatherapy, this first-class spa offers a truly special experience. For more details, see Chapter 7.

Grand Floridian Changing Lounge

This area is located by the pool, where the health club used to be. Created for early arrivals and late departures, the facilities here include a lounging area, changing rooms, lockers, and showers. If you arrive before your room is ready or you have a late plane out, this convenient lounge will allow you to freshen up, change clothes, or go swimming.

Recreational Activities at the Grand Floridian

- One large, heated swimming pool, open 24 hours
- One large hot tub
- White sand beach on Seven Seas Lagoon
- Marina complex with watercraft rentals
- Grand Floridian Spa and Health Club
- In-room massage, by appointment
- Jogging and walking path
- Wingfield tennis courts
- Golf shuttles to golf courses throughout the day
- Children's activity center
- Video arcade
- Fireworks cruises

OUR IMPRESSIONS OF THE GRAND FLORIDIAN

- The Grand Floridian is an enchanting and romantic resort. The rooms are luxurious, and a stay here will have you feeling special and pampered.
- The downside is that the Grand is expensive. Specials and discounted rooms are available, but rates are rarely outstanding. The exception to this rule is the Magical Holiday Package.

RECOMMENDATIONS FOR RESERVATIONS

- For a good view of Cinderella Castle, the best views are from Boca Chica, which is a smoking-optional building. The next best view is from Conch, with rooms ending in 25 to 31. After that, Big Pine rooms ending in 41 to 47 have great views. Both Big Pine and Conch are no-smoking buildings.
- Make your reservation for Victoria and Albert's when you reserve your room. The Chef's Table is unforgettable.

ROMANCE AT THE GRAND FLORIDIAN

- Unsurpassed theme, service, accommodations, and ambience: ♥♥♥♥
- Restaurant selection (the best in the World): ♥♥♥♥
- The Honeymoon suite or Turret room: ♥♥♥♥
- A lagoon-view room: ♥♥♥♥
- Breakfast in bed: ♥♥♥♥
- High tea at the Garden View Lounge: ♥♥
- Eating at Flagler's: ♥♥♥
- An intimate dinner at Victoria & Albert's: ♥♥♥♥
- The Romance Dinner: ♥♥♥♥
- Watching the fireworks or Electric Water Pageant from one of the swings on the beach: ♥♥♥♥
- A late-night swim in the pool or hot tub: ♥

The Wilderness Lodge

Located in the woods near the Magic Kingdom is the Wilderness Lodge. It is one of Walt Disney World's latest and most majestic creations. It is a magnificent tribute, both architecturally and thematically, to the great lodge houses built by the U.S. Park Service around the turn of this century. The Wilderness Lodge has been created with great care, and the mood it achieves is impressive.

Near the resort's front entrance, a topiary buffalo and calf graze. The Lodge's bellpersons wear the costumes of Park Service Rangers, from knotted kerchiefs to hiking boots. Once inside the great doors, you will know that you have made the right selection. The cavernous lobby soars eight stories above you and surrounds you with balconies of log railings. Two colossal totems face off across the huge expanse, and a shaft of sunlight enters through a circular window high among the timbers. There is a faint and delicious scent of smoke in the air.

The lobby of the Wilderness Lodge will take your breath away. Its grandeur and its detailing are stunning. The decor is American Indian, and the lobby is a showcase of native craftwork. Behind the front desk is an exhibit of authentic Indian cradleboards, while around the lobby are glass showcases of feathered headpieces, the intricate handiwork of native American artisans. In a far corner is a fireplace that befits the grand scale of the Lodge. The stonework of its massive chimney rises over 80 feet to the beamed ceiling above. A multitude of hued layers simulate the bedrock of

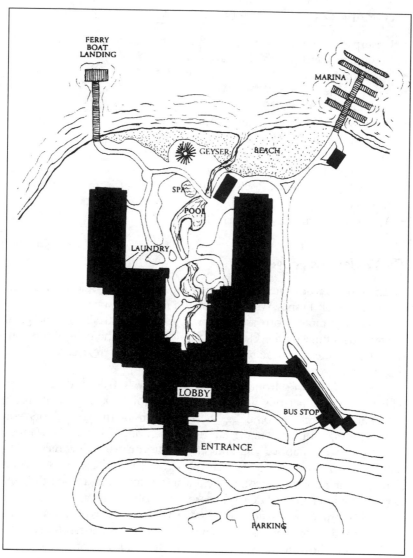

The Wilderness Lodge

the Grand Canyon. The forged iron hearth is artwork, and its hinges are carefully tooled to resemble quivers, each one full of iron arrows.

As grand as it may be, the Lodge is a place for people, too. Comfortable sitting areas, cozy corners, and fireplaces invite you to linger a while. This is a place of creature comforts, with sofas, ottomans, and hearthside rockers. It's a place for holding hands and for sitting quietly together by the fire. Spectacular and huge, the Lodge manages to be intimate and inviting. It may take you days or it may take you only a few moments, but you will discover that the charm and the rustic ambience of the Wilderness Lodge are unrivaled at Walt Disney World.

From a distance, the Lodge resembles a frontier fort. The hewn log walls and green roofs of its great central building turn gracefully into two long wings. The swimming pool is formed by a man-made hot spring that bubbles up in the lobby and flows out into the Lodge's rocky courtyard. As the stream builds to a torrent, it becomes a waterfall, splashing noisily over huge artificial granite boulders and tumbling into the pool.

The resort overlooks Bay Lake and Discovery Island. Every evening, the Electric Water Pageant passes by; with its music and lights, it is the perfect end to each magical day. The Disney imagineers have even provided a steaming geyser that erupts hourly.

The pool at the Lodge is themed and beautiful. During the summer months, there is one hot tub and one cold tub. During the cooler seasons, the cold tub is heated. The lakefront forms a small, sandy swimming beach, and its marina rents a variety of boats and bicycles. Walking, jogging, and cycling paths will take you around the lake to Fort Wilderness or to River Country.

Rooms at the Wilderness Lodge

The standard rooms at the Lodge have a high-timber, western sensibility. Though a bit smaller than those of the other premium resorts, the rooms are comfortable and well appointed. Each is woodsy and charming. The furniture is simple and natural and includes two queen beds and a colorful "quilted" spread. There is a large pine armoire with ample drawer space and a large television set. A small table and several chairs provide the ideal place for intimate dining. The bathroom is fairly standard, with a twin vanity and the usual tub-shower.

Each room at the Wilderness Lodge has its own balcony, and there are a variety of views. Standard-view rooms overlook small parking areas, while woods-view rooms open onto the dense forest surrounding the resort. Our woods-view room was on the side of the resort that faces the Magic Kingdom. At night, we were able to see the fireworks above the treetops.

Courtyard rooms provide views of the courtyard and pool, while lake-view rooms enjoy magnificent vistas of Bay Lake. Most of the standard rooms come with the usual dual queen-size beds, and two other offerings are available in limited numbers. There are about 40 rooms with single king beds. These have been designed for the physically challenged, and they are handsome rooms. Some rooms also offer a single queen bed and a bunk bed. These seem to capture the western feeling of the Lodge and are ideal for families.

1997 Room Rates for Wilderness Lodge

Accommodation	Regular Season	Value Season	Holiday Season
Standard view	$180	$165	$195
Woods view	$199	$184	$214
Courtyard view	$230	$210	$245
Honeymoon "suite"	$230	$215	$245

Suites at the Wilderness Lodge

A small assortment of suites is available at the Lodge. On the top balcony of the lobby are four charming Honeymoon "suites." While not really a suite, each has a king-size bed and a large bathroom with Jacuzzi tub. These rooms are special, intimate, and private. They are the only ones on this floor, high atop the vast lobby, and you will enjoy the feeling of being away from and above the rest of the world. Priced reasonably, a Honeymoon suite is a real bargain at $230 nightly.

The Junior suite costs about $300 per night and is even less during value season. This suite has a standard bedroom with two queen beds or one king and a small sitting room and wet bar. A standard adjoining room may be added to this suite. During value season, this two-room combination may be available for less than $400 per night with a Magic Kingdom Club discount.

The remaining two suites here are the Yellowstone and Yosemite, which are the presidential and vice-presidential suites, respectively. We think both are among the best-themed suites here at Walt Disney World and, at $665 and $560 per night, they are something of a bargain. The Yellowstone features an elegant, Western motif. From the suite's double doors and large foyer with elkhorn chandelier to the lavish, marble bath, this place is first class all the way. The suite's four-poster king bed is a unique sculpture of wood, and the spacious suite of rooms is furnished with a large, wooden dining table, stuffed leather chair, and antique books. The Yosemite is nearly as large and enjoys much more of a cowboy sensibility. Rawhide curtains, branding-iron towel racks, and saloon doors on the kitchen/wet bar are just a few of the memorable and whimsical details. Either suite comes with a large whirlpool tub (the Yellowstone's is bigger). We have promised ourselves to stay in one of these suites but, as yet, have not been able to decide which one.

Transportation and Convenience

Convenience is not, we are sorry to tell you, one of the strong suits here at the Wilderness Lodge. Still, transportation is acceptable, although we still hear an occasional complaint.

- To the Magic Kingdom, Fort Wilderness, River Country, Discovery Island: by boat, arrivals and departures from the lakeside dock; the Magic Kingdom can also be reached by bus via the Ticket and Transportation Center (TTC) and monorail
- To Epcot, Disney–MGM Studios, Blizzard Beach: direct bus
- To Typhoon Lagoon, Pleasure Island, Village Marketplace: 8 A.M. to 4 P.M., by bus to TTC and transfer; after 4 P.M., direct bus

Dining at the Wilderness Lodge

The Lodge has three western-themed restaurants; two have table service, and one has fast food. The Artist Point ♥♥ is the Wilderness Lodge's premier eating place. Dinner specialties are the freshest of meats, seafood, and game from the Pacific Northwest. The Artist Point also features a character breakfast.

The all-purpose restaurant is the Whispering Canyon Cafe. It's a fun place to eat and the food is good. Each of the day's hearty meals is served family-style and all you care to eat. For reviews and more information about these restaurants, see Chapter 6.

The Lodge has a themed counter-service eatery called the Roaring Fork. Open 24 hours, this self-serve restaurant offers a selection of breakfasts, sandwiches, salads, and desserts. There's even a buffalo burger. During the breakfast hours, a continental-style breakfast bar is offered in the lobby. It's called the Coffee Express and it features a selection of beverages, muffins, and bagels from 6:30 A.M. to 10:30 A.M.

The Lodge also has 24-hour room service with a menu that includes barbecued ribs, pizza, grilled fish, and prime rib. Foods come from either the Artist Point or Whispering Canyon. Wines, beers, and mixed drinks are also available. Room service also features the Romance Dinner for Two. For an evening to remember, this full-course dinner includes a keepsake floral arrangement, choice of entrees, wine or champagne, a personalized cake, specialty coffees, and two hours of child care at the Cub's Den.

Lounges at the Wilderness Lodge

The picturesque Territory Lounge is located adjacent to the Artist Point and serves a selection of microbrewery beers, specialty drinks, and wines from 11 A.M. to 1 A.M. The Trout Pass Pool Bar enjoys a nice view of the lodge and of the lake and beach.

Shops at the Wilderness Lodge

There's only one shop at the Lodge, but it's a good one. Just outside the front door of the Lodge Mercantile sits one of the comic sites of the Lodge: a totem pole of Disney characters. Inside, you will discover one of the nicest on-property places to browse. Besides some handsome Lodge logo merchandise, you'll find an impressive array of western craft items as well as quality fashions and the usual assortment of sundries.

Recreational Activities at the Wilderness Lodge

- Swimming pool with small water slide
- One hot and one cold spa
- White sand beach and marina with assorted boat rentals
- Bicycle rentals
- Video arcade
- Fishing excursion
- The Cub's Den children's activity center

OUR IMPRESSIONS OF THE WILDERNESS LODGE

- A beautifully themed resort. The fantasy element here is so powerful that a visit will be a real adventure. As elusive as romance is, we'd have to say that the Lodge has it.

- The selection of restaurants here could be better. Some real improvements have been made in offering a la carte items at the Whispering Canyon, but if you are visiting for a week, you might get tired of the eateries here.
- The Lodge is an outstanding value. It falls in cost somewhere between the premium resorts and the more modestly priced ones, yet it offers extraordinary theming, well-decorated rooms, and most of the services found at the more expensive places.
- The four Honeymoon suites could be the best on-property room bargain.
- The pool is a bit small for a hotel with nearly 800 rooms. Even during the winter months, two hot tubs are simply not enough.
- A car would come in handy here, especially for going to dinner at other resorts.

RECOMMENDATIONS FOR RESERVATIONS

- If you want to have your room located in the main lobby building, ask for it when you make your reservation. A room that is on one of the lobby's balconies is considered a woods-view room.
- Courtyard-view rooms will likely be noisy.
- Some of the lower-floor lake-view rooms have stunning balconies of "granite."

ROMANCE AT THE WILDERNESS LODGE

- Resort theming: ♥♥♥
- The Honeymoon "suite": ♥♥♥
- Having your morning cup of coffee in front of the fireplace on the third-floor landing above the main door: ♥♥
- The Artist Point restaurant: ♥♥
- The Territory Lounge: ♥
- Taking a stroll or a bike ride over to Fort Wilderness: ♥
- Searching for the sixteen hidden Mickeys in the lobby: ♥
- The Romance Dinner for Two (arrange with room service): ♥♥♥♥

Shades of Green

This resort, once known as the Disney Inn, is now reserved for use by active and retired military personnel, employees of the Department of Defense, and members of the National Guard and military reserves. On

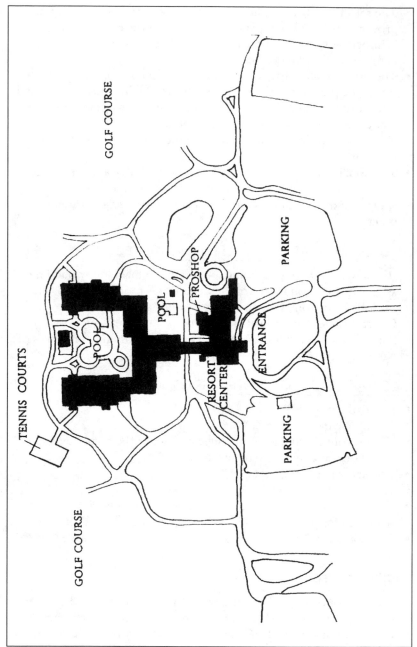

Shades of Green

long-term lease to the U.S. government, Shades of Green provides an affordable Disney vacation for the men and women of the U.S. armed services and their families.

This lovely resort is nestled between two of Disney's championship golf courses, the Magnolia and the Palm. It features a woodsy and quiet ambience. Rates are based on rank and range from very reasonable to downright deserving. Special passes are available to guests at a discount, and Shades of Green restaurants offer meals at reduced prices. Every effort at Shades is made to make the Disney experience an affordable one for our people in uniform.

The long entry drive at Shades of Green seems more like one to an exclusive country club than to a Disney resort. The grounds are beautifully landscaped, and the resort is handsome and well maintained. Theming isn't an element here, but the atmosphere is unmistakably Disney. While guests at Shades of Green do enjoy Surprise Mornings, they do not get Disney resort ID cards.

The staff members at Shades of Green are not Disney employees. We found them to be genuinely dedicated to delivering the best service possible. Employees have all been trained by Disney so that the magic Disney hospitality is definitely present.

Special arrangements can easily be made for small weddings at the resort's own garden gazebo. Family reunions and modest parties are also easily arranged by the resort's eager staff. Arrangements can be as grand or as modest as you can afford, and the many rules and regulations regarding such events at Disney resorts are not a consideration here. Staff members make a real effort to get to know their guests, and we suspect that repeat customers are the rule rather than the exception.

No taxpayer funds are used to support this resort. Shades of Green and all other Armed Forces Recreation Centers are self-supporting.

Rooms at Shades of Green

The resort consists of one large building with two three-story wings. Guest rooms face either the pool courtyard or the golf course. There is no such thing as a bad view here, and the rooms, at 450 square feet, are among the largest standard rooms in Disney World. Furnishings are light oak, and bedspreads are a floral pattern. Of the 290 rooms, 287 have two queen beds. Two of the remaining three rooms have one queen-size bed, and the last is a large suite. Each room has a daybed/sofa, small table and chairs, and balcony or patio. A large, remote-controlled color television occupies a colonial armoire, and the bathroom has twin vanities and a separate shower. Shades of Green is every bit a luxurious Disney resort.

The one suite at Shades of Green has a living room, master bedroom, and a large bath. There is a four-poster king bed in the bedroom and a foldout queen-size sofa bed and two Murphy beds in the living room. This suite can accommodate up to seven persons and has two full bathrooms, one with a small Jacuzzi and bidet.

Suite furniture is of light pine with a ceiling that features varnished, decorative beams. Baskets of crisp linens and objects of art make this lovely suite quite elegant. At $180 per night (regardless of rank), this is an excellent opportunity for honeymooners. It is spacious, luxurious, and romantic. The large patio overlooks the golf course.

Shades of Green is such a bargain that demand is beginning to exceed room supply. We have heard reports that overbooking has caused some Shades of Green guests to be relocated to other Disney resorts, such as the All-Star Resorts, which although they are bargains at $57 per night, are no match for the accommodations at Shades of Green. Other guests have been located at other resorts, mostly the moderately priced resorts such as the Caribbean Beach or Dixie Landings. These resorts are much nicer than the All-Star Resorts. Due to increasing demands for rooms at Shades of Green, still other guests are being put up at the Hotel Plaza resorts.

Shades reservation personnel have assured us that those guests who are going to stay at a resort other than Shades will be told so at the time of reservation. Since this resort is so nice, we suggest that you make your reservations as early as possible to avoid staying someplace less luxurious.

Valid military ID or current LES and Department of Defense (DOD) pay grade verification is required at check-in. Room rates at Shades of Green are based on rank and civil service rate and double occupancy:

- E1–E5: $57 per night
- E6–E9, O1–O3, WO1–CW3, GS1–GS10, NF1–NF3, widows, disabled veterans: $81 per night
- O4–O6, CW4–CW5, GS11–GS15, NF4–NF5: $89 per night
- O7–O10, retired DOD civilians, NF6: $98 nightly

Special package rates are now available. For information, call (800) GO ARMY-1. Reservations can be made by calling Shades of Green reservationists at (407) 824-3600.

Transportation and Convenience

Transportation to all Disney destinations is by Shades of Green buses. These are not Walt Disney World buses. They run on a schedule that is available at the front desk. Service is on par with that of Disney, and having a printed schedule should take the guesswork out of travel.

Dining at Shades of Green

There are two restaurants at Shades of Green. The Garden Gallery has a delightful garden decor with large potted trees. It features American cuisine in a table-service setting. Breakfast here is an unusual buffet, a sort of help-yourself meal with a la carte pricing. Dinners and lunches include sandwiches, steaks, seafood, and pastas.

The poolside sports bar and eatery is called Evergreen's and has the usual selection of snacks and specialty drinks as well as a good selection of sandwiches. The hamburger is one of the best at Disney. Decor here is interesting, with a collection of antique sports equipment and a tennis court, complete with players, fixed to the ceiling. It's popular with golfers. Both restaurants are open to the public for lunch, and the Garden Gallery offers discounted dinner prices for Shades guests. For reviews and more information about these restaurants, see Chapter 6.

Special Ticketing to Disney Attractions

Along with the usual selection of Disney tickets and passes (all discounted), Shades of Green also offers its own Length of Stay Pass called the Stars and Stripes Pass. It's good for your whole visit and will admit you to all of the Disney attractions. A three-day pass is $115 for an adult, and each successive day adds about another $20. Compared to the Length of Stay Pass, this is a considerable savings.

Services Available at Shades of Green

- Room service from 7 A.M. to 11 P.M.
- Coin-operated laundry facilities
- Small refrigerators ($4 per day)
- Video camera rentals $6 for 24 hours
- Travel Services

Recreational Activities at Shades of Green

- Two large standard swimming pools
- Two tennis courts
- One kiddie pool
- A children's playground
- A small health club
- Video arcade

Shops at Shades of Green

One small Army-Air Force Exchange Store features a selection of Disney merchandise at discount prices. Also available are a generous selection of sundries, magazines, and books. Military and DOD identification cards are required to purchase goods at this shop. There's also Made in the Shade, which features popular souvenir items.

OUR IMPRESSIONS OF SHADES OF GREEN

- This is a very nice resort and provides an affordable way for military personnel to visit Walt Disney World and to stay on-property.
- There is no hot tub here at Shades, but the management has assured us that plans are underway to have one built. Just how long the government wheels of progress will grind before this happens is anyone's guess.

ROMANCE AT SHADES OF GREEN

- Resort theming: ♥
- The suite: ♥♥♥

The Epcot Resorts

The Yacht and the Beach Clubs

Next door to Epcot and along the shores of Crescent Lake lie two of Disney's most enchanting creations. Both are visions of nineteenth-century luxury where guests are immersed in a setting that is perfectly exciting, lavishly relaxing, and splendidly romantic. The gray and blue clapboard buildings of the Yacht and the Beach Clubs perfectly evoke a bygone era of grace and hospitality. These picturesque resorts share

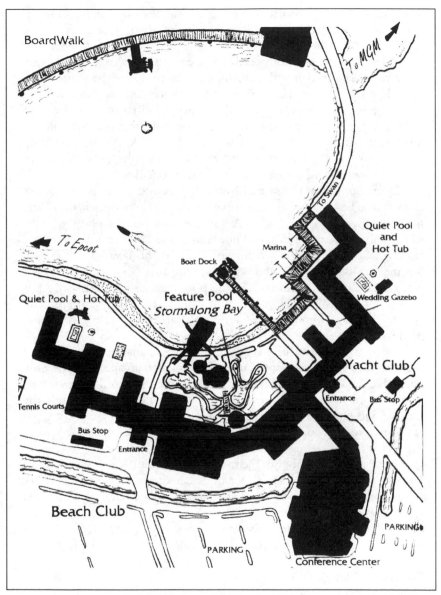

The Yacht and the Beach Clubs

a quaint, turn-of-the-century New England seaside theme. One reflects a more formal nautical charm, while the other radiates the casual ambience of the shore.

Lakeside, a rope-slung boardwalk, beached shipwreck, lighthouse, and a white sand beach with colorful cabanas complete the seaside illusion. The Disney magic is everywhere, from the antique "woody" station wagon at the front door of the Beach Club to the detailed ship models in the Yacht's elegant lobby. The overall effect is classy and unforgettable. Both the Yacht and the Beach are first-rate resorts from top to bottom. Their intimate and relaxed atmospheres will embrace you both, enhancing the chemistry for your romantic escape.

Stormalong Bay, the shared water playground, is an extraordinary and magical place. It seems more like a river than a pool as it meanders from the Beach to the Yacht. Along the way are bubbling springs, whirlpool eddies, waterfalls, and hot tubs nestled in surrounding rocks. It even features a sand beach for children. At the Beach Club end of Stormalong Bay is a wild and winding slide that begins in the crow's nest of the shipwreck and ends in the pool with a sudden splash. After a morning of Disney excitement, you will be ready to spend a blissful afternoon here, swimming and sunning. Each resort also has a quiet pool with a hot tub.

Along with Stormalong Bay, the resorts also share a common area that includes Periwig's Salon and Barber, a video arcade, and the Ship Shape Health Club with its old-fashioned indoor spa. Along the waterfront, the Yacht Club features a marina of rental watercraft, while the Beach Club enjoys a lazy stretch of white sand. These areas are separated by a long wooden pier. The charming lighthouse at the end of the pier is one of the signature sights of these idyllic resorts.

The landscaping at the Yacht and Beach Clubs is a showcase of Disney's penchant for details. Colorful gardens and manicured shrubbery will prove an inspiration to home gardeners. Long stretches of trimmed lawns lead gracefully to the lake. On one of them is the lovely gazebo used by Disney Fairy Tale Weddings. Amidst beguiling gardens of roses and the carved, wooden cupids, happy couples tie the knot, Disney-style.

The Beach Club

The relaxed and romantic atmosphere at the Beach has lured us back time and again. We like to think of this place as our home away from home. We confess that staying elsewhere has been done with some reluctance. The casual atmosphere here is elegant yet informal. For us, the Beach Club is simply inviting.

The Beach's lobby is a canvas of pastels, pink marble, and fine woodwork. Large windows facing the lake make the lobby airy and bright. Comfortable wicker furnishings are everywhere on plush carpets of floral designs, and wooden bird cages and large potted palms add just the right touches of warmth.

Around the resort are porches with rockers, beaches with cabanas, and lovely gardens with benches. Enjoying the Disney attractions for a few hours at a time will not be hard. After a morning in the parks, you'll be ready to return.

Rooms at the Beach Club   The "seaside" rooms here are sunny and bright. Ensconced amidst the light pastels and luxurious furnishings, you will not for a minute forget that you are enjoying a romantic vacation at the beach. The verdigris-finished bedsteads and seahorse lamps seem weathered by their "years" at the seashore. Pink and white carnival-striped drapes perfectly mime the beach cabanas of yesteryear. This is a place of creature comforts; it is your own intimate and private retreat. You have landed in the lap of luxury and, if you are like us, you will not be anxious to depart.

Beach Club rooms are indeed inviting. With a choice of either a single king or double queen beds, each room features a large vanity area with twin sinks. The attractive armoire is of light wood. Inside it you will find not only the usual television but also a stocked minibutler. Each room has a small table and several chairs—just the place for breakfast or intimate dining. Many rooms include a daybed/sofa. Balconies are either full-size, with patio furniture, or standing room only. Ground-floor resort rooms all have patios.

There is the usual Disney complement of views. Standard-view rooms look out onto well-landscaped gardens, beyond which are the resort's parking lots. Ground-floor, standard-view rooms have charming little patios that open onto beautiful gardens. Water-view rooms at the Beach overlook Stormalong Bay or the quiet pool area. Other rooms command views of the various gardens on the lakeside of the building, and some rooms provide excellent views of Epcot and IllumiNations, the laser light show.

1997 Room Rates for the Beach Club

Accommodation	Regular Season	Value Season	Holiday Season
Standard view	$244	$229	$259
Garden view	$280	$260	$295
Water view	$315	$295	$330

Suites at the Beach Club   From the luxurious to the lavish, the Beach Club offers a variety of suites. The Newport is this resort's Presidential suite. It features a king bedroom with a large vanity, bath, and large Jacuzzi tub. The formal living room is arranged around a fireplace and includes a spacious dining area, wet bar, and room enough for a small party. Located on a corner of the fifth floor, the Newport has a narrow balcony that runs the entire width of the living room and bedroom. The view of Stormalong Bay and of the lagoon is commanding. So is the price: $900 nightly.

The Nantucket is the Beach's Vice-Presidential suite. With a beautiful king bedroom and a smaller and less formal living room, it seems better suited for a honeymoon or anniversary. Located on the second floor, the Nantucket overlooks a pleasant garden area. It is charming and is conveniently located near the lobby. Price is $635 nightly.

The Beach also offers several Junior suites. At $445 nightly, there are two varieties, each with a large king bedroom. Junior A features a sitting area that is part of the bedroom, and Junior B offers a separate sitting area with French doors and a daybed. Junior B is a nice choice for a family with one child.

The Yacht Club

The lobby of the Yacht Club showcases its nautical theme. A large antique globe sits in the center of the elegant splendor. You will wonder where the Disney folks get things like this. There are intricate ship models in glass cases that invite more than just a casual glance. Ornate brass chandeliers, polished hardwood floors, and decorative ropework recalls the finery of New England's old yachting establishments. Tufted leather sofas and chairs will tempt you with the promise of luxurious comfort. Muted reds, whites, and blues herald the colors of the grand old yacht clubs of Cape Cod, Marblehead, and Bar Harbor.

This lobby area is more formal but is no less inviting than that of the casual Beach Club. There is a certain classiness to this place and, as one of our mothers said when we arrived, "Now, this is the style I'm accustomed to!"

Rooms at the Yacht Club   Like the rooms at the Beach, guest rooms at the Yacht Club are light and airy. The furnishings have a bit more formal charm, though. Bedsteads and armoires are of white antiqued wood; the lamps are of polished brass. The nautical decor is made complete with fabrics of pale reds, whites, and blues. Like her sister ship, the Yacht Club will embrace you with the luxurious comforts found only at first-class hotels: large, soft towels, signature toiletries, and a host of other details.

Each room at the Yacht Club has a vanity area with twin sinks. There are chairs and a small table, and some rooms even have daybeds. Every room has a large balcony with several chairs and a small table where you can sit and enjoy an early morning breakfast, read the newspaper, or simply sit and watch Disney World awaken.

Most rooms at the Yacht Club are configured with two queen beds, but like the Beach, it has a number of king bedrooms. Here at the Yacht, the assortment of views is the same as that at the Beach, except that no rooms here provide a view of Epcot.

Concierge Service at the Yacht Club   While both the Yacht and the Beach offer a variety of suites, only the Yacht Club features concierge service. All of the rooms and suites on the concierge level's fifth floor enjoy this wonderful service.

Concierge guests enjoy the upgraded room amenities, which include terry bathrobes and special toiletries, and they also enjoy use of the luxurious lounge overlooking the lagoon. The continental breakfast each morning features pastries, croissants, cereals, and muffins. Midday snacks are of chips and salsa, fruit, and cookies and milk. Late afternoons mean wine and cheese and a vegetable tray and, in the evening, cordials and desserts are offered.

Suites at the Yacht Club   Our favorite Yacht Club suite is the Commodore. It is charming and romantic—the perfect accommodation for a honeymoon, anniversary, or a romantic getaway. The Commodore is large and lavishly furnished. With a comfortable sitting room, a large bedroom with a king-size sleigh bed, and concierge service, a stay here will make your time dreamy and idyllic.

The Commodore's bathroom is spacious and luxurious, more of a room than a bath. Complete with television, vanity areas, walk-in shower, and Jacuzzi tub, it is world-class. If you can afford the $635 per night price tag, we are sure that it will not disappoint you.

The Turret suites occupy the first three floors of the resort's beautiful tower-like structure. Each includes an octagonal sitting room in the turret, a large bedroom, and a spacious living room. The Turret room is sunny and bright, offering a thrilling panorama of Stormalong Bay and Crescent Lake. At over $555 per night, these accommodations are unique and lavish.

If you're looking for something really spectacular, there is the Presidential, which is the fourth floor of the Turret suites. Highlights include a large dining area, Jacuzzi tub, and two full balconies. The basic suite is around $880, with an additional double-queen bedroom adding nearly another $425.

The Yacht's premier suite is the Captain's Deck. It is one of only a handful here on Disney property that offer such luxury. We have taken to calling it "Arnold's Room" after one of its celebrity guests. The Captain's Deck includes furnishings more lavish than even those found in the other Yacht Club suites. Furniture is dark and varnished. There is enough room here for a large family or a small meeting. In the dining room, the table will easily seat a dozen, and the wet bar is designed to be a serving area for a large room-service event.

The dark wood theme is carried throughout, with a large armoire and four-poster king bed in the master bedroom. The bath has an oversized shower and tub. This suite of rooms also has a forty-foot wide patio, which opens onto its own secluded garden and pond. An additional five rooms can be connected through adjoining doors. We know that Arnold must have liked this place: when he left, he surely said, "I'll be back." At nearly $1,000 per night, we have no doubt that he can afford it.

1997 Room Rates for the Yacht Club

Accommodation	Regular Season	Value Season	Holiday Season
Standard view	$244	$229	$259
Garden view	$280	$260	$295
Water view	$315	$295	$330
Concierge garden view	$399	$380	$415
Concierge lagoon view	$415	$395	$430

Transportation and Convenience at the Yacht and the Beach

Both the Yacht and the Beach are only minutes from almost any Disney destination. Whether by boat, foot, or by bus, transportation to anywhere is about as easy as it gets.

Reaching Disney–MGM Studios or Epcot from either resort is by Friendship motor vessel. Arrivals and departures are from the lighthouse dock on the beach side of the resorts. The trip to Epcot takes only a few minutes by boat and even less time by foot. All other Disney destinations, except Discovery Island and River Country, are reached by direct buses. Each resort has a bus stop near its front entrances.

- To Disney–MGM Studios: short boat trip from resort dock
- To Epcot: short walk or boat ride to International Gateway
- To Magic Kingdom, Village Marketplace, Typhoon Lagoon, Pleasure Island, Blizzard Beach: direct bus
- To Discovery Island, River Country: bus to Magic Kingdom and boat to either

Dining at the Yacht and the Beach

One of the many advantages here is the outstanding dining. Because these are "Siamese" resorts, guests at either the Yacht or the Beach will find that strolling over to dine at the other resort will be both pleasant and convenient. Each resort boasts its own array of themed restaurants and lounges.

At the Beach, you will find two dining places: the Cape May Cafe and Ariel's. Both offer table service. The Cape May has a delightful beach decor and serves breakfast and dinner, both buffet-style. Breakfast is a character affair, and dinner is a New England clambake. Ariel's serves dinner only and specializes in seafood.

At the Yacht are the Yacht Club Galley and the Yachtsman Steakhouse. The Galley serves a large and varied menu for breakfast, lunch, or dinner, including a wonderful breakfast buffet. The Yachtsman is open only for dinner with its specialty of fine cuts of prime beef. Other entrees include lamb, grilled seafood, and poultry.

In and around the pool area are two other restaurants: Beaches and Cream Soda Shop and Hurricane Hanna's. Beaches is one of our favorite things about these resorts. This delightful fifties-style soda fountain offers a mean double-chocolate ice cream soda, and it has no equal in or around Walt Disney World. Hamburgers and Disney's finest hot dogs are also featured here. Hanna's is the Y & B's poolside bar and eatery, serving an assortment of counter-style drinks and sandwiches. Either of these places is ideal for a light meal while you relax around Stormalong Bay.

The Yacht Club Galley is the source of in-room dining at both resorts. We have made good use of it on our numerous visits and have always found both the food and the service outstanding.

For more details and our reviews of the table-service restaurants, see Chapter 6.

Lounges at the Yacht and the Beach

Each resort has two lounges. One is adjacent to the lobby and the other is near its signature restaurant. In a quiet corner in the lobby of the Beach, you will find the Rip Tide Lounge. Complimentary coffee and a tea are offered during breakfast hours. Martha's Vineyard Lounge is the Beach's other lounge and is located adjacent to Ariel's. It offers an outstanding choice of spirits as well as an award-winning selection of wines. Martha's is a charming and quiet hideaway. Its soft lighting, wicker furnishings, and rose hues create an atmosphere that is intimate and romantic. In the evenings, wine tastings and a tempting selection of appetizers from Ariel's make Martha's a place not to be missed. We've even enjoyed a light dinner here.

At the Yacht, you'll find the Ale & Compass in the lobby. Varnished brightwork and polished brass are the decor here. Plush sofas and chairs invite you to sit awhile and sample the outstanding selection of imported ales and beers. Complimentary tea and coffee are offered each morning. It is a comfortable place to sit and to make plans for your day's adventure.

The Crew's Cup Lounge is next door to the Yachtsman Steakhouse. Offering a complete selection of beers, wines, and mixed drinks, the Crew's Cup features a clubhouse ambience. Comfortable booths, sofas, and plenty of varnished wood and polished brass make it charming and inviting. There's even a rowing shell overhead. With a varied offering of appetizers, finger foods, and sandwiches from the Yachtsman, this is a place to consider for lunch or a light evening meal.

Shops at the Yacht and the Beach

Each resort features its own shop. The Atlantic Wear and Wardrobe Emporium can be found at the Beach Club, and Fairings and Fittings is over at the Yacht. Both shops offer a large selection of sundries, character merchandise, and gifts. Each features its own line of logo resort wear and a unique line of men's and women's apparel. There's some very nice stuff at these shops, making them two of our favorite shopping places. Check out the sale racks.

Recreational Activities at the Yacht and the Beach

- Stormalong Bay pool complex ♥♥
- Five hot tubs/spas ♥♥♥
- Two quiet pools ♥
- Sand beach on the lake (no swimming) with cabanas
- Lafferty Place video arcade
- Fireworks cruises ♥♥♥
- Complimentary tennis courts (at the Beach Club)
- Jogging and walking paths (map available at the front desk)
- Ship Shape Health Club, state-of-the-art fitness center with sauna and spa
- Bayside Marina with a variety of rental boats
- Volleyball (ball at health club)
- Bocci ball and croquet court (at the Beach Club)

OUR IMPRESSIONS OF THE YACHT AND THE BEACH

- These are lovely, charming, and romantic resorts.
- With such convenience to Epcot and Disney–MGM and the excellent transportation, a stay at either resort will have you only minutes from anywhere.
- Dining is outstanding. To these choices add the convenience of the restaurants at Epcot, the Swan, Dolphin, and the BoardWalk, and you'll have to narrow your choices down from nearly 30 restaurants, all within walking distance.
- Our penchant for hot tubs is most certainly satisfied here. There are two lovely hot tubs near Stormalong Bay, one more at each of the quiet pools, and one in the health club.

RECOMMENDATIONS FOR RESERVATIONS

- Standard-view rooms on the ground floor of the Yacht and the Beach enjoy quiet garden areas. Parking lots are not very visible from them. This is not true for upper-floor standard-view rooms. Ground-floor standard rooms at the Beach are smoking rooms.
- The fifth floor at the Beach used to be concierge service. The rooms are a bit different and feature a few added amenities and upgraded fabrics.
- If you want real convenience to Epcot, ask for a room near the Beach's quiet pool.
- If you wish to be in one of the upper-floor rooms facing Epcot, ask for it when you reserve and again when you check in.
- Real versus tiny balconies at the Beach Club are hit or miss. On your reservation and at check-in, be sure to request a room with a real balcony.
- Some of the rooms can be a walk from the main elevators. If this is not to your liking, mention it at check-in.

ROMANCE AT THE YACHT AND THE BEACH

- Overall resort theming: ♥♥♥♥
- Room ambience: ♥♥♥
- Yacht Club concierge service: ♥♥♥♥
- The Commodore suite, with concierge service: ♥♥♥♥
- Stormalong Bay pool area: ♥♥
- Room-service breakfast in bed: ♥♥♥♥
- A "Wine Flight" at Martha's Vineyard: ♥♥♥
- Hot tubs at day's end or late night: ♥♥♥
- Taking a stroll over to France for espresso and dessert in Au Petit Cafe before IllumiNations:♥♥
- Taking a swim in Stormalong, then going to Beaches and Cream for a double-chocolate ice cream soda: ♥
- The *Breathless* IllumiNations Cruise for Two (see Chapter 7 for more information): ♥♥♥♥
- Watching IllumiNations from the beach: ♥♥♥

Disney's Caribbean Beach Resort

When we first arrived at the Caribbean Beach and were greeted by a valet dressed like a Nassau policeman, we knew that we were about to really

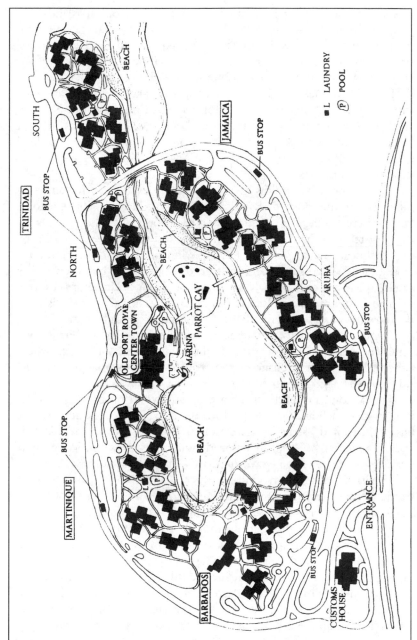

Disney's Caribbean Beach Resort

go somewhere. Having spent many months on tropical islands, we were able to appreciate the details of this costume. From the starched, white jacket and brass whistle to the braided epaulets and knee socks, here, we knew, was a bit of the authentic Caribbean. Once out of our car, the fragrances of jasmine and blossoming foliage embraced us.

Like all fantasies, this Disney creation will take a bit of willing participation. You will need to bring along a bit of imagination. Not too much though, because this fantasy is real enough. From check-in right to the door of your own little piece of this relaxing paradise, you will both be entering yet another of Walt Disney World's perfectly rendered themed resorts.

When you arrive, follow the signs for Guest Check-In, and you will arrive at the front door of the Customs House. The Customs House re-creates the lobby charm of an old-world island hotel. Trust us when we tell you that these places are few and far between even in the real Caribbean. Disney's knack for this kind of re-creation is uncanny. Ceiling fans, potted palms, and shuttered windows are but a few of the details typical not only of the Customs House but of the entire resort.

The Caribbean Beach Resort has been created as five small "island" villages with names that recall the exotic ports of call of the Caribe: Martinique, Aruba, Barbados, Jamaica, and Trinidad. Each offers its own white sand beach, pool, playground, and shaded courtyard. Everywhere is the lush and exotic foliage of the tropics: hibiscus, mango, jasmine, and palms. The scents of the islands are in the air.

The buildings of each village are distinctive in both color and design, to give each area a feeling of uniqueness. Two-story and stucco, these "tin-roofed" structures are rich with a taste of the tropical islands. The variety of brightly colored buildings and whimsical gingerbreads reminds us of some favorite down-island destinations.

The island villages surround Barefoot Bay, a 50-acre lake. Old Port Royale Center Towne, a Disneyesque version of a bustling West Indies village, is the resort's central hub. Colorful, gay and lively, this little "town" is home for the Caribbean's shops, restaurant, food court, water playground, and marina. Enjoy a soak in the hot tub or a dip in the pool, hop on a bike, rent a boat, or lounge around the Banana Cabana pool bar to the strains of Jimmy Buffet. It is a fun place to be.

In the middle of the lake is Parrot Cay, an island connected by foot bridges to the villages on one side of the lake and Old Port Royale Center Towne on the other. Narrow paths, live parrots, gazebos, a kiddie playground, and picnic area are all set against a lush backdrop of dense bamboo and a tropical garden. It is just the place for a quiet breakfast or a romantic evening stroll.

The colors, the foliage, and the ambience will relax you. Take your time to savor this place and your time here. The Caribbean Beach does exactly what the best of resorts anywhere do and what Disney resorts do better than anyone: it takes you above the everyday and transports you to that unforgettable place called "vacation."

Rooms at the Caribbean Beach

Our king bedroom was located in the island village of Aruba. Some resort rooms with king-size beds are located on the corners of the buildings. This gave our sitting area two windows, one on either wall, rather than the usual single window. With the curtains open and the sheer drapes drawn, the room was bright and airy.

While color schemes vary from one island village to another, the room furnishings are similar. Our room had pale sage walls, bordered at the ceiling by a strip of flowered wallpaper. Its deeper greens and hints of pinks matched the flowered bedspread. The posts of the wooden bedstead featured carved wooden pineapples, the symbols of hospitality.

A large armoire with television was opposite our bed. Next to it was placed the minibutler, stocked with soft drinks, beers, wines, and lots of snacks. One bonus was a coffeemaker, complete with a daily filter pouch of coffee. For us, having our first cup of coffee while still in our room (or bed) was heavenly.

The vanity area featured double sinks and a large mirror. Plenty of room for both of us to get ready for an evening out. The bathroom, a bit on the small side, had the usual shower-tub combination.

Overall, the room was pleasant and comfortable, and we enjoyed our time there. Everything seemed rather new and extremely well maintained, even though this resort is not one of Disney's newest. This, you will find, is the trademark of all Disney resorts.

There are two basic room configurations at the Caribbean Beach: rooms with king-size beds and rooms with twin double beds. All of the king bedrooms here at the Caribbean have connecting doors to adjoining rooms with two doubles. If you are visiting Walt Disney World with your children, this may be an enticing choice.

There are a small variety of views here. Water view rooms overlook either the lake or the pool. Since pool views seem to look onto the walls that surround the pools, we suggest that if you are looking for a water view you should opt for one of the lake; ask at check-in. Standard view rooms feature views of either the courtyard or the parking lots. When you check in, we suggest that you ask for (and be prepared to wait for) a courtyard view. Our courtyard view was quiet and beautiful, and it greatly enhanced our visit here.

1997 Room Rates for the Caribbean Beach

Accommodation	Regular Season	Value Season	Holiday Season
Standard view	$124	$114	$134
Water view	$139	$129	$149
King bed	$139	$129	$149

Transportation and Convenience

Service from this resort is quite good, with buses running at least every 20 minutes throughout the day and every 10 minutes during peak hours.

• To all Disney destinations: by bus

Dining at the Caribbean Beach

If there is a drawback to this resort, it is the limited dining options. At Old Port Royale Center Towne is a single table-service restaurant and a food court. The Captain's Tavern is open only for dinner, from 5 P.M. to 10 P.M. It is a small but quaint table-service restaurant and is moderately priced. For reviews and information about this and other restaurants, see Chapter 6.

The Old Port Royale food court is called Market Street, and it is a rather cute little avenue of food shops. Decorated with palms, colorful kites, and other Caribbean artifacts, these exotic storefronts come complete with balconies and "roofs." The effect is delightful. Counter-service shops have names such as Cinnamon Bay Bakery, Montego's Deli, and Bridgetown Broiler.

The seating here is more comfortable and private than most food courts, and with the choice of eating outside on a pleasant porch, we think that this place rates well for a Disney fast-food outlet. Open from 7 A.M. to midnight, Market Street serves a large variety of foods for each of the day's meals.

While the Caribbean Beach does not offer room service, it does offer the same delivery service available at most limited-amenities Disney resorts.

Shops at the Caribbean Beach

Several shops are located in Old Port Royale Center Towne. The Straw Market offers a selection of Caribbean Beach logo merchandise and a variety of tropical and "piratical" souvenirs and toys. Also found here is a nice collection of tropical sportswear, as well as a small selection of fruits and snacks and Jamaican Blue Mountain coffees.

Adjacent to the Straw Market is the Calypso Trading Post, where you will be able to purchase the usual variety of Disney character merchandise, postcards and stamps, books and newspapers, and a variety of snacks, souvenirs, and sundries such as sunblock and nonprescription medications.

Recreational Activities at the Caribbean Beach

Recreational activities are one of the Caribbean's strong suits. In addition to a themed main pool area are six more private pools. The central pool at Old Port Royale boasts a themed swimming area that includes a spa, water slide, and kiddie pool. The surroundings are an "old" Spanish fort, complete with turrets, cannons, and waterfalls. A short slide runs from the ramparts to the water. The pool is exactly the kind of thing that we love so much about Disney resorts: it resembles a movie set more than a hotel pool. The hot tub is, unfortunately, rather small. Although the Caribbean offers sparkling white sand beaches, no lake swimming is allowed. With chaise lounges, cabanas, and some nice hammocks, the beaches are attractive places to catch some sunlight or moonbeams.

The Caribbean also offers a selection of motorized and nonmotorized boats, bikes, and "surrey" pedal cars. A family length-of-stay recreational package is available for $105, providing unlimited use of bikes and boats. Considering that most motor boats are $20 for half an hour, this package is a great deal if you make use of it.

OUR IMPRESSIONS OF THE CARIBBEAN BEACH

- Guest Services is located far away in the Customs House, and dining options are minimal. This is more of a problem at breakfast time, when the food court is the only option.

- A car would be of some advantage here, especially for traveling to other resort areas to dine.

RECOMMENDATIONS FOR RESERVATIONS

- Barbados and Trinidad South are a bit far from the central resort area and should probably be avoided (or resort guests in these areas should be given complimentary bicycles). We prefer either Jamaica or Aruba. Both are a short walk from the central areas, and the walk takes you across Parrot Cay. We found this stroll pleasant and, in the evenings, even a bit romantic.

ROMANCE AT THE CARIBBEAN BEACH

- Resort theming: ♥♥
- Courtyard-view room: ♥♥
- King bed resort room: ♥♥
- Early picnic breakfast on Parrot Cay: ♥♥
- Late-night swim at a quiet pool: ♥♥
- Beach hammock by starlight: ♥♥♥♥
- Evening stroll around the resort: ♥♥

The Swan and the Dolphin

Here's a story we have heard about these two places. The Walt Disney Company had worked out a deal with the Sheraton and Westin Hotels to permit them to operate a dual hotel complex on Disney World property. John Tishman, representing both the owners and his construction company, had overseen the selection of the architectural plans. Before construction began, Michael Eisner came aboard as Disney CEO. Shown the plans, he was unimpressed.

"Come meet my architect," he was reported to have told Tishman. Eisner's architect was the world-renowned Michael Graves. What ensued was a competition to see whose design would win the most accolades. This contest resulted in the construction of what has been termed a masterpiece of "entertainment architecture." Whatever you may think about them, the Swan and the Dolphin are unlike any hotels that you have ever seen. While located in the very heart of Walt Disney World, neither is run by Team Disney. The Swan is a Westin resort, and the Dolphin is managed by Sheraton.

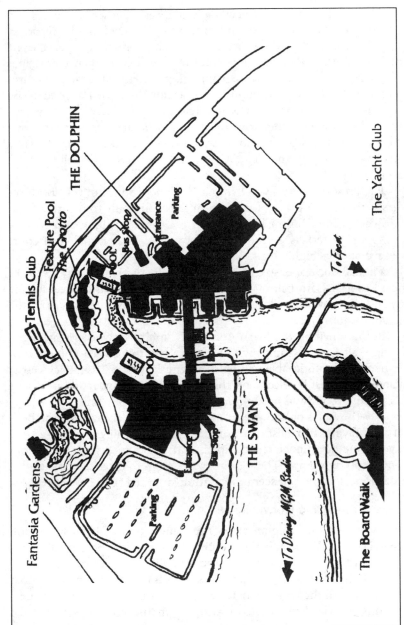

The Swan and the Dolphin

These two resorts sit perfectly aligned, set together like sisters and nestled neatly between Epcot and the Disney–MGM Studios. Separate, yet part of a greater whole, these two share something special. The coral and aquas of their exteriors and the perfect convergence of shapes tell us that there is a juncture happening. These fantastic structures were designed from the ground up to occupy each other's space, to be seen together and from each other. The theme of these resorts is fantasy and fun. Everything from the fifty-foot swans perched atop one resort to the nine-story cascading waterfall at the other serves to evoke a feeling of whimsy and delight. A visit here after dark will work its magic spell.

Each resort has its own Olympic "lap" pool with hot tub. Both resorts share a water playground that ranks second only to the Yacht and the Beach Clubs' Stormalong Bay. The Grotto is a long and narrow lake/pool. Waterfalls, secluded hot tubs, and a water volleyball court are several of its highlights.

Virtually no expense has been spared in the landscape design of these resorts. Date palms, magnolias, and other well-tended foliage abound. Driveways, walkways, and paths are all integral pieces in the big and beautiful picture.

Because neither the Swan nor the Dolphin is owned or managed by the Walt Disney Company, there are a few things that you will not get here. Most noticeable will be the Length of Stay Pass. Each resort maintains a Guest Services desk that offers the usual selection of tickets and passes. Your Swan or Dolphin resort card will be limited to charging at both resorts only. Aside from these, you will enjoy all of the benefits of staying at a Disney resort: Surprise Mornings, preferred tee times, same-day dinner reservations, and guaranteed park admission, to mention only a few. These two resorts seem to cater to conventions and businesspeople and seem more adult-oriented than Disney resorts.

Transportation and Convenience

The Swan and the Dolphin enjoy the same wonderful transportation that serves the Yacht and the Beach Clubs and the BoardWalk. This group of resorts is the most convenient of all Disney resort areas.

Both the nearby Epcot and Disney–MGM are reached by boat from a dock on the walkway between the resorts. All other Disney destinations are via direct buses, leaving from the bus stops near each front entrance.

The Swan

The Swan was the first Disney resort that we visited without our kids. We hadn't been to Disney World in more than 10 years when we arrived at the Swan. We'd never seen Epcot, and Disney–MGM Studios had just opened. We had no idea what to expect and were ready for just about anything. What we got was a few days of intimate and relaxing fun. We had a wonderful time strolling around and discovering the parks and we had an even more memorable time at this classy resort. We enjoyed hot tubs, swimming, and fine dining, all accented with occasional touches of Disney magic. We were hooked.

On this first trip, we slowed our car as we approached the Swan. We marveled at the elaborately complex landscaping and ornate cast-iron street lamps. Above and around us loomed a building the likes of which we had never seen. The huge, twin swans sitting on its roof were not even its most unusual details. The resort's paint job seemed more like a giant mural: huge, aqua waves broke on hues of coral. The balconies included ironwork so intricate that it appeared to have been carved.

So intriguing was this place that we felt more like exploring than registering. The tropical theme of the grounds and building were carried gracefully into the interiors. A fountain of swans and a flock of parrot chandeliers were but a few of the many delightful decorations. The furnishings featured carved swans, and even the sand in the ashtrays was imprinted with the seal of the swans. Hallways, windows, and porticos were all in symmetry. This confluence, we were to discover, was one of the essentials of Michael Graves' design.

Rooms at the Swan   Our first room at the Swan had two queen beds. It would take a few more visits before we would discover king-size sleeping accommodations. The room's bright array of tropical colors was cheerful and gay. Woodwork was lightly colored and trimmed in pastel aquas and pinks. Our balcony looked out onto a small lake and, across it, to an as yet unfinished Dolphin. A quick look around our room revealed a large armoire with a color television, a massage showerhead, and a basket of luxurious toiletries. In the closet were bathrobes with embroidered swans. The level of luxury, we knew at once, was something that we were going to get very used to.

Many of the resort rooms look out onto the Dolphin, which is a very attractive and impressive sight. From some upper-floor rooms, guests can get an impressive view of IllumiNations. Many more have views of Disney–MGM Studios, and others look out over the swimming areas. There really aren't any bad views here, simply better ones. Rooms are available with either a king-size bed or two queens. Not all rooms, however, have balconies. Value season at the Swan is considerably longer than it is at Disney resorts and includes summer.

1997 Room Rates for the Swan

Accommodation	Regular Season	Value Season
Standard view	$295	$265
Lake view	$340	$285
Resort view, no balcony	$360	$300
Resort view, balcony	$380	$315
Royal Beach Club (concierge)	$410	$385

Concierge Service and Suites at the Swan   Concierge service at the Swan is known as the Royal Beach Club and is located on the exclusive east end of the twelfth floor. A continental breakfast is served each morning, and beverages and fruit are offered at midday. Hors d'oeuvres and cocktails begin before dinner, and cordials and coffee are served in the evening. Alcoholic beverages are served at reduced prices. In all, you receive a day's worth of delights. The Swan's dedicated concierge staff is available to assist with all of your reservations and special needs. There is even a complimentary shoe shine service. All you have to do is ask.

There are five different suite designs at the Swan. Each has something unique to offer. The Junior suite is the most affordable. Each comes with a lavishly furnished bedroom, a king bed, desk, and sofa and chairs. The ample living room and dining area feature a round table and four cane-back chairs. Cloth robes, private bar, and live plants are a few of the indulgences.

The color scheme of these suites is that of the resort: aqua and rose. Fabrics are soft and plush. Each occupies the end unit of the Swan's wings. This corner position provides for many windows and an outstanding panorama. At $315 during value season and $380 during the regular season, the Junior suite has a lot going for it. A stay here will be indulgently romantic.

From this modest start, the suites become considerably more expensive. Beginning with the Grand suite at nearly $1,000 per night, followed by the Governor's suite at nearly $1,300, and reaching all the way to one of the two incredible Presidentials at around $2,000 nightly, these suites are well suited to those able to afford them. The two Presidential suites each feature a theme. One is the Oasis room, the other is the Southwestern room. With over 1,000 square feet, these multiroom suites each feature a marble entryway, grand piano, fully stocked bar, king-size bed, Jacuzzi tub, and full kitchen stocked with assorted beverages. Furnishings are lavishly extravagant. It is hard, even for us, to imagine traveling in this style.

Dining at the Swan   As we have mentioned, dining options at this resort are exceptional. With memorable eating places at the neighboring BoardWalk and the Yacht and the Beach Clubs as well as those at the nearby countries of Epcot, the choices begin to look limitless. And they are. For convenient, varied, and outstanding dining, this is the corner of Walt Disney World to be in.

The Swan offers its guests three interesting table-service eateries. The all-purpose restaurant is the Garden Grove, which serves every meal in a pleasant garden gazebo. At dinner, it becomes Gulliver's Grill, featuring seafood and steaks. Disney character breakfasts are served here on weekends, and a variety of dinnertime entertainment, including characters, is featured throughout the week.

Palio offers fine Italian dining in a romantic atmosphere. Featuring strolling musicians and outstanding food, Palio is one of our favorite dining spots at Disney. The Splash Grill and Deli is the Swan's convenience-food location. Located near the lap pool, this small restaurant features a variety of lunches, dinners, and snacks. Even more convenient is the Swan's 24-hour room service. Its large menu can furnish snacks, meals, beverages, or the makings for intimate in-room dining. For reviews and information about these and other restaurants, see Chapter 6.

Lounges at the Swan   Kimonos is a beautiful and stylishly created retreat that features an Oriental flair. Relax and watch the sushi chefs perform their graceful art. Kimonos is a romantic place to have some fine sushi, tempura, or a drink.

Cappuccino's is the lounge that accompanies Palio. Fine wines and cognacs are the specialties of the house. This is the place to go for gourmet coffee and the World's best pastries and desserts. The dessert counter at Cappuccino's is so good that it should be designated a deadly weapon.

The Lobby Court Lounge, besides offering a selection of wines and spirits, also offers the best cup of coffee in Disney World. Open in the morning and again in the evening, the Lobby Court Lounge also features a decadent assortment of pastries and chocolate desserts, more than enough to tempt the stalwart. This is a delightful place to sit in the evening and listen to the lounge's player piano.

Shops at the Swan Disney's Cabana is the Swan's souvenir and Disney character merchandise store. It also offers a large selection of casual men's and women's sportswear.

Services Available at the Swan

- Valet parking
- Full bell service
- Valet and laundry service
- Beauty salon
- Concierge desk
- Nightly turndown service
- Pay-per-view movies
- Refrigerators

Recreational Activities at the Swan

- Lap pool with spa, and the Grotto (a three-acre water playground)
- Kiddie pool
- White sand beach with watercraft rentals
- Swan Health Club
- Jogging and walking path
- Tennis club and basketball court
- Camp Swan and Camp Dolphin children's activity centers
- Video game room
- Fantasia Gardens miniature golf

RECOMMENDATIONS FOR RESERVATIONS

- Since this resort is managed by Westin Hotels, reservations are handled not only by Disney Central Reservations but also by Westin and the Swan. For reservations, call Swan reservations at (800) 248-7926; Westin reservations at (800) 228-3000; or Disney Central Reservations at (407) 934-7639. For brochures and information, write:

The Walt Disney World Swan
1500 Epcot Resorts Blvd.
Lake Buena Vista, FL 32830-2653

- Throughout the year, Westin Hotels runs a variety of specials and packages, including romance and honeymoon packages. Ask about them when you call. Summer specials are frequent.

ℛOMANCE AT THE SWAN

- Resort theming: ♥♥♥
- Room amenities: ♥♥♥
- Fine dining: ♥♥♥
- Breakfast on your balcony: ♥♥♥
- Dinner at Palio, listening to the music of a strolling violinist: ♥♥♥
- Hot tubs: ♥♥♥
- Evening walks to BoardWalk, Epcot countries, and the Yacht and the Beach Clubs: ♥♥
- Watching IllumiNations from your balcony: ♥♥♥
- Beach hammock, under the stars: ♥♥♥

The Dolphin

Water is the theme of this resort, and it is everywhere. From rows of fountains at the front gate to trickles that flow down the stone walls of the foyer, the pleasant sound of rushing water is music for Dolphin guests. One of the sights here is the waterfall on the Swan side of the resort. Overlooking Crescent Lake, this giant fountain cascades along nine stories of huge, shell-shaped levels and into a 60-foot-wide clamshell.

The scale of everything here is grand. The most prominent part of the resort's main building is the 27-story pyramid that has become a fixture of the Disney skyline. Nearby sit the two 56-foot dolphin statues that celebrate this resort's aquatic theme. Next to the Statue of Liberty, they are the tallest free-standing sculptures in the U.S. From their perch high atop the resort, they stand watch upon a colossal creation of tulip-shaped floral fountains that adorn the tower wings. At night, this array seems too large to be real.

Keeping to the color theme of the two resorts, the building's coral hues are swathed in painted, turquoise banana leaves. Reaching from ground level to the tenth floor, this outrageous mural took six months to complete. It creates a fantasy aura that is part of the Dolphin's mystique.

The lobby too is whimsical and entertaining. Brightly colored fabric hangs from its ten-story ceiling to create a cavernous tent. Flowering vines climb trellises that encircle the lobby floor, and, arranged symmetrically around the central fountain are clusters of sofas and chairs. You see artwork everywhere: murals, paintings, and sculptures; the works of Picasso, Matisse, and Rousseau. Even the elevator seems bright and tropical.

Rooms at the Dolphin   The rooms are bright and cheerful. A large and well-appointed vanity and a cozy sitting area will make you feel at home. From the floral drapes to the coral and turquoise bedspread, your romantic Disney vacation will take on the fun and tropical theme of the Dolphin. One look out the window and you know that you are in the middle of all of the magic that Disney has to offer.

The variety of resort rooms at the Dolphin come with a choice of either one king bed or two doubles. That is two doubles, not two queens. As with hotels everywhere, the more spectacular the view, the more spectacular the price. Our favorite room at the Dolphin is called the King View Premier. Located on the ends of the wings of the main building, these charming rooms look out in two directions with an unmatched view of the lake, the Swan, Epcot, and Disney's BoardWalk. Each has a king-size bed and twin balconies. A coffeemaker will make mornings a pleasure. At $380 during the brief peak season, this room enjoys many specials during the remainder of the year.

Value season at the Dolphin does not mimic Disney's. It is much longer and runs from early January to mid-February and again from mid-April to the end of the third week in December.

1997 Room Rates for the Dolphin

Accommodation	Regular Season	Value Season
Standard view	$295	$265
Lake view	$340	$285
Resort view, no balcony	$360	$300
Resort view, balcony	$380	$315
Club level (concierge)	$410	$385

Concierge Service and Suites at the Dolphin   The 77 spacious and lavishly decorated guest suites of concierge service are located in the Dolphin Tower. Private check-in will begin your journey here, and along the way you will learn the meaning of "pampered." As Tower guests, you will receive champagne and a complimentary gift upon arrival. You'll be treated to a host of luxurious toiletries, Dolphin bathrobes, hair dryer, special stationery, and coffeemaker.

The plush Tower Lounge is available exclusively for the use of Tower guests. This area features a large entertainment center, magazines and newspapers, and a small library. A continental breakfast will be the perfect way to start each day. If you desire, fresh coffee and orange juice can be delivered to your room. Hors d'oeuvres and cocktails service are offered before dinner. After dinner and before your romantic evening out, don't forget to stop by and have a dessert while you watch the fireworks. There is a charge for all concierge alcoholic beverages.

Complimentary use of both the Dolphin's health and fitness center and the tennis courts are also part of your romantic Dolphin Tower visit. A light pressing service is also available upon request. And, of course, the concierge staff eagerly awaits your every request.

The Dolphin boasts that it offers more suites than any other resort at Walt Disney World. While this may be true, many of them are better suited for business purposes. The two suites worth mentioning are the Junior suite and the Presidential.

The Junior suites are in various places throughout the resort. Each consists of a parlor connected to a regular resort room with either a single king bed or two doubles. The parlor offers a sitting area with a pull-out sofa bed and several comfortable chairs.

While you might not feel the need for an extra room, you might find it a good place for the kids if they are with you. During the brief peak season, a Junior suite will cost around $610 per night. Most of the year, the same suite is $525.

There are four Presidential suites at the Dolphin. Each has been extravagantly decorated with its own exotic personality. At nearly 3,000 square feet, these suites are larger than many private homes. Named Los Presidentes, the Pharaoh's suite, the Emperor's suite, and Caesar's suite, each is the final word in luxury. Service even includes a round-the-clock butler. These two-bedroom suites offer a large entertainment center, gold-plated bathroom fixtures, ten telephones, four VCRs, and a fully stocked kitchen. Some of the famous persons who have occupied these rooms are Dustin Hoffman, Macauley Culkin, Eddie Murphy, Dolly Parton, and Michael Jackson. This suite costs $2,500 nightly.

Dining at the Dolphin   As guests of the Dolphin, you will enjoy a large variety of eateries. Five table-service restaurants provide everything, from the poolside Cabana Bar and Grill to the seafood and steaks of exotic Harry's Safari Bar and Grill. The Coral Cafe is the Dolphin's all-purpose restaurant and features a mix of buffets and a la carte offerings throughout the day. The Dolphin Fountain is a 1950s-style soda shop with a menu of American classics, while Juan and Only's offers Mexican cuisine. A replacement for the now-closed Sum Chow's is expected some time in 1997. For more details and reviews of these restaurants, see Chapter 6.

The Dolphin offers the option for fast food too. Tubby Checkers Buffeteria is a cute little cafeteria that offers a pretty standard selection of convenience foods. Snacks, breakfasts, lunches, and dinners are the offerings, and there is even a small convenience store that offers a variety of sundries.

Room service at the Dolphin should not be overlooked as a dining option. The menu is large. We love having our dinner served to us on a white tablecloth right in the privacy of our own room. We suggest that you give it a try. Also available for delivery are Chinese food and pizza. To order breakfast the night before, turn your television set to Channel 88 and follow on-screen directions. A Japanese-style breakfast is also available.

Lounges at the Dolphin   When it comes to nightlife, only Pleasure Island and the BoardWalk have more to offer than the Dolphin. The Copa Banana is the Dolphin's nightclub. Dance the night away to the rhythm of the islands and enjoy a fruitful selection of tropical drinks. Harry's Safari Bar and Juan's Bar and Jail are two other exotic lounges to visit. Both offer a large selection of wines, beers, and cocktails. Have a yard of ale at Harry's or sip a rare tequila at Juan's while you listen to live flamenco guitar. Both are fun and colorful places and well worth your time.

You shouldn't have any trouble finding the Lobby Lounge. Drop by this quiet bistro for a glass of wine or aperitif while you enjoy the music of a live pianist. And at poolside, you can enjoy beer, wine, or tropical cocktails at the Cabana Bar and Grill.

Shops at the Dolphin   There are four shops in the lobby of the Dolphin. From gourmet chocolates to jewelry and fine apparel, these shops should provide some interesting browsing and even something special to celebrate your visit here.

Services Available at the Dolphin

- Valet parking
- Full bell service
- Beauty salon
- Multilingual concierge
- In-room massage
- Valet and laundry service
- Pay-per-view movies

Recreational Activities at the Dolphin

- Heated pool, and the Grotto (a three-acre water playground)
- Kiddie pool
- White sand beach with watercraft rentals
- Body by Jake Health Club
- Jogging and walking path
- Tennis club and basketball court
- Camp Dolphin and Camp Swan children's activity centers
- Video game room
- Fantasia Gardens miniature golf

RECOMMENDATIONS FOR RESERVATIONS

- For brochures and other printed information, write:

  The Walt Disney World Dolphin
  1500 Epcot Resorts Blvd.
  Lake Buena Vista, FL 32830-2653

- For reservations, call Sheraton Central Reservations at (800) 325-3535; Dolphin Reservations at (800) 227-1500; Disney Central Reservations at (407) 934-7639.
- The Sheraton offers many discounts and vacation packages throughout the year.
- Being a member of the Sheraton Club will give you such perks as late check-out and free room upgrade. It may be worth joining. Call the Sheraton reservation number for details.

ROMANCE AT THE DOLPHIN

- Resort theming: ♥♥♥
- Room amenities: ♥♥

- Premier King View room: ♥♥♥
- Breakfast in bed: ♥♥♥♥
- Hot tubs: ♥♥♥
- Evening walks to BoardWalk, Epcot countries, the Yacht and the Beach Clubs: ♥♥
- IllumiNations from your balcony: ♥♥♥

Disney's BoardWalk

There are a lot of things we love about the BoardWalk: the turn-of-the-century Americana, the Victorian elegance, and the seaside ambience are but a few. These themes are some of our favorites, and they come together here in a way that is magical, exciting, and romantic. Directly across Crescent Lake from the Yacht and the Beach Clubs, the BoardWalk is the perfect creation to cohabit this small corner of Walt Disney World. It is a first for Team Disney: an area that features lodgings, shops, nightclubs, and restaurants, all fused into one perfectly themed and splendidly exciting destination. It has almost instantly become Disney's destination of choice for visitors.

The BoardWalk features two very different resorts connected by a bustling, barrel-vaulted Victorian lobby. The entrance recaptures a bygone American era. This is the 1930s Atlantic seaside, and here you'll be transported to that age when Americans vacationed on the shore amidst the splendor of sprawling resorts and the excitement of oceanside promenades. Such names as Coney Island, Atlantic Beach, and Luna Park evoke the memories of these grand summer excursions.

The lobby's centerpiece is a magnificent miniature carousel, 70 years old and perfect in every minute detail. Overhead, the indescribable "electrolier" chandelier weaves its magical spell of wonder and delight. Overstuffed sofas, large potted palms, fan-back wicker chairs, and the old photographs and curious relics of this period's long-vanished amusement parks create a powerful sense of nostalgia. Disney's knack for this kind of re-creation remains unmatched.

The BoardWalk Inn and the BoardWalk Villas are this area's two resorts. The Inn is Disney's smallest and most intimate. With only 378 rooms, this romantic, Victorian-style resort features well-appointed rooms, awning-covered balconies, private courtyards, and a host of unforgettable "seaside" and garden views. Explore the Inn's hallways to discover cozy sitting areas and fascinating artifacts from the amusement

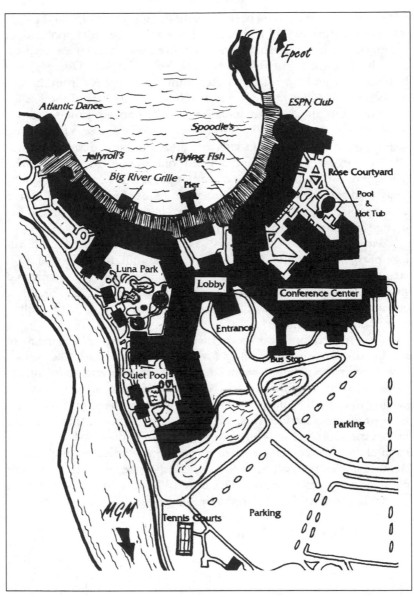

BoardWalk

parks of this era. Everything has a tale, and we urge you to spend the time learning the story behind this place. The Inn has one quiet pool and an accompanying hot tub/spa, both set in a lovely and peaceful garden area.

The 532 rooms of the BoardWalk Villas fall into Disney's new home away from home category. Accommodations range from the single-bedroom studios to the luxurious Grand Villas. Part of the Disney Vacation Club, these accommodations will be both for time-share sale and for rental. All of the Villa's lodgings feature some sort of cooking facility; most offer both full kitchens and laundries. A stay here will allow you to eat "at home" and dine out only as often as you wish. The Villas have two pool areas: one is a quiet pool with a community clubhouse and another more resembles an amusement park. Luna Park is a exciting place, featuring a roller coaster–like water slide, a carousel lounge and eatery, and a carnival-like children's play area.

More than a resort, the BoardWalk's charm is that of a seaside village of the mid-Atlantic. Its grounds are beautiful, hospitable, and relaxing. Mowed lawns, picket fences, beguiling gardens, and manicured shrubbery carefully accentuate its varieties of architecture. The effect enhances the sensation that this place evolved over time, that it truly *is* a small coastal town.

Once settled into your room, the excitement begins. The magic of the BoardWalk comes alive after dark. Its lively Promenade features a world that you have only imagined. You see shops, restaurants, nightclubs, sidewalk vendors and entertainers, and boats arriving and departing from the Promenade Pier. There are magicians, games of skill, fire-eaters, and portrait artists. Everywhere is the magic that you have been expecting, and it is all right outside your door. Walk hand-in-hand along the Promenade, then enjoy a quick snack or fine dining. Rent a bicycle "surrey," stroll to Epcot, dance the night away, or simply sit and enjoy the nightlife. The BoardWalk is right in the middle of everything, and we are certain that it will become *the* place to stay.

Rooms at the BoardWalk Inn

This is one of Disney's deluxe resorts, and a stay here means that you'll be immersed in both the luxury and magic of Disney. The Inn is a showpiece of Victorian charm, featuring an eclectic blend of elegant furnishings styled to create the ambience of a bed and breakfast. Iron and brass bedsteads, antique photographs of old seaside resorts, vintage furniture, and papered wainscoting all evoke an enchanting sense of the past. Accommodations at the Inn feature either twin queen beds or a single king. Standard rooms are large (390 square feet), and most feature child-size daybeds. Marble baths are roomy, and spacious vanities feature large mirrors and dual sinks. Draperies have been created using the images of actual postcards of this period. The Inn's rooms feature the colors of blue and white, with bedspreads of botanical specimens accented with floral greens and pastels.

All rooms at the Inn have balconies; those with standard views overlook the front of the resort and its reception area. From the water view rooms, you'll be right on the Promenade, enjoying all the charm and romance of the BoardWalk. Lodgings here are surprisingly quiet when the balcony doors are closed. The Inn's garden view rooms are adjacent to the lovely Rose Courtyard, one of the most unique and quiet places at Walt Disney World. Here, among flower-covered trellises and picket-fenced gardens, in the shadow of Epcot's Eiffel Tower, your Disney romance will come to life. Sit a while amidst this garden splendor or take a dip in the quiet pool. The Rose Courtyard only *seems* a world away from the excitement of the nearby Promenade.

1997 Room Rates for the BoardWalk Inn

Accommodation	Regular Season	Value Season	Holiday Season
Standard view	$244	$229	$259
Garden view	$280	$260	$295
Water view	$315	$295	$330
Concierge	$410	$390	$425
Concierge Deluxe	$460	$440	$475
Garden suites	$595	$595	$615

Concierge Service and Suites at the BoardWalk Inn

Known as the Innkeeper's Club, the Inn's concierge service is small and sublime. From our own blissful experience here, we know you'll relish the plush bathrobes, the luxurious lounge, and the highly personal service. A continental breakfast with coffees, teas, and a variety of pastries, bagels, fruit, and cereals will be the perfect beginning to each morning. Available throughout the day are a variety of beverages and snacks, ready for your nibbling. After 3 P.M., enjoy tea, sandwiches, and pastries. Late-afternoon snacks include wine, cheese, and an appetizer from one of BoardWalk's fine restaurants. The friendly and helpful concierge staff will be most pleased to make all your arrangements. After dinner, you'll want to return to the lounge's balcony to sip cordials, nibble desserts, and enjoy IllumiNations. This is romantic Disney at its finest.

Standard concierge rooms differ only slightly from the Inn's regular accommodations. The Innkeeper's Club offers only three king beds among its standard rooms. The remainder have two queen beds. Concierge Deluxe rooms feature two queen beds and a large sitting area with a pull-out queen. Junior suites, at around $560 nightly, each have a king master bedroom and Jacuzzi tub with adjacent parlor room featuring a plush sitting area, pull-out queen, and second bath.

The Inn's presidential suite is called the "Steeplechase," and it is the most elaborate and grandest on the property. Extravagant furnishings, a Promenade view, and its incredible size combine to make this suite of rooms ($1,135 per night) something unique even among presidentials. Canopied king bed, giant Jacuzzi tub, and a full patio with potted palms are but a few of its many memorable features. The Sonora, at $930 nightly, is the vice-presidential suite, and though scaled back a little, it is nearly as stunning.

The Inn's Garden suites are some of the most unique on-property accommodations. Perfect for any honeymoon or romantic getaway, each features a private entrance through the gate of its own unique rose garden. Complete with birdhouse, mailbox, arbor, and picket fence, each suite is the quintessential love nest. Just a bit secluded, all 14 Garden suites offer downstairs sitting areas and upstairs king bedrooms with couple-sized Jacuzzi baths. Furnishings are typically luxurious and follow color schemes similar to standard rooms.

Except for several of the Concierge Deluxe rooms on the third floor and the Garden suites, which are in the Rose Courtyard, all suites and concierge rooms are located in the fourth floor's exclusive Club area. All Garden suites and Concierge Deluxe rooms, regardless of location, include concierge access.

Rooms at the BoardWalk Villas

The sunny seaside cottage accommodations of the Villas come in a variety of shapes and sizes, each with a roomy balcony. These bright and colorful lodgings all offer a simple decor of casual comfort. Floral prints, brass fixtures, and gleaming white woodwork reminisce the family vacation house at the beach. Ceiling fans, large tiled baths, and cozy creature comforts will have you feeling right at home.

The studio features a single king bed and a queen sleeper/sofa. A small wet bar provides refrigerator, microwave oven, and coffeemaker.

Request a toaster from housekeeping, if you like. Some studios also offer a child-size day bed, providing enough sleeping space for four adults and one child.

The other accommodations are known as vacation villas. The Grand Villa is a luxurious, three-bedroom apartment. It includes two baths, a living area with sleeper/sofa, dining room, complete kitchen, master bedroom with a four-poster king, and a large Jacuzzi tub.

The spacious one-bedroom villa is one of our favorite accommodations at Disney. It is the perfect place for a small family, a romantic escape, or both. These villas each feature the complete villa kitchen with dishwasher, toaster, blender, range, refrigerator, and enough equipment to cook just about any meal you might desire. The living area features an entertainment center with VCR and TV as well as several chairs and a pull-out queen sleeper. Let's not leave out the breakfast bar, dining area, washer and dryer, or the rest of this splendid place. The master bedroom's king bed adjoins the tiled bath and its Jacuzzi tub. This villa's comfortable 720 square feet and its location at the BoardWalk make it one of the World's most attractive accommodations.

The two-bedroom villa is simply a one-bedroom villa with a connected studio added on. As you might imagine, the BoardWalk Villas can provide an outstanding alternative to getting several rooms (for couples traveling with children) or a kitchen (for those wishing to prepare some of the day's meals).

There is the usual assortment of views here at the Villas. The standard view overlooks the front of the resort and parking areas; preferred views can be either overlooking the BoardWalk or one of the pool areas.

1997 Room Rates for the BoardWalk Villas

Accommodation	Regular Season	Value Season	Holiday Season
Studio			
Standard view	$244	$229	$259
Preferred view	$280	$260	$295
One-bedroom Villa			
Standard view	$315	$295	$330
Preferred view	$360	$340	$375
Two-bedroom Villa			
Standard view	$415	$395	$430
Preferred view	$465	$445	$480
Grand Villa	$995	$985	$1045

Transportation and Convenience

Located in our favorite corner of Walt Disney World, the BoardWalk shares the same transportation system as the Yacht and the Beach Clubs and the Swan and the Dolphin. Whether by foot, bus, or boat, you'll feel next door to every Disney destination. From the Promenade Pier, *Friendship* launches sail regularly for the brief and relaxing voyage to either the studios, the other resorts around the lake, or Epcot. Rather walk? Epcot's International Gateway is a short and pleasant stroll away. Direct buses depart frequently for all other Disney destinations. However or wherever you are headed, we think that you'll find transportation at the BoardWalk about as easy as it gets.

- To Disney-MGM Studios: short boat trip from the Promenade Pier
- To Epcot: short walk or boat from Promenade Pier
- To Magic Kingdom, Downtown Disney, Typhoon Lagoon, Blizzard Beach: direct bus
- To Discovery Island, River Country: bus to Magic Kingdom, then boat

Dining at the BoardWalk

Dining choices here at the BoardWalk are so good that you might not care to venture elsewhere for a meal. But if you do, be ready to make a decision, because there are more than 20 good restaurants within walking distance.

At the BoardWalk, try the fine dining and imaginative cuisine of the Flying Fish restaurant. This is one of the World's hottest places for a great meal and one not to miss. Spoodle's and its "cuisine of the sun" is another outstanding BoardWalk eatery. Featured here is an outstanding breakfast menu and Mediterranean tapas and wood-fired pizzas for both lunch and dinner. There's more, too: try the super sandwiches, pastas, and salads at ESPN Club or the Big River Grille and Brewing Works' pleasing selection of pub pies, salads, gourmet burgers, and five handcrafted beers. For more detailed information and reviews of these and other Disney eateries, see Chapter 6.

The BoardWalk also offers 24-hour room service, delivering food from its variety of restaurants. If you don't see what you feel like eating on the menu, ask for it. Room service also features a sumptuous assortment of themed "amenities baskets" such as might be left in your room while you are out. Just a few of these treats include a chef's special chocolate turndown, elaborate welcome baskets, and cookies and milk.

The BoardWalk Promenade also features an interesting and often amusing selection of treats more suited to a nibble, a quick lunch, or snack. The BoardWalk Bakery will tempt you with muffins, bagels, croissants, and a luscious offering of pastries. The Bakery also manages a selection of juices, coffee, milk, espresso, and cappuccino. Seashore Sweets is the Promenade's old-fashioned sweet shop. Saltwater taffy, hand-dipped gelato, and a selection of beverages and coffees make this a place to check out. Spoodle's sidewalk cafe even has an "express" breakfast window, which becomes a pizza cafe after 5 P.M.

In the evening, along the Promenade are a host of vendors and carts offering an entertaining variety of treats: popcorn, hot dogs, shaved ice, crepes-on-a-stick, and fresh fruits and juices. There's even a coffee cart with a variety of excellent specialty coffees and pastries.

Lounges and Nightlife at the BoardWalk

Besides the entertainment district of the Promenade, the BoardWalk is home to two lounges. The BelleVue Room is the Inn's 1930s-style sitting room. Drop in here to enjoy a dessert sampler, a glass of wine, or the full-service bar. Cozy and quiet, it is open from 11 A.M. to midnight, with the nostalgic music and radio shows of the 1930s. Leaping Horse Libations is the pool lounge at the Villas. Looking more like a carousel, the Leaping Horse offers an assortment of sandwiches and alcoholic or nonalcoholic specialty drinks.

Entertainment at the BoardWalk

The Promenade is one of Disney's newest entertainment areas, and there's so much happening here that we'll simply mention a few of the highlights and tell you more in Chapter 5. The Atlantic Dance offers big-band dancing, appetizers, and a full-service bar. The ballroom's 10-piece orchestra will keep you in the "swing" of things from 8 P.M. to the wee hours. Jellyroll's is definitely not a bakery. Drop in on this nightclub to enjoy the zany antics of the dueling pianos; sing, dance, clap, and have a drink and a good laugh. Jelly's is open from 7 P.M. to 2 A.M. ESPN Club is another BoardWalk hot spot, and we admit to being a bit puzzled where to put this in our guide: with a restaurant, full-service bar, and a video sports center, it almost transcends categories. Look for ESPN in both Chapters 5 and 6.

There's lots more happening along the Promenade: a small amusement arcade, a fire-eater, juggler, magician, portrait artists, and a host of other period entertainment. It's *the* fun place to be and one you'll not want to miss wherever you are staying at Walt Disney World.

Shops at the BoardWalk

Adjacent to the lobby is Dundy's Sundries, the place for BoardWalk logo merchandise and the usual variety of film, souvenirs, and gifts. Looking to take home a soap dish like the one in your room? Find it here. The Promenade's Screen Door General Store is just the place for drinks, snacks, and beverages. Looking for a little something to fix in your Villa kitchen? Check out the modest grocery section here. Thimbles and Threads is the BoardWalk's source for character merchandise, swimwear, and resort apparel.

For the serious collector and interested browser alike, Wyland Gallery displays and sells a truly amazing collection of stunning marine artwork. Both sculptures and murals here are not to be missed.

Recreational Activities at the BoardWalk

- Luna Park swimming area with the 250-foot-long Keister Koaster water slide and large pool
- Two quiet pools
- Three hot tub spas, one at each pool area
- Muscles and Bustles Health and Fitness Center
- Children's playground at Luna Park
- Lil' Toots Harbor Club, evening and daytime children's activity center
- Bicycle rentals at the Villas Community Hall
- Surrey rentals on the BoardWalk Promenade (four-wheeled pedal cars for two, four, or six persons)
- The BoardWalk Rolling Basket Tour
- Two lighted tennis courts (equipment and lessons available)
- Rentals at Villas Community Hall: video movies, bikes, pool floats
- Fantasia Gardens miniature golf (see Chapter 7 for details)
- BoardWalk two-hour guided bass fishing excursion (see Chapter 7)
- BoardWalk fireworks cruise
- Sideshow Games video arcade

OUR IMPRESSIONS OF THE BOARDWALK

- The Inn is luxurious and romantic—a first-class establishment in every way
- The Villas offer unique and comfortably homelike accommodations. The one-bedroom villa is a real gem.
- Overall, this resort is really something special: beautifully themed, romantic, and exciting. There is so much to do here that you could keep busy without ever visiting a single theme park. One of Disney's premier destinations.

RECOMMENDATIONS FOR RESERVATIONS

- At the Inn, go for either water or garden views. The garden view is the most romantic.
- For couples with children, try a one-bedroom villa or a Junior suite.
- Try a one-bedroom villa to save money on meals. Look for off-season specials.
- If you want a room with a Jacuzzi: go for a one-bedroom villa, Junior suite, Garden suite, Steeplechase, or Sonora

ROMANCE AT THE BOARDWALK

- Overall theming: ♥♥♥♥
- King bed at the Inn: ♥♥♥
- A stay at the Innkeeper's Club: ♥♥♥♥
- A Garden suite: ♥♥♥♥
- Dinner at the Flying Fish: ♥♥♥
- Rent a surrey for two and ride around the lake: ♥♥♥
- A night of dancing at the Atlantic Dance: ♥♥♥♥
- A nightcap and radio show at the BelleVue Room: ♥♥♥
- A late night swim at the quiet pool or hot tub: ♥♥♥
- A drink and appetizer on the outside patio of the Atlantic Ballroom: ♥♥♥
- Breakfast in bed: ♥♥♥♥
- IllumiNations from the second-floor outside balcony of the Atlantic Dance: ♥♥
- If you're on your honeymoon, be sure to mention it on your reservation

The Village Resorts

Port Orleans and Dixie Landings

It's not the mighty Mississippi, but it's a river and it's known as the Sassagoula. It wends its way from Lake Buena Vista through the Disney Village Resort area. If you hop a boat at the Village Marketplace and head upstream past the grand old paddle wheeler Empress Lilly and past the Disney Institute, you might just imagine yourself on the Ol' Mississippi. Upriver, you'll make harbor at Disney's Port Orleans resort. This quaint and colorful little city, with its narrow, cobbled streets, gas lights, and relaxed French Quarter ambience, will make you feel as though you've gone back in time to walk the streets of old New Orleans.

Further up the Sassagoula, you'll enter Magnolia Bend, part of Disney's Dixie Landings resort. The banks of the river here are lined with stately magnolias and graceful willows. Here and there, an occasional footbridge crosses the waterway, leading off to the grand "old mansions" of the resort.

A bit farther upstream, the boat will bring you to Alligator Bayou. Now you've entered the back river country and another part of Dixie Landings. Here, the resort more reflects the rural charm of the bayou. The rustic resort buildings are nestled amidst a dense forest of slash pines. Shaded footpaths crisscross in all directions past small ponds and along tiny streams. At night, the crickets "sing" in the bushes, compliments of the Disney imagineers.

This is what you'll find along Disney's Sassagoula River: three delightfully different areas that together are the Port Orleans and Dixie Landings resorts. While they combine for over 3,000 rooms, the feeling here is anything but that of hustle and bustle. Along the banks of the Sassagoula, you will enjoy a sense of privacy and harmony.

We have grouped Port Orleans and Dixie Landings together not because they are so alike but because, together, they make up this Disney picture of "life on the river." What they have in common is that they are both moderately priced and beautifully themed resorts.

Port Orleans

This lovely resort evokes the ambience of the old French Quarter. The delight begins the moment you pass through the iron gates and into the

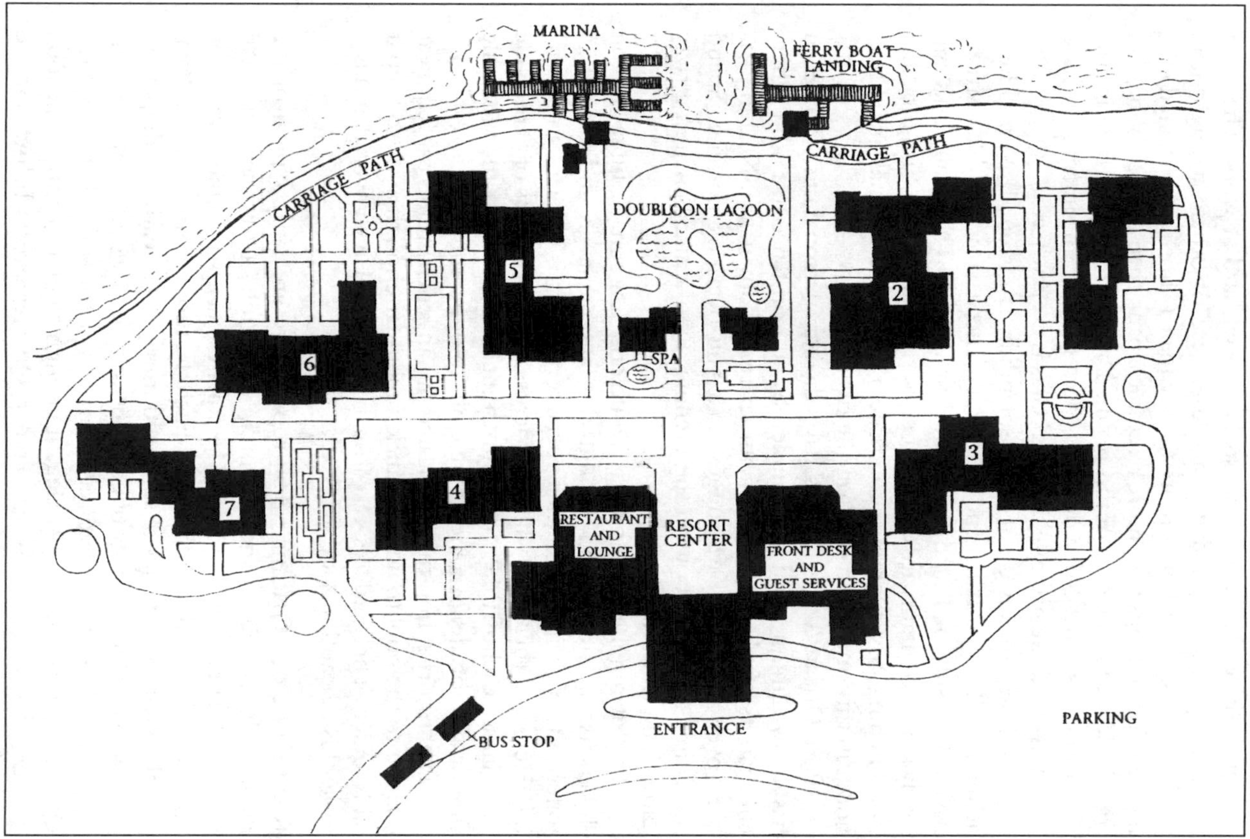

MARINA

FERRY BOAT LANDING

CARRIAGE PATH

CARRIAGE PATH

DOUBLOON LAGOON

SPA

1

2

3

5

6

7

4

RESORT CENTER

RESTAURANT AND LOUNGE

FRONT DESK AND GUEST SERVICES

ENTRANCE

BUS STOP

PARKING

Port Orleans

tree-lined drive. The Disney artists have been hard at work. The main building is the Mint, and it is a masterpiece of ornate wrought-iron work and glass. Check-in is more fantasy than a chore. The vaulted ceilings and iron railings here more resemble a bank than a hotel lobby, and friendly service is the coin of this realm. The hotel staff is attired in perfect period costume. Not a detail has been missed. The imagineers have been busy, and the promise of Mardi Gras is everywhere.

The Port Orleans grounds are splendidly landscaped. A stroll here at night will be relaxing and romantic. The narrow, cobbled streets have names such as Rue d'Blues and Rue d'Baga. The small parks and lovely stone fountains are enchanting. Narrow sidewalks, gaslights, and iron hitching posts combine to create a real sense of small neighborhoods in this small "old city" on the river.

Port Orleans's row houses have distinct personalities, too. Each has its own unique yard, surrounded by an iron fence just a bit different than its neighbor's. The quaint charm is convincing. Nothing has been overlooked, and we suggest that you overlook nothing. Spend some time strolling about in the evening. Find a nice bench in a cozy garden and sit awhile.

The swimming pool here is Doubloon Lagoon. A huge dragon slithers its way around and through this fantasy playground, forming a water slide with its long and slippery tongue. It is colorful and exciting. Here and there you will come across colorful statues of "crocodile musicians," each with a musical instrument. Don't miss the crocodile shower at poolside for a memorable photo opportunity.

The resort's hot tub is located in an enchanting garden near enough to the pool to invite a quick dip but far enough away to keep it fairly quiet. The garden's cast-iron benches and ivy-covered trellises make this a beautiful spot after dark.

Rooms at Port Orleans   The rooms here are fairly typical of the moderately priced Disney resorts. Although a bit smaller than Disney's luxury resort rooms (314 square feet), we found ours to be both spacious and comfortable. Each features a small vanity area, complete with two pedestal sinks and mirrors. Beneath the drapes are genuine wooden Venetian blinds. The antiqued wood furniture, ceiling fan, and formal armoire enhance a sense of the old French Quarter. Our room was just elegant enough to be romantic. One look out the window and onto the French Quarter streets below, and we knew that we were someplace special.

Most of the rooms at Port Orleans have two double beds, but there are also 62 king bedrooms. These rooms are a bit more expensive, but we always find a double bed to be rather small. King bedrooms here at Port Orleans are all corner rooms, making for a slightly larger sitting area.

1997 Room Rates for Port Orleans

Accommodation	Regular Season	Value Season	Holiday Season
Standard view	$124	$114	$134
Water view	$139	$129	$149
King bed	$139	$129	$149

Transportation and Convenience   Port Orleans is fairly convenient to the rest of the World. There is one large bus stop in front of the resort. Buses run every 20 minutes and even more frequently during the busier hours.

A boat service runs to Pleasure Island and the Village Marketplace. The small launches are fun and will take you through parts of Walt Disney World that you would never have a chance to see otherwise. Don't miss this trip.

- To Village Marketplace, Pleasure Island: by boat or bus
- To Magic Kingdom, Epcot, Disney–MGM Studios, Typhoon Lagoon, Blizzard Beach: by bus

Dining at Port Orleans   There is one table-service restaurant at Port Orleans, Bonfamille's Cafe, and a Mardi Gras–themed food court called the Sassagoula Floatworks and Food Factory. Bonfamille's is a delightful garden courtyard restaurant that serves both breakfast and dinner. The cuisines here are American and Creole. For more information and our review of Bonfamille's, see Chapter 6.

The Sassagoula Floatworks is a warehouse full of Mardi Gras props. Giant masks and colorful floats are suspended from the ceiling. Food-wise, the choices are many with a definite New Orleans flair. The variety of "shops" offer everything from scrambled eggs and muffins to burgers and Creole chicken with red beans. There's even fresh pasta and pizza. Don't miss the traditional French Quarter treat, beignets, at the bakeshop.

While Floatworks seats 300, the resort has over one thousand rooms. Of course, this means that if you eat at the more traditional times, you're likely to find it crowded. If the two of you are like us, you may not like to spend mealtimes in such an atmosphere. An alternative is to take your trays into one of the pleasant outside sitting areas or out by the pool.

Another meal alternative is Sassagoula Pizza Express, which delivers pizza, salads, beverages, and desserts from 4 P.M. to midnight.

Lounges at Port Orleans   Scat Cat's is a delightful little lounge adjoining the lobby. It has a full bar and, in the evening, frequently features live entertainment. Hors d'oeuvres are available from the kitchen of Bonfamille's. Mardi Grogs is the poolside bar, serving a variety of nonalcoholic and specialty cocktails during pool hours. Also on the menu are snacks and deli sandwiches.

Shops at Port Orleans   Jackson Square Gifts and Desires offers the usual selection of Disney character merchandise as well as a line of clothes and accessories with the Port Orleans logo. This shop also has a variety of general store items as well as offering authentic Creole condiments and New Orleans chicory coffees.

Recreational Activities at Port Orleans

- Doubloon Lagoon, a themed swimming pool with water slide
- Hot tub (spa)
- Boat and bike rentals
- Walking or jogging paths
- Video arcade

OUR IMPRESSIONS OF PORT ORLEANS

- Of the moderately priced resorts, we think that Port Orleans is the most romantic. After dark, it is simply enchanting.
- The boat service to Pleasure Island and the Village Marketplace is delightful. It turned our routine trip into an adventure. It is especially pleasant around sunset.
- If you are heading over to Dixie Landings, whether to look around or to have a meal, you'll find that it is a short walk away via a delightful footpath that runs along the river.

RECOMMENDATIONS FOR RESERVATIONS

- If you can, avoid the standard parking lot view. The beautiful part of this resort is inside the courtyard.

- Pool-view rooms are convenient for swimming, but you may find that you have sacrificed peace and quiet.

ROMANCE AT PORT ORLEANS RESORT

- Overall theme: ♥♥♥
- Room with king bed: ♥♥
- Doubloon Lagoon: ♥♥
- Bonfamille's Cafe: ♥♥
- Taking food from food court to the outside area: ♥
- Taking a nice, long hot tub at day's end: ♥♥♥
- Taking an evening stroll to Dixie Landings: ♥♥♥
- Taking a late-night swim: ♥♥
- Enjoying a sunset cruise to Pleasure Island and the Village Marketplace: ♥♥
- Renting a boat or bicycles and exploring: ♥♥

Dixie Landings

With a bit of the old Disney magic, Dixie Landings manages to be two very different resorts in one. The Magnolia Bend area of Dixie Landings reminisces the plantations of the Old South. Stately courtyards, charming fountains, and formal gardens re-create the sweeping grandeur of the antebellum South. Resort rooms here are in large mansion-like buildings with winding stairways and imposing columns. The weeping willows and sloping lawns of Magnolia Bend give way to dense thickets of pine and Florida maple at Alligator Bayou. Here, the "weathered" resort buildings are quaint and small. Their tin roofs peek through the treetops. Footpaths seem narrow and winding and the charm is more rustic and homey.

While Dixie Landings has over 2,000 rooms, the resort is so spread out that it does not feel so large. Still, a visit to the central building, the Sassagoula Steamboat Company, will serve to remind you that this is indeed a big place. During the busier times of day, there is a lot of traffic here.

The Steamboat Company re-creates a small port on the river with docks, warehouses, and a water-driven cotton mill. The Disney penchant for detail is everywhere. Even the bathrooms in the lobby have old-fashioned cisterns and wooden toilet seats. Talk about theming.

Check-in will be the beginning of your Dixie adventure. The reservationists wear the costumes of clerks, and they will help you

Dixie Landings

"book passage" on your trip upriver. The front desk resembles a steamship office more than a hotel. Piles of old steamer trunks and exotic ports of call create a pleasant sense of fun.

The Sassagoula Steamboat Company is home to the Dixie Landings restaurants, lounge, general store, and food court. Also located here is Guest Services. The guest buildings of both Alligator Bayou and Magnolia Bend surround Ol' Man Island, a three-acre water recreation area with pool, playground, spa, and a stocked fishing hole.

Ol' Man Island has one large pool with a short water slide. There are also five quiet pools located around the resort. These are convenient to most rooms, and if you are looking for something a bit more intimate, you're in luck. There is only one hot tub here at the Landings, and we feel that it is not enough. It is located right in the middle of things at Ol' Man Island, minimizing peace, quiet, and privacy.

Rooms at Magnolia Bend   Magnolia Bend is made up of four "parishes." With such names as Parterre Place and the Acadian House, each is really a large resort building housing more than 250 guest rooms. The feel here is a bit big for our tastes, especially in the standard rooms that look out onto the parking areas. Views from the river side of the complex are infinitely more relaxing and private.

The rooms at both Magnolia Bend and Alligator Bayou are the same general size and shape. With 314 square feet of space, each is adequate and comfortable. While the rooms at both the Bend and the Bayou are the same dimensions, they are worlds apart in decor. The ambience at Magnolia Bend is definitely more formal. French Provincial furniture, brocade upholstery, and an antiqued, mirrored armoire are suited perfectly to the antebellum grand manor. Each room has a ceiling fan, a small sitting bench, table and chairs, and a spacious and well-lit vanity area. There are two pedestal sinks and each has its own mirror, giving you both a place to get ready for your evening out. Rooms feature either two double beds or one king.

Rooms at Alligator Bayou   Alligator Bayou offers much more of a down-home feeling. Instead of four large mansions, the same number of guest rooms are spread out among 16 rustic and weathered buildings, each housing about 60 rooms. The look here is "backwater cracker" but the ambience translates into something more intimate. The Bayou's buildings are tucked away in a small forest. Each feels a bit hidden and the sensation of being in a large resort is lost.

The Bayou rooms manage an aura of homespun comfort and warmth. The log bedstead frames, patchwork "quilts," and other details give the rooms a feeling of fantasy and fun. In-room theming is at its best here in Alligator Bayou. Rooms with twin doubles also feature a trundle bed. This is the only moderately priced resort that has accommodations for more than four persons.

1997 Room Rates for Dixie Landings

Accommodation	Regular Season	Value Season	Holiday Season
Standard view	$124	$114	$134
Water view	$139	$129	$149
King bed	$139	$129	$149

Transportation and Convenience   Transportation at Dixie Landings is the same as at Port Orleans. Dixie Landings, though, has four bus stops situated around the perimeter of the resort. The same wonderful boat service runs to the Village Marketplace, and travel to all other Disney areas is by bus. Service here is quite good, although the buses get crowded during the peak morning and afternoon travel hours.

- To Village Marketplace, Pleasure Island: by boat or bus
- To all other Disney destinations: by direct bus

Dining at Dixie Landings   The restaurants at Dixie Landings are all located in the resort's large central area. While the guest accommodations are organized around this area, it can be a trek from some of them. While we found that this made for a pleasant morning stroll, you might want to locate yourselves according to your own needs.

At the Landings, you will find one table-service restaurant, Boatwright's Dining Hall, and a colorful food court with five counter-service food outlets. Boatwright's serves hearty breakfasts and dinners, and the food is surprisingly good. For reviews and information about this and other restaurants, see Chapter 6.

The Dixie Landings food court is called the Colonel's Cotton Mill, and it offers a good selection of fast foods for the day's meals. It even manages to provide an interesting ambience. Breakfast offerings run the gamut from a muffin or bagel to French toast or eggs, while the other meals get a hearty treatment of burgers, sandwiches, pizza, and Cajun specialties.

If you need to escape the noisy food court atmosphere, go out by the pool and sit at one of the tables there. They are well-shaded and comfortable. In the early morning hours, you are likely to encounter only the occasional swimmer or landscape workman. The Cotton Mill is open from 6 A.M. to midnight, with hours varying for some of the shops. Like its "sister resort," Port Orleans, Dixie offers pizza delivery.

Lounges at Dixie Landings   There are two lounges at Dixie. In the central building is the Cotton Co-Op. Its long mahogany bar looks like something out of a movie. Besides the usual beverage offerings, the Co-Op also features a small variety of finger foods prepared at Boatwright's. There is also a live entertainer in the evenings. Muddy Rivers is the poolside bar.

Shops at Dixie Landings   Fulton's General Store is located in the main resort building and will be your source for Dixie Landings logo merchandise as well as a fairly good selection of other character stuff. It has a country store feel with a large penny candy counter. It has the usual sundries as well as an interesting selection of wines and liquors.

Recreational Activities at Dixie Landings

- Five quiet pools throughout the resort complex
- Ol' Man Island, a 3 1/2-acre themed water recreation area
- One hot tub
- Marina with boat and bicycle rentals
- Guided fishing excursions on the river

RECOMMENDATIONS FOR RESERVATIONS

- For the sake of convenience, you may wish to request a particular building when you reserve your room. Oak Manor would be our choice at Magnolia Bend, and in Alligator Bayou, buildings 14–17 or 27 are our suggestions. All are nearest the central building and Ol' Man Island.

ROMANCE AT DIXIE LANDINGS

- Overall theming: ♥♥
- Rooms with king-size beds: ♥♥
- Late night swim in a quiet pool: ♥♥
- An evening stroll to Port Orleans: ♥♥♥
- Sunset boat ride to Marketplace and Pleasure Island: ♥♥
- Renting a boat or bicycles and exploring: ♥♥
- Taking the boat to Port Orleans and eating at Bonfamille's: ♥♥♥

Old Key West Resort

Old Key West is Disney's venture into time-sharing and, since it is also available as a nightly rental, we thought we'd give it a try. We must admit to being a bit skeptical. It seemed large and not particularly close to anything, and it looked like condos. Whatever reservations that we'd had, however, were quickly put to rest when we arrived at our one-bedroom vacation home.

The Key West theme is executed as only Disney can do it. The Florida Keys should look this nice. The pastel villas, with their "tin" roofs and gingerbread gables, are scattered in clusters throughout the area known as Conch Flats.

Landscaping at Old Key West is lush and tropical. The villas are surrounded by dense stands of foliage and flowering trees, providing a feeling of privacy that you will find hard to equal elsewhere in Walt Disney World. Plants are larger than life. If you are from a northern clime, you will marvel at the variety of greeneries, most of which you've probably only seen as potted house plants. Like much of Walt Disney World, this place is one big garden. Palms, crepe myrtle, blossoming hibiscus, and spider lilies abound. Quaint and narrow Key West streets wander gently among the Florida cracker-style villas. Southern porches, iron streetlamps, and old-fashioned bus stops add the finishing touches to the little taste of Key West created by the Disney imagineers.

Driving, we followed Old Turtle Pond Road to our villa. Parking was a few steps from the front door. Once inside, our curiosity turned to sheer delight. Our villa was not only surprisingly large but surprisingly beautiful. The ambience was definitely Florida Keys–style, open and airy, bright, and casually comfortable. Greeted by a mix of pastels, a splash of florals, and an expanse of open spaces, we hurried from room to room to survey our new abode. Ceiling fans, numerous large windows, and a king-size bed were just the beginnings. The vacation home had a huge living room/kitchen where we found a comfortable chair, love seat, and sofa with queen-size, foldaway bed. Handsome watercolors of island scenery, silk "tropical plants," and a carved wooden conch combined to give our villa a lived-in, at-home feeling.

The kitchen was integral with the living area, just the way we like it. Furnished with the best of appliances, it surpassed our expectations. It was handsomely tiled and was not only functional but beautiful. The kitchen featured a large refrigerator, microwave, dishwasher, stove, toaster, coffeemaker, and enough basic culinary gear to cook up whatever we might have cared to. There was even a blender and an electric hand-mixer. In the drawers and cupboards were mixing bowls, quality utensils, and dinner service for eight. With the cloth placemats, terry napkins, and napkin rings provided, we could easily have entertained. There were even wine glasses. The kitchen and the living room were separated by a tile-topped island that held a large-screen television and VCR.

There was also a lovely patio overlooking water. Featured here were another ceiling fan, a table, and chairs. Surrounded by dense growths of tropical plants, it had the feel of privacy.

The master bedroom for our vacation home was comfortable and beautifully appointed. The king-size bedstead was made of decorative, enameled iron. The floral "quilt," was a wedding-ring pattern, and the armoire was an antiqued white. Here we found yet another television set. In one corner of the bedroom, we found a wicker chair and ottoman; in another corner, we discovered a glass door that opened onto the tiled patio. This was beginning to look like paradise. And then we entered the bathroom.

We knew that we'd arrived. The Jacuzzi was easily large enough for two. Next to it, louvered shutter doors opened onto the sleeping area. A charming pedestal sink and beautiful tile work tied everything together neatly. As big as the tub was, the bathroom itself was even larger. Adjoining it was yet another room, with toilet, large walk-in shower, and another sink and vanity area. There was even a laundry room, complete with full-size washer and dryer, a small supply of laundry detergent, and iron and ironing board.

What made this place so nice was not merely its list of furnishings. Distinguishing this casual elegance from the usual was the caliber of furnishings. Everything from the beautiful prints to the varnished-wood venetian blinds spoke of quality. It was a completely and beautifully furnished little apartment, a place where almost anyone would be glad to live. A few hours after we'd arrived, we were happily calling it "home."

Accommodations at Old Key West

There are three basic types of lodgings here at Old Key West: the studios, the vacation homes, and the Grand Villas. The studio offers a single room with two queen beds, an outside patio, and a small kitchen with microwave oven, wet bar, and mini-refrigerator. One of these added to our one-bedroom vacation home would make a two-bedroom vacation home, able to accommodate eight persons.

The three-bedroom Grand Villa is a two-level townhouse, something quite different altogether. Accommodations are for twelve. The master bedroom still has the king bed and Jacuzzi tub, but upstairs are two queen-size beds in one room and two double beds in the other. The fine furnishings of the Grand Villa and its cathedral ceiling create an impressive effect.

1997 Room Rates for Old Key West

Accommodation	Regular Season	Value Season	Holiday Season
Studio	$229	$209	$244
One-bedroom Vacation Home	$305	$285	$320
Two-bedroom Vacation Home	$410	$390	$425
Three-bedroom Grand Villa	$843	$825	$860

Transportation and Convenience

We are pleased to tell you that getting places from Conch Flats is fast and easy. To make things even better, the buses follow a schedule, which you receive in your check-in packet.

• To all Disney Destinations: by bus

Dining at Old Key West

There is one table-service restaurant, Olivia's Café, and two counter-service snack shops, Good's Food-To-Go and the Turtle Shack. Both Good's and Olivia's are located in the resort's central area, adjacent to the main swimming area. The Turtle Shack is in one of the outlying pool areas. Both fast-food outlets offer a selection of sandwiches and snacks.

Olivia's serves breakfast, lunch, and dinner, offering an intriguing menu of Key West cuisine. It also features a character breakfast on

Sunday and Wednesday. Old Key West features room service from Olivia's. For a review of Olivia's and other restaurants, see Chapter 6.

Shops at Old Key West

The Conch Flat General Store will be your source for just about everything at Old Key West. There is even a substantial grocery section. Every room comes equipped with a grocery check-off list that you can drop off at the General Store. They'll do the shopping and deliver the goods for a mere buck. Now we're talking vacation.

Recreational Activities at Old Key West

- One themed central pool area with sauna and hot tub
- Three quiet pool areas, one with a hot tub
- 1.5-mile biking, jogging, walking, biking path
- Children's playground and kiddie pool
- Marina with rental watercraft
- Bicycle rentals
- Tennis, basketball, and volleyball
- Fitness center
- Video game room
- Complimentary video tape library
- In-room massage, by appointment

RECOMMENDATIONS FOR RESERVATIONS

- Forget the Studios, which are nice but nothing compared to the luxury and space of the villas.
- The one-bedroom vacation home is an ideal place for a family, especially during value season when the prices come down.

ROMANCE AT OLD KEY WEST

- Resort theming: ♥♥
- Villa amenities: ♥♥♥♥
- Jacuzzi: ♥♥♥♥
- Taking a bike ride or walking on the path to the Village Marketplace, and taking a look at the Treehouse Villas, too: ♥♥
- Taking a boat to the Village Marketplace: ♥♥

The Villas at the Disney Institute

Once known as the Disney Village Resort, this area offers a unique variety of lodgings, all set in the quiet and secluded surroundings of the Lake Buena Vista golf course and the Disney Institute.

Rooms at the Villas at the Disney Institute

There are five basic types of accommodations: bungalows, townhouses, Treehouse villas, Fairway villas, and Grand Vista Homes. They all belong to the home away from home category and provide some sort of kitchen facility. Most provide living space for more than the usual four persons as well as fully furnished kitchens. If you plan to visit Walt Disney World with a large family, then one of these may be just the place for you. All Villa accommodations feature daily maid service that includes dish washing.

Bungalows   These one-bedroom, L-shaped suites are scattered around the shores of one of the Institute's lakes. Each has a living room and a wet bar area with refrigerator, coffeemaker, and microwave. The separate bedroom features double queen beds and a small vanity and small bath. The two-story rustic buildings feature patios or balconies for each suite. The recently refurbished bungalows are comfortably furnished and are quite cozy.

Townhouses   Available as either one- or two-bedroom units, these well-furnished, split-level apartments feature living rooms, full kitchens, and upstairs sleeping quarters. With a pull-out sleeper downstairs, the one-bedroom unit can sleep four, while the two-bedroom model can accommodate up to six guests. Adjacent to the Institute and on the shores of Lake Buena Vista, the townhouses overlook Downtown Disney.

Treehouse Villas   Some of the most interesting accommodations at Walt Disney World, these octagonal lodgings are built deep in the woods along the canals that crisscross the Lake Buena Vista area. Called "treehouses" because they are built on stilts, they feature simple, rustic exteriors. Inside, they are modern and luxurious. The Treehouse area seems more like a national park than a Disney resort. It is peaceful and secluded. There are even a handful of peacocks that roam the grounds.

The upstairs area of each Treehouse has two bedrooms, each with a queen bed. It has a small kitchen and living room, and it is almost

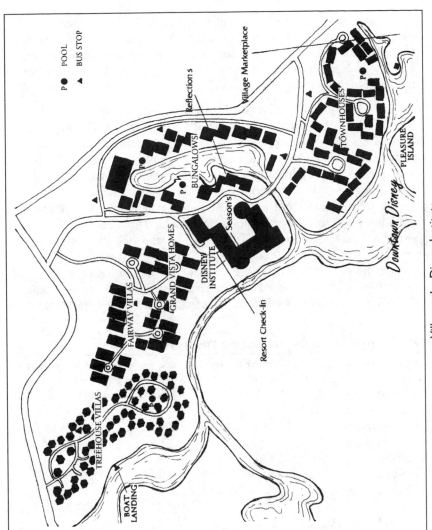

Villas at the Disney Institute

completely surrounded by a large, elevated deck. It's the perfect place to relax or dine under a canopy of trees. Downstairs is another bedroom with one double bed and a laundry room with washer and dryer. Each "home" has its own driveway and yard. Other Treehouses are barely visible through the dense woods.

Fairway Villas and Grand Vista Homes   Both of these types of accommodations offer even more luxury for a large family. The modern, cedar-sided villas are located right along the golf course. Each features two bedrooms and a large living room with cathedral ceiling. With a single queen in one bedroom, two doubles in the other, and a sico bed in the living room, there's sleeping space here for eight.

The Grand Vista Homes were originally designed as model homes for a Disney development that never developed. There are only four of these lavish places: two two-bedroom homes and one three-bedroom home. The two-bedroom homes can accommodate six, while the three-bedroom home can lodge eight. Each comes with a golf cart and bicycles. Refrigerators are stocked upon arrival with snacks, beverages, and milk. Nightly turndown service and newspaper delivery are standard.

1997 Room Rates for the Villas at the Disney Institute

Accommodation	Regular Season	Value Season	Holiday Season
Bungalow	$215	$195	$230
One-bedroom Townhouse	$305	$285	$320
Two-bedroom Townhouse	$340	$320	$355
Treehouse Villa	$375	$355	$390
Two-bedroom Fairway Villa	$400	$375	$415
Two-bedroom Grand Vista Home	$975	$975	$995
Three-bedroom Grand Vista Home	$1,150	$1,150	$1,185

Transportation and Convenience at the Villas at the Disney Institute

The Villas are not centrally located. Despite this, it is an easy matter to reach virtually any Disney destination. Buses run every 30 minutes but make a great many stops throughout the Villas. For travel within the Villas area, rental golf carts are available for $24 per day or $36 for 24 hours.

- Transportation to all Disney destinations: by bus, every 30 minutes

Dining and Shops at the Villas at the Disney Institute

There are two restaurants nearby at the Institute. Season's Dining Room features all-day dining with an interesting menu for each of the day's meals. See Chapter 6 for details. Reflections is a small, lakeside shop that features gourmet coffees, outstanding pastries and muffins, and a selection of quality sandwiches. The Reflections poolside patio is a pleasant stop for lunch.

With nearby Downtown Disney, you'll will not want for a selection of either restaurants or shops. If you are staying in the Treehouses, Fairway villas, or Grand Vista Homes, you will find a car will come in handy. Both the townhouses and bungalows are within walking distance to Downtown Disney.

Recreational Activities at the Villas at the Disney Institute

- Six swimming pools
- Two hot tubs
- Rental bikes and canoes
- Several outstanding walking or jogging paths

OUR IMPRESSIONS OF THE VILLAS AT THE DISNEY INSTITUTE

- It's hard to believe you're at Disney World out here. It's woodsy and quiet.

RECOMMENDATIONS FOR RESERVATIONS

- During the slower seasons, both the Treehouses and the bungalows enjoy generous discounts.

ROMANCE AT THE VILLAS AT THE DISNEY INSTITUTE

- Resort ambience: ♥
- Treehouse villas: ♥♥
- Taking a walk or a bike ride: ♥

The Studio Resorts

Disney's Coronado Springs Resort

In his quest for the fabled seven cities of Cibola, Spanish conquistador Francisco de Coronado should have come to Florida. While he wouldn't have found the legendary lost cities of gold, he would have discovered 16 of the most fanciful resorts in the New World, the latest of which bears his name.

Disney's Coronado Springs features the flavor and architecture of the Southwestern U.S. and Mexico and is set on 125 wooded acres between MGM Studios and the Animal Kingdom (expected to open in spring of 1998). Spread lazily around Lago Dorado, a picturesque 16-acre lake, Coronado Springs features three "villages," each a unique taste of the old Southwest. Disney's first moderately priced resort to include a convention center, Coronado Springs offers a colorful diversity of resort experiences all wrapped neatly into one.

Scheduled to open in August of 1997 (long after this book goes to print), Coronado Springs is yet another master stroke of theming, brought to you by those ever-improving Disney imagineers. In order to give you a good picture of what this currently unfinished resort will be like, we have visited the site, spoken at length with the resort's manager, and seen renderings and room mock-ups.

If you arrive here with just the right amount of imagination, you'll find yourselves journeying to another place and time. The resort's entranceway leads over a small stone bridge and up to the central building's grand and tent-like porte cochere, where you are greeted by the Mayan-costumed staff. The cars and vans of arriving guests seem oddly out of time amidst the palms, cacti, and sunwashed terra-cotta. Once inside, you are beneath the lobby's great tiled dome. White clouds float above you on a blue painted sky. On the sunburst tile floor of the rotunda, a fountain whispers softly; beyond, through an expanse of glass, you see a panorama of the lake. On Lago Dorado's other shore, you see what appears to be the ruins of an ancient Mayan pyramid, peeking above dense vegetation. The magic and mystery of this lost kingdom begin to take hold. The gentle gurgling of water and the sunny Southwest atmosphere are Coronado Spring's stock-in-trade. Tile floors, Indian throw rugs, and massive wooden ceiling beams accent this great hacienda. Large chandeliers, tile-

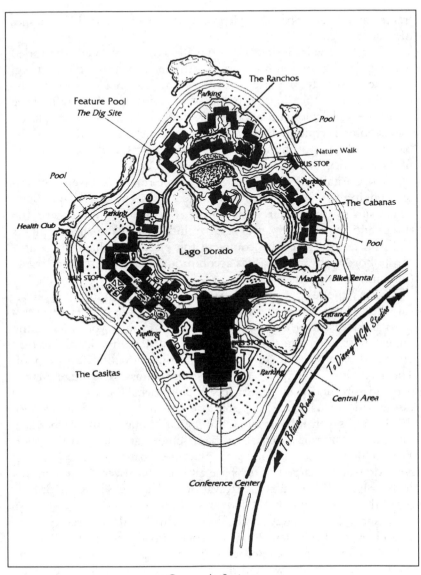

Coronado Springs

framed arches, and Spanish-style ironwork are all accented by splashes of aquas and corals.

Your Coronado Springs odyssey will take you through the varied geographic areas of Southwestern North America. From the bustling, city-like Casitas to the arid arroyos of the Ranchos and on to the coastal Cabanas, the trip is both diverse and engaging. Throughout the resort are gaily colored fountains set amidst quiet and shaded plazas. Landscaping is typically Disney: perfect in its detail, relaxing in its ambience, and transporting in its effect. Cacti, palms, and the vegetation of the region all enhance the resort's motif.

The Casitas lodgings are adjacent to the resort's convention center and lobby. These terra-cotta structures seem urban and busy. Their sun-splashed courtyards and flower-filled patios accent the three- and four-story Spanish-style architecture. Palm-shaded plazas and iron-crested balconies complete the picture of this little south-of-the-border city. The Casitas accommodations are intended largely for convention guests.

Across the lake, Coronado Springs takes on another mood altogether. Gone now is the hustle and bustle of the city. Here, just a short and pleasant stroll from the resort's central area, you will find the bungalow-style lodgings of the Ranchos and Cabanas, a wildlife preserve and nature walk, and Coronado Springs' exciting feature pool. The Dig Site's centerpiece is impossible to miss. The huge Mayan pyramid surrounded by ruins appears only partially unearthed. Water cascades down its precipitous staircase and into the swimming pool that lies at its feet. From behind, the Jaguar Flume whooshes its riders through nearby ruins, beneath a giant jungle cat, and into the pool. The children's wading pond and play area, patio, volleyball court, poolside bar, and large hot tub have all been "uncovered" here in this enchanting and entertaining "excavation." The Dig Site is the discovery of the Lost Kingdom of Gold come to life.

A short distance away and behind the small wetlands preserve runs an arid riverbed. Hidden along this rocky streambed are the Pueblo-style Ranchos. Both secluded and picturesque, these rustic lodgings feature a dozen or so two and three-story stucco buildings. Scattered about the dry riverbed and quiet pool area, the Ranchos are the picture of the rural Southwest.

Farther along this mythical journey are the coastal Cabanas. Surrounding a rocky shore, these two-story bungalow-style buildings appear to have roofs of thatch. There is a south-of-the-border seaside mood at work here, accented by palms, low-lying cacti, and a splendid lakeside vista. Half of the Cabana rooms feature water views, where the romantic panorama includes the ruins of the pyramid and, after dark, the dazzling lights of the Casitas across the lake.

Each of the three village areas has its own quiet pool; a network of walkways and footbridges connects them to each other and to the Dig Site. Besides the volleyball court and pools, there's bicycle and non-motorized boat rentals available at the lakeside marina. Coronado Springs also features La Vida (a health club) and a hair salon, both located in the Casitas. There's also the beautiful Esplanade walkway, which runs completely around the lake. It's perfect for a romantic evening stroll.

Rooms at Disney's Coronado Springs Resort

This is a moderately priced Disney resort, and rooms here are all comparable to other resorts of this category. With 314 square feet, you should find them spacious for two and fairly comfortable for a small family. Each has a large vanity with a single sink and the usual shower-tub bathroom. All of the rooms at this resort feature coffeemakers and irons and ironing boards. Small refrigerators are available for a small daily charge. There is the usual mix of single king beds and twin double beds.

Each of the three villages features its own special decor that has been created to enhance its theme. Rooms at the Casitas are casually formal and accented with turquoise and salmon. Bedspreads are a colorful Mexican pattern and bedstead and armoire are antiqued aqua accented with Mayan sunbursts. Rooms at the Ranchos have a decidedly Indian motif. Blues, golds, and the triangular patterns of Southwestern Native American artistry accentuate these rustic lodgings. The ambience of Old Mexico comes alive in the bright and comfortable Cabana rooms. Bedspreads are of reds and golds, while the Spanish-style furnishings are antique gold with brightly painted accents.

Because this resort features a large convention center, it also offers an assortment of suites. The Junior suites, VIP suites, and Executive suite seem to us, though, to be aimed largely at the convention market. Suite offerings here, we feel, are not aimed at either families or couples.

1997 Room Rates for Disney's Coronado Springs Resort

Accommodation	Regular Season	Value Season	Holiday Season
Standard view	$124	$114	$134
Water view	$139	$129	$149
King bed	$139	$129	$149

Transportation and Convenience

Transportation to all Disney World destinations is by bus. There is one bus stop at the central area and another few bus stops around the resort. Because of its location in Walt Disney World, we'd have to guess that service to the Magic Kingdom and to the nearby Studios and Animal Kingdom will be very good. With a bit more of a drive to Epcot, that ride may take a few minutes longer.

Dining and Lounges at Coronado Springs

Restaurant options here will depart a little from what is normally offered at moderate Disney resorts. Because of the convention trade, the table-service restaurant at Coronado Springs will be a bit more upscale than those at sister resorts. The Maya Grill will feature a cuisine of grilled seafood and meats. Seasonings will be of the Southwest; the stylish decor will use Mayan themes. Mexico has made some significant culinary contributions, most notably with corn, potato, tomato, and, of course, chocolate. We very much look forward to the romantic potential of this dining experience.

The Pepper Market will be the Springs' food court and will indeed be something unique. This indoor marketplace of "street vendors" will offer the usual assortment of counter-service staples plus an interesting variety of Southwest regional specialties. Carts, tables, and atmosphere will all be festive and vibrant. Service here will not be the usual paper plate and plastic flatware, however. China dishware and stainless silverware will make this much more of a restaurant experience. We would expect prices to be a bit higher than other food courts. Coronado Springs will also offer limited room service with such items as continental breakfasts, taco and Caesar salads, deli subs, and pizzas. Francisco's Lounge will be in the resort's central area, and there will be another themed lounge by the Dig Site, poolside.

Shops at Coronado Springs

Panchito's Gifts and Sundries will offer the usual assortment of Disney character merchandise and sundries such as film, candies, newspapers, and magazines. This will also be the place to purchase resort logo goods and, we would guess, offerings such as Southwestern and Mexican foods and condiments and regional resortware.

Recreational Activities at Coronado Springs

- One feature pool area, the Dig Site, with water flume
- Hot tub/spa for 22 persons
- Three quiet pools
- La Vida Health Club
- Two video arcades: the Jumping Bean and the Iguana Arcade
- Children's wading pool and playground area
- Jogging and walking path (0.9 mile)
- Rental bicycles, paddle boats, and canoes
- Nature walk in preserved wetlands

OUR IMPRESSIONS OF CORONADO SPRINGS

(These impressions are based on what we have seen so far.)
- This is another star in the firmament of Disney resorts.
- The central area and the Casitas are where the action is. Expect both the Ranchos and Cabanas areas to be much more laid-back and quiet.
- The central area, with restaurants and guest services, is not as convenient to the Ranchos and the Cabanas as to the Casitas. We would expect that the pleasant walk will make up for this.

RECOMMENDATIONS FOR RESERVATIONS

- For a romantic experience, we'd suggest a king bed in either the Ranchos or Cabanas.
- For proximity to the Dig Site, stay in the Ranchos or Cabanas.

ROMANCE AT CORONADO SPRINGS

- A stroll along the lakeside walkway
- Breakfast in bed

- Late-night hot tub or swim
- Cabana with water view and king bed
- Dinner at the themed restaurant

All-Star Resorts: Music and Sports

The All-Star Resorts are Disney's foray into the budget market. Rooms here are the most inexpensive on-property and, as you would expect, the All-Star Resorts are one of Disney World's busiest destinations.

Each carries its lively and colorful themes all the way from landscaping and architecture to the details of room furnishings. The All-Star Resorts feature nearly 4,000 rooms.

The road to the All-Star Resorts takes you right past Blizzard Beach, Disney's newest water park. A peek at this fantastic playground will definitely get you in the mood for the bright and comic-strip-like All-Stars. These resorts are larger-than-life and we mean a lot larger than life.

The resort buildings here are dwarfed by the sculptures that decorate them. The All-Star Resorts will dazzle you with five-story footballs, soaring surfboards, towering trumpets, mammoth maracas, and dozens of other uniquely large objects. Not for a minute will you forget that you are on vacation and that the theme is fantasy.

Both Music and Sports are further divided into smaller areas, each comprised of two buildings with a more specific theme. Our room was at Jazz Inn. Jazz has a definite New Orleans feel to its fountains, cast-iron benches, and walkways. The railings around the upper-floor walkways are musical scales, appropriately decorated with colorful notes and clefs. Piped-in music around the grounds has a jazz flavor, and the tops of the buildings are edged in silhouettes of musicians.

Other areas in All-Star Music are Calypso, Country Fair, Rock Inn, and Broadway Hotel. Each is imagineered with its own theme from top to bottom. Calypso, for example, is decorated with brightly colored palm leaves, four-story-tall conga drums, and spectacular, rainbow-like marimbas. The music here is the lively beat of the tropics. Taking a walk around this resort is a musical adventure.

Over at the All-Star Sports, things are much the same. Which is to say that they are quite different. The theme there is sports, and

All-Star Resorts

the areas have names such as Center Court, Hoops Hotel, and Touchdown.

While the actual buildings are the same, the theming has created a whole different atmosphere. The courtyard area at Touchdown is arranged like a football stadium, complete with gigantic helmets, a playing field, goal posts, and towering "floodlights." Over at Surf's Up, the landscaping will take you to the seashore. Here, the grounds around the pool resemble grass-covered sand dunes. Mounds of pampas grass and thickets of palms complete the picture.

Music and Sports each have a central area with front desk, Guest Services, a food court, shop, video arcade, and lounge. The central areas are called Melody Hall at Music and Stadium Hall at Sports.

If you elect to stay at the All-Star Resorts, whether Music or Sports, we suggest that you take a stroll around both properties. There are a lot of wonderful little touches that have been created to delight you. And they will.

Rooms at the All-Star Resorts

There are two basic types of rooms, standard with two double beds and rooms with a single king bed. The king room is also the room equipped for handicapped people. All-Star rooms are on the small side, 260 square feet, which is to say that they are about the same size as most budget motels. The room furnishings are decidedly more Disney than off-property rooms but, by Disney standards, they are pretty modest.

Our king bedroom at Jazz Inn lacked many of the amenities of even the Disney moderately priced resorts. The room decor was festive and modern. The "quilted" bedspread and bathroom wallpaper both featured patterns of jazz musicians, and the drapes were decorated with musical scales. The room furniture is similar throughout the All-Star. Modern and cartoon-like, it seemed entertaining. The theming in the rooms was simple. Creature comforts were minimal. One thing that we did like about our room was the environmental system, which we found very quiet.

Each room at the All-Star has a rather small vanity. Our king bedroom had only a shower. Wonderfully designed for the use of those physically challenged, it was very spacious with a handy seat right under the water. The double room has the more conventional shower-tub. King bedrooms each come with a small refrigerator.

1997 Room Rates for the All-Star Resorts

Accommodation	Regular Season	Value Season	Holiday Season
Standard view	$79	$69	$84
Landscape view	$84	$74	$89

Transportation and Convenience

With so many rooms here, we were concerned that transportation would be slow. We are delighted to report that service to all Disney destinations is quite good. Both Music and Sports each have their own bus fleets, and we found service to be frequent and convenient.

• To all Disney destinations: by bus

Dining at the All-Star Resorts

Both the End Zone Food Court at Sports and the Intermission Food Court at Music offer a complete array of food for breakfast, lunch, and dinner. All of the food served here is cooked on the premises, and much to our surprise, it was considerably better than many other Disney food court offerings. The hamburger was actually very good.

The dining areas here, like most food courts, are noisy and at peak hours are crowded. Try taking your trays the few steps out to the pool area and eat at a table, under an umbrella.

There are several other interesting options for eating at All-Star. One is ordering out. There is a pizza delivery at All-Star, and while this pizza is nothing to write home about, it is decent. The menu also includes beers, wines, salads, and subs. There are also food trucks that drive around during the day, hawking breakfast stuff in the morning and sandwich goodies later.

Lounges at the All-Star Resorts

Each central area has a lounge that serves beers, wines, and specialty drinks, both alcoholic and nonalcoholic. The Singing Spirits Pool Bar is the lounge at Melody Hall, and at Sports, it's the Team Spirits Pool Bar. As their names imply, each is adjacent to the main pool.

Shops at the All-Star Resorts

Sport Goofy Gifts and Sundries is at All-Star Sports, and Maestro Mickey's is at Music. Each offers a selection of its own logo merchandise, and both have the usual Disney character products, sportswear, gifts, souvenirs, sundries, and even a small selection of liquor. Also available is a small offering of magazines, books, and newspapers. And if you are planning to snack in your room, each shop has a modest selection of chips, beverages, and groceries items.

Recreational Activities at All-Star Resorts

Music and Sports each have two pools—one large main pool and one smaller, less centrally located pool. At All-Star Music, the large pool is shaped like a huge guitar. An island in the center features a frolicking gang of sculptured Disney characters who occasionally spray near-by swimmers with jets of water. It is a delightful sight gag. The quiet swimming area at Music is the Piano Pool and is—you guessed it— shaped like a huge piano. At Sports, the main pool is called Surfboard Bay and is located amidst the beachside landscaping of Surf's Up. It has a California beach theme. A bit farther away is the quieter swimming area, the Grand Slam Pool. Each main swimming area also has a nice kiddie pool.

OUR IMPRESSIONS OF THE ALL-STAR RESORTS

- For the cost-conscious, the All-Star Resorts are an affordable way to stay on-property. Each is a charming and themed Disney resort, albeit a bit spartan.
- Many of the rooms are a hike from the parking lots. The luggage assistance system is awkward and runs on its own schedule, not yours. A stay here will teach you the real meaning of LUGgage. Plan on carrying your own bags to your room unless you simply cannot. If so, speak with the front desk upon check-in.

RECOMMENDATIONS FOR RESERVATIONS

- At Music, the Calypso area is closest to Melody Hall and is adjacent to the main pool. It is also the noisiest area. Country Fair is the most secluded but it is a hike from the parking area. Rock Inn, Broadway Hotel, and Jazz Inn seemed to be the most convenient, are relatively quiet (for this resort), and are near the quieter pool. We would recommend that you request one of these areas if you are staying at All-Star Music.
- At Sports, the busier area is Surf's Up. All other areas seemed quiet by comparison. Touchdown and Home Run Hotel would be our

recommendations. Both are convenient to the quieter pool area and to parking.

ℛOMANCE AT THE ALL-STAR RESORTS

- Separate room for the kids: ♥♥

Fort Wilderness Campground Resort

Fort Wilderness Campsites and Homes

If you have never been to Fort Wilderness, you'll find that there's a lot more going on out there than a campground. More than any other Walt Disney resort area, Fort Wilderness is a world unto itself. With 750 beautifully wooded acres, Fort Wilderness would have little trouble drawing guests even without the nearby Disney attractions. What this amazing place has to offer includes a sandy beach, two swimming pools, a host of watercraft, sports activities, a petting farm, a water park, a popular dinner show, a themed restaurant, and a couple of shops. And besides offering a real variety of quality campsites and motor home hookups, Fort Wilderness even has its very own lodgings, the Wilderness Homes. To say that Fort Wilderness is a campground would be like calling the Magic Kingdom an amusement park. Fort Wilderness is a campground, but it is much, much more.

Fort Wilderness has a distinctly western flavor. Weathered log buildings, rough hewn timbers, split-rail fences, and meadows filled with wildflowers are set amidst a shady forest of slash pine, cypress, and live oak. Fort Wilderness does not feel much like Florida.

There are two basic types of accommodations at Fort Wilderness: campsites and the Wilderness Homes. Each offers something quite different. A Wilderness Home is a Disney resort lodging. The campsites, of course, furnish a place to either pitch your tent or to hook up your motor home or trailer.

Fort Wilderness Campsites

Fort Wilderness is Disney, and that means everything will be something special. The campsites, whether for tents, motor homes, or travel trailers, are all fairly large and relatively private. Each comes with either a full or partial hookup. Full hookups include water, sewer, electric,

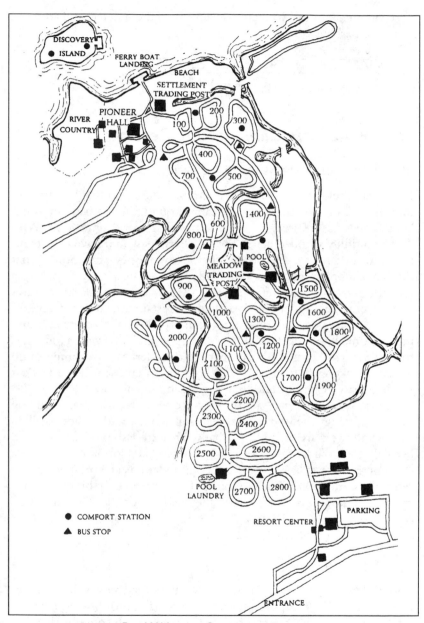

Fort Wilderness Campground Resort

and cable television. Partials supply only electric and water. All offer ample space, a small barbecue grill, and a picnic table, and all provide 110 and 220 electricity.

Wherever your campsite is, you won't be far from an air-conditioned Comfort Station. Each of these features private showers and restrooms, an ice machine, and a coin-operated laundry. They are all clean and well maintained.

There are a small number of campsites where guests are allowed to have pets. Availability is limited, and these sites are all partial hookups. Cost is $3 per night for each pet. If you want to bring your pet on a Disney adventure, be sure to reserve one of these when you make your reservation: loops 1600–1900.

Fort Wilderness Homes

The Fort Wilderness Homes are something altogether different. Each is really a small, air-conditioned 12- by 50-foot mobile home. Each has a full kitchen with utensils, pots and pans, a microwave oven, and a dishwasher. Every home includes a color television with cable, a ceiling fan, and a bathroom. A living area has a pull-down, double Murphy bed, and the homes are offered with a choice of one of two different bedroom designs. One style features a double bed and a set of bunk beds; the other has one double bed. Each Wilderness Home has a raised, outside deck, a picnic table, and an outdoor grill.

While certainly not equal to the luxury found at Old Key West, the Wilderness Homes have their charm. Furnishings are quaint and homey. Chairs and table are woodsy and rustic. The overall feeling is surprisingly pleasant. Each is large: 504 square feet.

If you are visiting Disney with your children, a Wilderness Home can provide the privacy for your romantic Disney holiday. Being able to prepare many of your own meals will save you some serious money as well. Maid service is included with the Wilderness Homes and, amazingly, it includes dishwashing. So cook up a storm and leave the cleaning to Disney.

Location, Location, Location

As the old adage goes, there are three important elements to real estate. The same is true for Fort Wilderness. The central area is around Pioneer Hall. It is here that you will find the resort's restaurants, Guest

Services, the Settlement Depot, the beach, River Country, and most of the other recreational activities. We suggest that you locate yourselves as close to it as possible in one of the preferred campsites.

Fort Wilderness is large. The roads here wind lazily through the resort's 700 forested acres. The campsites and homes are all located on small "loop" roads that connect to the larger streets. There are nearly thirty such loops. Some are closer to things than others. Some offer a bit more seclusion. Others offer convenience to the pools or to the beach or bus stops. Each loop is numbered, with the series beginning at Loop 100 and ending with Loop 2800.

Loops 100 through 500 are the Preferred Campsites, and you will pay about $6 more per night to stay in one. They are all full hookups. It is well worth the extra expense, and we suggest that you request one when you make your reservation. We also suggest that you make your reservation as far in advance as possible. These puppies go fast.

If you are planning a stay in one of the Wilderness Homes, you'll be a bit farther away. These homes occupy loops 2100 through 2800. The partial hookup campsites are also a little farther out, occupying loops 1500 to 2000.

1997 Accommodation Rates for Fort Wilderness

Accommodation	Regular Season	Value Season	Holiday Season
Wilderness Home	$215	$185	$230
Preferred Campsite	$58	$49	$64
Campsite, full hookup	$52	$43	$59
Partial hookup	$44	$35	$49

Occupancy rates are based on two adults per accommodation with children under 17 years of age at no extra charge. A maximum of six persons are allowed in each Wilderness Home and 10 persons maximum at any one campsite. Extra adults at the homes are $5 each per night and $2 each per night at the campsites.

Transportation and Convenience

Transportation to the Magic Kingdom and Discovery Island is by boat and quite convenient. All other destinations are by bus to the Ticket and Transportation Center (TTC), followed by a bus transfer or, to Epcot, a monorail trip. If there is a problem with Fort Wilderness, this is it. Such trips are time-consuming, especially during the busy seasons.

There are two bus services at Fort Wilderness: one that carries guests around the resort, and another that takes guests to the TTC. Buses come and go about every 20 minutes. For complete bus directions, see your resort information and check-in newspaper, *The Gazette*.

Since Disney asks that you not drive your car around in Fort Wilderness except to arrive and depart, you'll want to give some thought to getting around this large resort. Rental electric carts are available either for your length of stay or by the day. At $23 per day or $36 for a 24-hour period, these carts are expensive, but if you are in one of the more distant areas, one will come in handy. There are also rental bicycles, available either by the hour or for $18 per day. With miles of peaceful, wooded paths, a couple of bikes would be nice. During our time at Fort Wilderness, we noticed many people riding around on their own bicycles. So, if you are driving and can bring your bikes along, do it. Don't forget a couple of good locks.

- To all Fort Wilderness areas: by internal bus
- To Magic Kingdom, Discovery Island: boat launch from Bay Lake dock
- To all other Disney destinations: bus to Ticket and Transportation Center, then transfer to other buses; monorail from TTC to Epcot

Restaurants and Eating at Fort Wilderness

Many guests staying at Fort Wilderness fix their own meals. Whether you are visiting in your motor home or staying in a Wilderness Home, a real advantage of Fort Wilderness is the ability to cook for yourselves and save a lot of money.

We suggest then, on your way through one of the surrounding communities, that you stop for groceries. There are two Trading Posts here at Fort Wilderness, and while they offer a decent selection of basic foodstuffs, they do so at Disney prices. If you are looking for a real supermarket, Gooding's at the Crossroads Plaza near the Marketplace is convenient.

There are three restaurants at Fort Wilderness, and two of them offer dinner shows: the Hoop-Dee-Doo Revue and the All-American Backyard Barbecue (see Chapter 6 for details). The third restaurant, Trail's End, is located next door to Pioneer Hall and features reasonably priced buffet meals for breakfast, lunch, and dinner. There's plenty of good food at each, and dinners even include hand-carved roast beef.

Recreational Activities at Fort Wilderness

- Two heated swimming pools and white sand beach
- Marina with rental craft
- River Country water park
- Two lighted tennis courts
- Jogging and walking paths
- Video arcade
- Swamp Trail nature walk
- Petting farm
- Horseback riding and nightly hayrides and campfire program
- Volleyball, tetherball, basketball
- Fishing excursions

OUR IMPRESSIONS OF FORT WILDERNESS

- No doubt, this is a super campground. The facilities are first-rate—sparkling and clean. Everything seems new. There is so much to do here that you hardly have to go anywhere for fun.

ROMANCE AT FORT WILDERNESS

- Taking an evening stroll around the resort: ♥♥
- Having a nightcap at Crockett's Tavern: ♥
- Taking a late afternoon dip in the lake on a hot summer day: ♥
- Having your privacy when you bring your family to a Wilderness Home: ♥♥
- Watching the Electric Water Pageant from the beach: ♥♥

The Hotel Plaza Resorts

Hotel Plaza is a group of seven on-property hotels located near the Disney Village Marketplace. None are owned or managed by Disney, but they provide an interesting alternative to staying in one of the Disney resorts. While these can be an economical alternative to the other on-property resorts, a stay in one of them will not provide the same benefits as a visit to one of the Disney resorts. Hotel Plaza resorts do not have Surprise Mornings, Length of Stay Passes, Resort Cards, or full use of Disney transportation. These are privately owned and independent hotels.

On the plus side, these resorts are infinitely more convenient than anything off-property and they are all quite nice. One is truly luxurious. Accommodations range from good to lavish.

Hotel Plaza has its own bus system, which ferries guests to most Disney destinations. It is important to note, though, that these buses do not drop off guests at the same bus areas used by Disney buses. While this amounts to a matter of a few dozen yards at both Epcot and MGM, it is more noticeable at the Magic Kingdom, where the purple and green Hotel Plaza buses leave guests at the Ticket and Transportation Center. On a busy morning, the trip from the TTC to the Magic Kingdom can take 20 minutes. Also, we have heard Hotel Plaza guests complain that bus service is slow and crowded. Hotel Plaza buses run every 25 minutes, a little less frequently than those of Disney.

Guests have convenient access to a selection of restaurants, lounges, and nightclubs at the resorts along Hotel Plaza Boulevard. Each of the hotels on the Boulevard has a Disney store that offers a selection of Disney character merchandise and the usual assortment of tickets and passes. Both Pleasure Island and the Disney Village Marketplace are within walking distance, as is the Crossroads Shopping Plaza.

Generally speaking, these hotels are attractive. While they really do not enjoy the theming found at such places as Dixie Landings, their rooms are well decorated, comfortable, and well maintained. Pools and grounds range from good to beautiful, but none begins to approach the likes of Stormalong Bay at the Yacht and the Beach Clubs or even Doubloon Lagoon at Port Orleans.

If you desire a Disney resort experience, look to be within arm's reach of the parks, or yearn to enjoy the magic of a themed resort room, then Hotel Plaza may not be for you. Pretty uniformly, these are regular hotels.

Price remains the most attractive element in the Hotel Plaza formula. These hotels often feature discounts, many of which are excellent. Even during Disney's regular season, competition on Hotel Plaza Boulevard can get downright cutthroat. All the better for you. Magic Kingdom Club members get discounts at all of the Hotel Plaza Hotels. Most of these hotels are featured in one or more of the packages offered by Delta Airlines and the Walt Disney Travel Company.

The Grosvenor Resort

Pronounced "Grove-nor," this 19-story hotel is one of the nearest to the Village Marketplace. Its 629 rooms are all well appointed and brightly decorated. Each room at the Grosvenor has a wet bar, coffeemaker, and VCR. Situated on 13 beautifully landscaped acres, this is a rather nice hotel. The British Colonial–style lobby is bright and airy. Of all the hotels along the Boulevard, the "very British" Grosvenor makes the best effort to give itself a theme.

Standard rooms begin at $170 during value season to $200 during the regular season, with a maximum of five persons per room. Specials and packages are seasonal, vary greatly, and will no doubt provide rooms for considerably less than these prices. AAA discounts apply. There are a few suites here at the Grosvenor; prices begin at $450 per night. For reservations, call Disney CRO at (407) 934-7639, or the Grosvenor at (800) 624-4109.

Restaurants and Lounges at the Grosvenor

Restaurants and lounges at the Grosvenor all enjoy the British theming that is evident in the lobby. Here, guests can drop by Crumpet's Cafe for a quick snack or bite to eat 24 hours a day. Pastries, muffins, hot and cold sandwiches, beverages, and espresso are a few of the cafe's offerings. Cricket's Lounge is also located in the lobby. This full-service bar offers espresso and cappuccino as well as a large-screen television.

Baskerville's is the Grosvenor's full-service restaurant and enjoys a pleasant Sherlock Holmes theme. It features Disney character breakfast buffets on Tuesday, Thursday, and Saturday and a character dinner on Wednesday. Dinners feature an a la carte menu, and on Saturday evening, Baskerville's presents the MurderWatch Mystery Theater and its signature prime rib buffet. There's even a Sherlock Holmes museum.

Baskerville's lounge is Moriarty's, named after the famous detective's infamous adversary. Neither restaurant nor lounge has an atmosphere that we would call memorable.

Barnacle's is the Grosvenor's poolside snack bar and lounge. Its menu includes drinks and a small selection of burgers, hot dogs, and sandwiches. Sunday afternoons feature live entertainment.

Services Available at the Grosvenor

The Grosvenor offers services found at most hotels, such as bell service, valet parking, 24-hour room service, valet service, on-property car rentals, ATMs, and baby-sitting service.

Recreational Activities at the Grosvenor

- Two heated swimming pools with kiddie pool
- Fitness center, whirlpool, hydrotherapy spa
- Tennis, basketball, shuffleboard, volleyball
- Video game room
- Video movie rental

Buena Vista Palace Resort and Spa

This, the most elegant of the Hotel Plaza resorts, is also one of the closest to the Village Marketplace. The lobby is rich with crystal chandeliers, broad expanses of glass, and plush furnishings. With more than 1,000 guest rooms, this 27-story multitower resort offers 130 suites and its Crown Level concierge service. Four rooms come with Jacuzzis, and every guest room has a minibar and a private balcony or patio and is lavishly furnished. Standard guest rooms feature either two queen beds or one king.

The Buena Vista's Palace Suites complex is located adjacent to the resort's recreational area. It is connected to the main building by landscaped walkways and houses 100 one- and two-bedroom suites. Standard here are minibars, coffeemakers, and hair dryers. A queen sleeper-sofa is in each living area, and a single king or two queen beds can be found in each bedroom. A microwave oven and small refrigerator are available upon request.

The Palace also offers twenty Evergreen Rooms. Hailed as "ecologically friendly," these accommodations are smoke- and odor-free. The very latest in technology has been applied to water and air filtration, and these rooms include nonallergenic pillows and blankets as well as undyed bathroom tissues and linens.

Nightly room rates at the Palace run from $120 to $220. There is no charge for children under the age of 18. AAA discounts are applicable, and special romantic packages and seasonal bargains are usually available. We suggest that you call the Palace's toll-free reservation

number, (800) 327-2990, or Disney Central Reservations to get the
most current offerings.

Restaurants and Lounges at the Buena Vista Palace

The Palace offers an outstanding assortment of dining places. Starting
at the top (the twenty-seventh floor, that is), you will find Arthur's 27,
an award-winning gourmet restaurant that features international
cuisine. The Outback Restaurant (no connection to the Outback
Steakhouse chain) specializes in grilled beef and seafood. The atmosphere is "down under" and includes waterfalls and palms. Overlooking
the lake is the Watercress Cafe. Open 6 A.M. to midnight every day, this
is the Palace's all-around eatery. Breakfasts here are Disney character
buffets. The Spa Courtyard offers spa cuisine in a pleasant courtyard
setting. There is even a poolside snack bar and 24-hour room service.

For afternoon happy hour or a late nightcap, the Palace features
four lounges, one of which is high atop this 27-story building.
Complimentary champagne is served there daily at sunset. The
Laughing Kookaburra Good Times Bar, a happening nightspot, features live entertainment and 99 brands of beer.

The Spa

This year, the Palace offers its guests a world-class spa experience, with
a complete array of body treatments as well as a hair salon and fitness
center. Featuring whirlpool baths, wet and dry saunas, a lap pool, and
state-of-the-art fitness gear, this spa is determined to keep pace with
the competition. For more details about Disney's three wonderful
spas, see Chapter 7.

Services Available at the Buena Vista Palace

The Palace offers full bell service, valet parking, a hair salon, children's activity center, laundry service, on-premises car rental, and
concierge desk.

Recreational Activities at the Buena Vista Palace

- Two swimming pools and kiddie pool
- European-style health spa and sauna
- Three lighted tennis courts and a volleyball court

- Complete health club and three-mile jogging and walking trail
- Children's activities

The Hilton at Walt Disney World Village

The very name of this hotel has come to be synonymous with fine accommodations. The Hilton is a Four Diamond, 800-room resort, located directly across the street from the Disney Village Marketplace. Of all the Hotel Plaza resorts, it is the closest to the Marketplace. The Hilton's list of amenities is nearly endless. Spacious and well-appointed rooms, 27 elegant suites, and seven restaurants and lounges make the Hilton one of Hotel Plaza's most outstanding travel destinations. The Hilton boasts a tropical theme, which is carried beautifully from the lush garden grounds to the tropical ambience of the guest rooms.

With either two double beds or a single king bed, each room features a comfortable sitting area, perfect for romantic in-room dining. Furnishings, though not themed, are first class. Prices run from $150 during the Hilton's off-season to $255 during the busy season.

Tower Level rooms, on the ninth and tenth floors, feature concierge service. Private lounge, plush bathrobes, continental breakfasts, hors d'oeuvres, and a late afternoon honor bar provide part of the personalized service that comes standard in this "hotel within a hotel." There are nearly 30 suites at the Hilton. They are large and luxurious. Each features a large dining table and chairs, full-size desk, minibar, coffeemaker, bath scale, and a host of other upgraded amenities.

The Hilton also offers a number of vacation packages that seem quite competitive with those of Disney. The Four-Night Romance Package Deluxe includes accommodations, airport transportation, a Four-Day Park Hopper Pass, welcome champagne, and one breakfast in bed. Prices begin at under $1,300 per couple. A golf package is also available.

For reservations and information, call the Hilton at the Village Marketplace at (800) 782-4414, Hilton reservations at (800) HILTONS, or Disney Central Reservations.

Restaurants and Lounges at the Hilton

The Hilton boasts a large number of restaurants even for a hotel of its size. Finn's Grill is its premier eatery, and it specializes in seafood and steaks. County Fair is more of an all-around place to eat. Guests can enjoy a la carte breakfasts, lunches, and dinners in the relaxed atmosphere of an old-fashioned country fair. Foods to go are offered at the County Fair Terrace, while the County Fair Buffeteria features breakfast and dinner buffets.

Other eateries include Rum Largo, the poolside bar and cafe, the Old-Fashioned Soda Shop, and a Benihana's Japanese Steakhouse. Disney character breakfasts are also on the menu here at the Hilton.

Services Available at the Hilton

The Hilton offers full bell service, 24-hour room service, curbside check-in, on-premises car rental, concierge desk, men's and women's apparel shops, American Express Travel Desk, special services for Japanese guests, and valet service.

Recreational Activities at the Hilton

- Two heated, outdoor swimming pools
- Tropical outdoor spa
- Complimentary Nautilus health club
- Children's activity center
- Preferred tee times at Disney golf courses
- Golf shop
- Video arcade
- Two lighted tennis courts

The Hotel Royal Plaza

By the time this book reaches you, the Royal Plaza's redesign and refurbishing should be largely complete. We're happy to tell you that all of this work has made it one of the freshest faces on the boulevard. While this hotel's restaurants are still being developed, the rooms, lobby, pool, lounges, and virtually every other area of this resort have been made "like new." From the poolside lanais to the Executive King bedrooms, the Royal Plaza has done the updating that is overdue at some of the other resorts along Hotel Plaza.

Room furnishings at the Royal Plaza have adopted a relaxing tropical look of coral hues with accents of greens and aquamarines. In addition to either two queen beds or a single king, all of the rooms include a pull-out sleeper/sofa and coffeemaker. Bathrooms have been enlarged to include a bathtub large enough for two, and every room on the top five floors has a Jacuzzi tub. Our favorite rooms here are the Executive Kings. These suites include large baths with Jacuzzis, and each has a comfortable parlor room with pull-out sofa and chairs. Each has an interesting, triangular king bedroom, and most include a wet bar with a refrigerator. The Royal Plaza features four different cost seasons, and during the peak season this room is only around $200, making it a bargain. A concierge floor and lounge are in the works for this resort as well as a variety of honeymoon packages that can include such goodies as his-and-her bathrobes and special room amenities.

This hotel's two eateries have yet to be refurbished, and definite plans have still not been made. Besides two restaurants, you'll find a snack bar adjacent to the lobby and two lounges, one poolside and the other in the main building.

Rooms at the Hotel Royal Plaza range in price from $75 to $200, making this hotel a good alternative to one of the Disney resorts and clearly better than something off-property. For reservations and inquiries, we suggest you call the Hotel Royal Plaza at (800) 248-7890 or make your reservations through Disney Central Reservations.

Services Available at the Royal Plaza

Guest services at the Royal Plaza include valet parking, bell service, car rental, laundry service, and room service until midnight.

Recreational Activities at the Royal Plaza

- Heated pool
- Large spa and sauna
- Four lighted tennis courts
- Table tennis
- VCRs
- Video arcade

The Travelodge Hotel

The Travelodge has a pleasant, tropical theme. Its lobby is colorful and bright. Cages of tropical birds add an exotic background rustling and chirping. The winding staircase, large potted trees and palms, wicker furnishings, and faux marble finish lend the lobby a comfortable and inviting feeling. A pleasant change indeed from many of the other nearby resorts, where lobbies tend toward cold and imposing.

While we found the rooms clean and well appointed, they seemed a bit tired. Standard rooms each have a private balcony with table and chairs and many command impressive views of Lake Buena Vista. Each includes in-room pay movies, hair dryer, minibar, free daily newspaper, coffee and tea maker, and either double queen beds or a single king. Room rates begin around $120 per night, but special offers should make rooms available at less than $100 year-round, with even larger savings during the off season.

Four suites are all located on the top floor. At around $200 to $300 per night (depending on the season), one of these suites would be on our list of bargains at Walt Disney World. Each suite includes a large master bedroom with king bed, a large sitting area with pull-out queen, a wet bar, coffeemaker, and large television set. What makes each so attractive is a large sunroom with glass ceiling. Complete with lovely wicker furnishings, this area makes the entire suite, and its panoramic view, quite attractive.

For reservations and information, call the Travelodge Hotel at (800) 578-7878 or Disney Central Reservations.

Restaurants and Lounges at the Travelodge

Trader's is this hotel's table-service restaurant. Its large expanse of glass opens onto trickling fountains and an attractive dining porch. Steaks and seafood are the specialties. With a breakfast buffet and an a la carte dinner menu, Trader's is a moderately priced eatery. Surroundings are pleasant, and the food is good.

Located near the lobby is the Parakeet Cafe, a counter-service restaurant, which features a variety of quick meals, snacks, beers and wines, and liquor. Homemade doughnuts, pizza, and "croissandwiches" are several of the offerings.

There are two lounges here at the Travelodge. The Flamingo Cove is the hotel's lobby bar. Upstairs is Topper's, a lively sports bar. Topper's offers several pool tables, free popcorn, and a commanding view of the neighborhood.

Services Available at the Travelodge

Included during your stay at the Travelodge are bell service, baby-sitting, room service until midnight, and a Guest Services desk for reservations.

Recreational Activities at the Travelodge

- Heated pool and children's playground
- Video arcade
- Disney Channel in all rooms

DoubleTree Guest Suites Resort

This modern resort rightfully claims to be the only all-suites hotel inside of Walt Disney World. Its lobby is large, and the restaurants are clean and colorful. The pool area is attractive yet unremarkable. Rooms at the DoubleTree are spacious, nicely furnished, and comfortable. Here comes the "but": this place is just like a thousand other nice hotels. It offers little or none of the fun, fantasy, and artfulness that is present in great quantities in virtually all of the Disney resorts.

Each "room" here is actually two, a living/dining area and a bedroom. Bedrooms come with a choice of twin doubles or a single king. The single bathroom is large and features a spacious vanity area with a hair dryer and television set. The living room includes a sofa bed, desk, dining area, refrigerator, microwave, coffeemaker, and television. Rates for the one-bedroom suites run from $129 to over $239, depending on the season (April to mid-December is considered the off-season). The DoubleTree also offers two-bedrooms suites, with prices beginning around $325 per night and hitting $425 during the winter holiday season. The DoubleTree also offers a variety of seasonal and special packages. For reservations and pricing of both the suites and packages, call the DoubleTree at (800) 222-TREE or Disney Central Reservations.

Restaurants and Lounges at the DoubleTree

Streamer's is the restaurant at DoubleTree. Adjacent to the atrium-style lobby, this eatery offers a large menu. Breakfasts include the usual entrees and a few specials such as the "Last Resort Breakfast." For dinner, choose among burgers, pizza, fajitas, shrimp tortellini, and Cajun swordfish.

DoubleTree also has a poolside snack bar and lounge. For those wishing to do for themselves, there is Streamer's Market. This place offers a very large selection of sandwiches, snack foods, and groceries. Given that each suite comes with a microwave and a refrigerator, this is an opportunity to throttle-back on dining expenses. Room Service is available.

Recreational Activities at the DoubleTree

- Tropically landscaped, heated pool with spa
- Separate kiddie pool
- Exercise center, tennis courts, and a jogging and walking trail
- Video arcade
- Children's activities

Marriot Courtyard at Walt Disney World Village

Here is yet another of Hotel Plaza's attractive yet bland offerings. The large lobby features tiered corridors in a surrounding atrium style. The lobby lounge is colorful and bright but features little, if any, real character. The grounds here at the Marriot are well maintained but nearly featureless, compared even to some of the other resorts at Hotel Plaza. The pool area is large and there is even a whirlpool hot tub. This 14-story hotel is clean, well kept, and well appointed.

There are 325 rooms here at the Marriot Courtyard. Two of them are large executive suites. Bedding choices are either twin doubles or a single king or queen. Each room has a coffeemaker, color television with pay movies, and small table and chairs. Furnishings are standard hotel fare. Bedspreads are floral and drapes are aqua. The guest rooms here are bright and new, though devoid of any interesting features. Rooms here could be in a hotel virtually anywhere. Room rates are $79 to $169.

For reservations and inquiries, call the Marriot Courtyard at the Village Marketplace at (800) 223-9930, Marriot Courtyard reservations at (800) 321-2211, or Disney Central Reservations.

Restaurants at the Marriot

The Courtyard Cafe and Grill is one of several places to eat at the Marriot Courtyard. This restaurant serves both breakfast and dinner. The Village Deli features pizza and frozen yogurt. Pizza is also available at the Courtyard Cafe.

Recreational Activities at the Marriot

- Two swimming pools with whirlpool spa
- Children's pool and playground

- Video arcade and in-room Nintendo
- Exercise room

OUR IMPRESSIONS OF HOTEL PLAZA

- The seven Hotel Plaza hotel/resorts are competently managed. The Boulevard itself is shady and beautifully landscaped. The hotels are all nice. None of them, however, offers the Disney magic that you come here for.
- We have heard many complaints about the slow bus service at Hotel Plaza. Given that each bus serves all seven of the hotels on each trip, we guess that such complaints may not be unfounded.

ROMANCE AT HOTEL PLAZA

- Dinner at Arthur's 27: ♥♥♥♥
- An evening stroll over to Pleasure Island or the Marketplace: ♥
- Buena Vista Palace Spa: ♥♥♥
- We didn't find much at Hotel Plaza that we found particularly romantic. The fantasy that we so enjoy at the themed Disney resorts is simply not an element here.

PART 2

What to Do Once You Get There

CHAPTER 3

Getting Started

Well, here you are—you've made it. After all of your careful planning and eager anticipation, you've finally arrived at Walt Disney World. What next?

One of you grabs the camera, and you both run out to the first park that strikes your fancy. With whatever you have left of the day, you try to get in as much as you can. You run from ride to ride and show to show. You stay out all day, racing from place to place, eating fast food, returning to your room at midnight to collapse exhausted into your bed. Your last thoughts before falling into a deep, comatose sleep are "Will we be able to see everything at Epcot tomorrow?"

We hope that this is not what you do. Let others turn Walt Disney World into a track and field event. We would like to head you in another direction, one that will be a lot more satisfying. Remember that the two of you have come for a special time together and to see the attractions too. Doing both, and staying in the mood, will be a simple matter of balance.

Look through this book for the heart symbols ♥. Intersperse your theme park adventures with enough time together doing what is blissful and intimate. Spend a morning at the Magic Kingdom, then go back to your resort for a few hours in the pool. Ride a bike or rent a boat. Relax, then go back out for an evening of dining and excitement. But remember, come home early for a nice soak in the hot tub and then some time together. Get the picture? All it takes is resisting the notion that you have to see as much of Disney World as possible.

Tools of the Trade

Things change constantly at Walt Disney World. We're talking not so much about the big things but about the small ones. Show times, performers, fireworks shows, parades, and even park hours are all subject to seasonal and even daily variations. The first thing you'll want to do after settling in is to get a handle on what's happening and when. There are several useful tools for this.

"The World Update"

At check-in, you should receive this colorful information sheet. It will give you the latest facts about Surprise Mornings and which rides will be running early. It will tell you about new attractions, special events, rehabs (which attractions are down for maintenance), and the operating hours of all the Disney attractions for the days that you'll be guests. There's lots more, too, and much of it will be helpful in planning your days.

Theme Park Guidemaps

Available for each of the theme parks, one of these detailed maps will be your guide to a ride or attraction, restroom, shop, or eatery. Updated weekly, the guidemaps also provide all the information you'll need to find out what's happening and when in any of the parks, including parades, fireworks, live entertainment, and special events. The guidemaps are available at the Guest Services of your resort, the entrance at each of the theme parks, and at most shops and vendors throughout the parks. We suggest you pick up all of them early in your stay to help you plan a relaxed and easy Disney visit.

More Good Stuff

There's more going on at Disney than even the guides can cover. Drop by your Guest Services and ask what specials or special events are going on at Pleasure Island, the water parks, and the Village Marketplace.

Getting Around at Walt Disney World

Walt Disney World is a big place. Getting around its nearly 40 square miles will be something that you will want to get good at. It will not be hard. The bus system at Disney runs an astounding 160 buses with nearly 600 drivers to keep them going. It is the third largest bus system in Florida.

We're not going to tell you that busing around Walt Disney World will be romantic. What we will tell you is that there are a lot of other ways to get around and that some of these are most certainly special and, yes, even a bit romantic. Besides the usual buses, there's the monorail, a fleet of boats, carriages, and trolleys. We encourage you to take the road less traveled.

Disney Bus Service

This past year has seen even more new strategies in Disney bus service. We are happy to report that there seems to be real improvement. During the Disney rush hours (9 A.M. to 11 A.M. and 5 P.M. to 7 P.M.), buses are running more frequently. With buses promised every 20 minutes, the reality seems more like every 10 minutes. Routes have been altered to make better use of buses. You will find that most buses make a roundabout series of stops, and some of them may surprise you. As you board a bus, always ask the driver if it will be stopping at your destination.

Bus service at Walt Disney World is really quite good. Buses can get just about anywhere in 10 or 15 minutes. Plan on five minutes to get to your bus stop and, along with a short wait for the bus, you can count on 30 minutes to actually arrive at your destination.

The Disney Fleet

If you both enjoy a pleasant outdoor trip, there is nothing like a boat ride. Dozens of watercraft ply the waters of the World, and as Disney resort guests you'll be free to use all of them. From the dock at the Magic Kingdom, boats make their arrivals and departures for the Wilderness Lodge, the Grand Floridian and the Polynesian resorts, Discovery Island, Fort Wilderness, and River Country. At Epcot's World Showcase Lagoon, catch a watercraft across the lagoon to either Germany or Morocco. At Epcot's International Gateway, *Friendship* water taxis carry passengers to the BoardWalk, to the Yacht and the Beach Clubs, and to the Swan and the Dolphin. Hop off at any for a meal or to catch a connecting boat to Disney–MGM.

The Disney Village Marketplace and Pleasure Island are both located on Lake Buena Vista, which connects to a series of waterways. Here, watercraft leave for trips up the Sassagoula to Port Orleans and Dixie Landings as well as to Old Key West.

The Monorail

There are three monorail spurs at Walt Disney World running on more than 13 miles of elevated track. Two spurs run around the Seven Seas

Lagoon. The express carries day guests to the Magic Kingdom from the Ticket and Transportation Center (TTC). The local, for Disney resort guests only, makes stops at the TTC, the Polynesian, the Grand Floridian, the Contemporary, and the Magic Kingdom. The third monorail line runs from the TTC to Epcot. This monorail line is long and scenic, but expect crowds in the early morning hours when Magic Kingdom resort guests flock to Epcot.

The best seats on the monorail are in the front car with the driver. Ask the monorail attendants if seats are available (only four or five can ride at a time). If not, try waiting for the next train. Better yet, try this on the Epcot spur. This is not a loop run, and whoever is in the front car will be getting out.

Trolleys and Tramways

There is a host of odd transportation throughout the World. These include the Walt Disney Railroad, horseless carriages, horse-drawn trolleys, the Skyway to Tomorrowland, and lots more. Each of these is waiting to take you on a pleasant fantasy ride.

Travel to Other Resort Areas

Getting to any of the attractions is simple. Traveling to other Disney resort areas is a bit more complicated, though, and you will likely want to do it for a Disney character breakfast, for dining, or for just looking around. If you have a car, then driving may be the simplest thing to do. But busing is not too difficult. During the day, the easiest way to get to another resort will be to go to any park and catch a bus returning to where you want to go. Frequent buses come and go all day long from all resorts. After park closing, this same technique can be used from the bus centers at the Village Marketplace and Pleasure Island. Buses to all Disney resorts arrive and depart from the Marketplace beginning at 10 A.M., and after 11 P.M. buses continue into the wee hours from the Pleasure Island bus area.

CHAPTER 4

$\mathcal{T}$he Attractions

Walt Disney World is home to an ever-growing number of attractions. It is best known for its three theme parks: the Magic Kingdom, Epcot, and Disney–MGM Studios. In spring of 1998, the Animal Kingdom, a fourth theme park, will open. There are other entertainment areas, too: Discovery Island, Typhoon Lagoon, Blizzard Beach, River Country, the BoardWalk Promenade, Downtown Disney, and the Disney Institute. From water parks to wildlife preserves, from nightclubs to shopping districts, Disney World offers more than just a *little* something for everyone.

If we were to give you one bit of advice about which of these to include in your visit, we'd tell you to keep an open mind. Consider everything, especially if you've never heard of it. Often, that small and unsung attraction is the one you will remember long after the thrill of Splash Mountain has faded. If you aren't interested in the thrill rides, there are countless other things to do. If you do enjoy the more exciting attractions, then fasten your seat belts and get ready for the most exciting rides in themedom.

In this chapter, we will give you an idea about what there is to do now that you have arrived. We'll provide just enough information so that you can discover what best suits your interests and avoid spending time at attractions that are not your cup of tea. As for the BoardWalk and Downtown Disney, we'll tell you about them in Chapters 5 and 7.

$\mathcal{T}$IPS FOR THE THEME PARKS

- Surprise Mornings are an important perk for Disney resort guests. Each morning, a different theme park opens an hour and a half before the public onslaught. Only certain attractions are open—you can find out what these will be in the World Update, which you should have received at check-in. The schedule repeats itself weekly:

- Magic Kingdom: Monday, Thursday, Saturday
- Epcot: Tuesday and Friday
- Disney–MGM Studios: Sunday and Wednesday

- The first few hours of the day in each park are usually the least crowded. Make use of them.
- The busiest days in each park are that park's Surprise Mornings. Most Disney guests arrive early and stay the day. Don't do this. Come early, but as soon as the park begins to get too busy, zip over to one of the other theme parks to take advantage of the first few hours of its day.
- Each park has a Tip Board near its entrance that provides up-to-the-minute reports of show times and estimated waits. Use them to avoid wasting time in lines.
- Signs at many of the shows will tell you how long the wait will be from a certain point. Always ask the cast members that patrol the line if you are waiting for the next show or the one after it.
- Many attractions have two aisles for their lines, and most people take the one on the right. Don't go with the flow. The left line is often faster.
- Try arriving at one of the parks an hour or two before closing. You may feel like salmon swimming upstream, but you'll be amazed at how much you can accomplish while most people are leaving.
- Storage lockers are located near the entrance to each of the parks. Small ones are $.50 for a day's use and larger ones cost $.75.

The Magic Kingdom

When most people think of Walt Disney World, they think of the Magic Kingdom. In fact, the Magic Kingdom is only a small part of what there is to do and to see at Walt Disney World. Children tend to think of it as the best part of Disney, which often leads adults to think that it is largely for children. Lately, we have found ourselves returning to the Magic Kingdom and enjoying it more and more. While there are many child-oriented attractions here, do not assume that the child in you won't enjoy them.

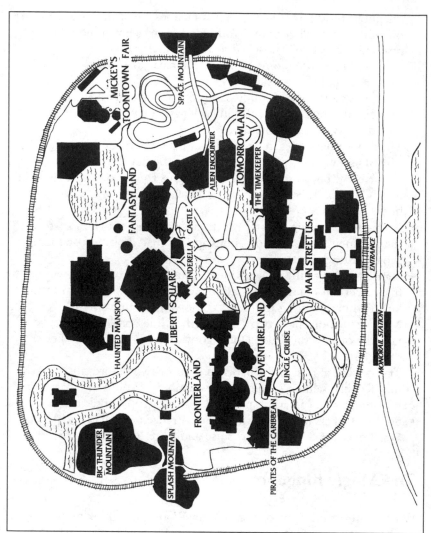

The Magic Kingdom

The Magic Kingdom is made up of seven different areas: Main Street USA, Adventureland, Frontierland, Liberty Square, Fantasyland, Tomorrowland, and Mickey's Toontown Fair.

MAGIC KINGDOM TIPS

- The most important thing to know about this theme park is that it is the busiest part of Walt Disney World.
- Don't try to see it all in one day.
- If you are interested in seeing the big-name attractions, we suggest that you make them your first effort. Start early. Surprise Mornings at the Magic Kingdom are on Monday, Thursday, and Saturday.
- Try the busier attractions during a parade or fireworks show.

Main Street USA

Main Street, a re-creation of a turn-of-the-century American town, is really a collection of shops, small eateries, and a movie house. The Victorian architecture is beautiful. Slate mansard roofs and carved gingerbread evoke the days of the horseless carriage. It is easy to run through this part of the Magic Kingdom on your way to the big-name attractions. While you probably will do so on your first few visits to the Magic Kingdom, you will find it worthwhile to slow down here eventually. Main Street opens at least half an hour before the actual park. Come early and browse, then head for the rides when the park opens.

Walt Disney World Railroad

This is a real steam-powered railway that huffs and puffs its way around the borders of the Magic Kingdom. These authentic old trains were discovered by the Disney people in Mexico, hauling sugar in the Yucatan. The ride takes a bit over 20 minutes and is an entertaining way to get a good overall view of the park. There are three stations, one on Main Street, one in Frontierland, and the other at Mickey's Toontown Fair. All aboard!

Harmony Barber Shop

Who would ever need to get a haircut at Disney? Well, Rick did, and we got a very pleasant experience as well as an exceptionally good haircut. It makes for a great photo, as the barbers are in period costumes. If you inquire first, you may find yourself in the barber chair while the Dapper Dans, Disney's barbershop quartet, gather 'round and harmonize.

Main Street Cinema

This theater features six small screens and nonstop animated classics. It's especially nice if you want to catch Mickey's debut in *Steamboat Willie*.

Transportation on Main Street USA

The trolleys, horseless carriages, and fire engine make a one-way trip up or down Main Street. They are interesting but hardly worth a wait in line.

Main Street Eateries

Main Street is bustling with food establishments. The Crystal Palace now features a pleasant garden atmosphere and character buffets for breakfast, lunch, and dinner. Both lunch and dinner are quite good. The art nouveau Plaza Restaurant is a quiet haven that offers a menu of good sandwiches. There's also Tony's Town Square with its traditional Italian cuisine. (For more on these restaurants, see Chapter 6.) There are lots of fast-food offerings, too: the Main Street Bakeshop, Plaza Ice Cream Parlor, and Casey's Corner, home of the all-American hot dog.

The Shops of Main Street

There are lots of shops along Main Street and, depending on your tastes, you should find at least something that interests you. Some of our favorites are Disneyana Collectibles, the Main Street Book Store, and Main Street Athletic Club, which features real sports memorabilia.

Adventureland

At the end of Main Street, hang a left and cross a small footbridge into another world. With dense jungle on your left and what appears to be Zanzibar on your right, you will head off into the heart of Adventureland. This has always been a favorite of ours. We enjoy strolling about, looking closely at all of the architectural details.

The Swiss Family Robinson Treehouse
✓ Walk-through exhibit
✓ Lasts about 30 minutes
✓ Line moves slowly

Talk about artificial plants. This attraction is a huge treehouse built in a man-made tree. The tree has 80,000 vinyl leaves on it, and the treehouse contains a variety of cute and interesting "inventions" created by the castaway Robinson family.

INTERESTING, but not enough to make it worth a long wait
Tip: Try this attraction when there is hardly any line. Don't attempt this one with cranky kids if there is a wait.

The Enchanted Tiki Birds: The Tropical Serenade
✓ Sit-down show
✓ Lasts 20 minutes
✓ Line moves fairly quickly

This is Disney's very first audio-animatronic attraction, featured originally at Disneyland. More than two hundred birds, plants, and statues all come to life with lots of music, special effects, and corny Disney humor.

QUITE GOOD, entertaining, and a nice cool place to relax

The Jungle Cruise
✓ Boat ride
✓ Lasts 10 minutes
✓ Line moves slowly

This boat ride through Africa (and India) is one of the Magic Kingdom's signature attractions. It is loaded with gags and audio-animatronic animals. Each boat's pilot gives the ride his or her own special brand of groan-a-minute humor. We did this ride once at night, in a misty rain. It was great.

EXCELLENT, especially at night—don't miss it

Pirates of the Caribbean
✓ Boat ride
✓ Lasts 8 minutes
✓ Line moves quickly

This is a terrific adventure, one of the best that the Magic Kingdom has to offer. It is a boat ride through a Caribbean town that is being plundered by a gang of fun-loving pirates. The special effects and audio-animatronics are some of Disney's finest despite the age of this attraction.

EXCELLENT, not to be missed
Tip: This ride may be too intense for very young children.

The Restaurants of Adventureland

With the closing of the Adventureland Veranda, food offerings here are now limited to several counter-service places. El Pirata y el Perico (the Pirate and the Parrot) offers Mexican items such as tacos, nachos, and taco salads. The nearby Sunshine Tree Terrace features drinks, coffees, and frozen yogurts; across the plaza, you'll find the Oasis and its refreshing beverages. Right near the Treehouse is the Egg Roll Wagon.

The Shops of Adventureland

Shopping is very good in Adventureland, and we recommend some browsing later in the day. Plaza del Sol Bazaar has an outstanding selection of tropical clothes, while other shops, such as Traders of Timbuktu, Elephant Tales, and Tiki Tropics, offer some interesting items. Drop by Lafitte's Portrait Deck for a souvenir FotoToon. You'll love it.

Frontierland

The Wild West comes alive in this area of the Magic Kingdom. It boasts several outstanding rides and a few good shows.

Splash Mountain
✓   Water-flume ride
✓   Lasts 10 minutes
✓   Line moves quickly

This is one of Disney's newer attractions and it is also one of the busiest. Waits here can run as long two hours. Themed after Disney's movie, *Song of the South,* this ride is essentially a log-flume trip through the world of Brer Rabbit. The music is a pure delight, and the ride tells the tale with more than 100 robotic characters. When you finish this ride, you will be pleasantly spritzed with water and humming "Zippity Doo Dah." We guarantee it. (Or, if you sit in the very front of the log, you may be half-drenched and singing "Blow the Man Down.")

EXCELLENT, not to be missed
Tip: Arrange, at nearby Splashdown Photo, to have your picture taken while you are on this ride. It will be one of your most memorable Disney photos.

Big Thunder Mountain Railroad
✓ Mild roller coaster
✓ Lasts 3 minutes
✓ Line moves quickly

This ride is one of those attractions that you can go on time after time and still see new things. It is a "runaway" mining train careening through an old-time mining camp and is loaded with thrills, fun, sight gags, and great special effects.

EXCELLENT, not to be missed
Tip: Try Big Thunder a second time after dark.

Country Bear Jamboree
✓ Audio-animatronic show
✓ Lasts 15 minutes
✓ Line moves slowly

This cute show features bears that sing, dance, and generally horse around. It is entertaining, and we recommend it.

GOOD, especially for children
Tips: Try this one during an afternoon or evening parade. There is a special Christmas version of this show.

The Shootin' Arcade
✓ Electronic shooting arcade
✓ Costs $.25
✓ Line moves slowly

We visited Disney World when our son was 12 years old. He spent virtually all of his time here sharpening his shooting skills. We checked up on him now and then to be sure that he was all right and even dropped by with an occasional hamburger.

OK, if you like this sort of thing
Tip: Walk by and take a look at the Hawken rifles.

Diamond Horseshoe Jamboree
✓ Combination restaurant and live show

This used to be a ticketed show. No longer. Now, the Diamond Horseshoe Jamboree is more like a saloon. There is live entertainment going on nearly continually, and all you have to do is stroll in and pull up a chair. A small counter-service restaurant is at the bar, featuring a pretty unremarkable selection. If you wish, you can simply sit and watch the shows. The entertainment varies, but some of it is quite good.

Interesting. **Check it out**

Tom Sawyer Island
✓ Walk-through playground
✓ No time limit
✓ Line moves slowly

This attraction, a raft trip to a small island, may not be high on our list of things to see, although it isn't such a bad place to bring an overactive child. It's basically an island-playground, complete with cave, fort, and lots of places to explore.

Mostly for kids
Tip: This could be a good place for tired parents to rest.

Frontierland Grub

Pecos Bill's is this area's big restaurant. It features an enjoyable sidewalk atmosphere that, unfortunately, gets pretty crowded. Barbecue, burgers, and hot dogs are on the menu. Keep an eye on the animals on the wall while you are eating. Aunt Polly's Landing, over on Tom Sawyer's Island, features a pleasant porch but only if you want a peanut butter and jelly sandwich or cold fried chicken. Westward Ho is a food cart that should be named Westward Ho Junk Food. During the busier seasons, you may find the Turkey Leg Wagon over by Pecos Bill's, which features an interesting lunch.

The Shops of Frontierland

The shops of Frontierland have a definite western flair. The Prairie Outpost and Supply and the Frontier Trading Post both have nice collections of Native American and frontier clothing. After that, there's the Trail Creek Hat Shop, the Briar Patch, and Frontier Wood Carving.

Liberty Square

This area, snuggled between Fantasyland and Frontierland, is a small slice of Revolutionary War Americana. Take a look at the Liberty Tree, complete with its 13 lanterns representing the original 13 states. This tree was actually moved here, with great difficulty, from another location at Disney World.

Liberty Square Riverboat
✓ Boat ride
✓ Lasts 15 minutes
✓ Line moves quickly

This magnificent re-creation of a paddle-wheel steamer was built right on Disney property. The ride makes a short loop on Frontierland's River of the Americas and provides a relaxing view of the attractions along it. This boat, by the way, is pulled along on an underwater track and is not a thrill ride.

GOOD, pleasant, can be cool and restful
Tip: Try queuing up just when the boat arrives, as it can hold virtually everyone waiting.

The Hall of Presidents
✓ Audio-animatronic show
✓ Lasts 25 minutes
✓ Line moves quickly

This show is neither exciting nor funny, but it is interesting, especially if you are history buffs.

INTERESTING, with good audio-animatronics

The Haunted Mansion
✓ Low-speed ride
✓ Lasts 9 minutes
✓ Line moves slowly

We won't tell you much about this one except to say that it is more fun than scary. We'll leave the rest for your delight.

EXCELLENT, do not miss

The Restaurants of Liberty Square

The Liberty Tree Tavern is a pleasant, colonial-style restaurant and offers a nice variety of lunches (entrees and sandwiches) and a character dinner buffet. Food is good and prices are moderate.

In addition, there are two other good places to eat here, both of them offering counter service. Sleepy Hollow has a selection of vegetarian foods, from avocado salad to pita sandwiches; we enjoy the offerings here. The Columbia Harbor House has a seafood theme, offering fish, chicken, and salads.

The Shops of Liberty Square

There is a lot to be said for the shops in Liberty Square. The assortment is unusual and the quality is good. This is not your usual array of theme park shops. The Yankee Trader is one of our favorite shops. It specializes in kitchen-related items. Other places of interest are the Silversmith, Old World Antiques, and the Heritage House.

Fantasyland

Cinderella Castle marks the main entrance to Fantasyland. The only structure at Walt Disney World that is taller is the new Twilight Zone Tower of Terror at Disney–MGM Studios.

Cinderella's Golden Carousel ♥

✓ Merry-go-round
✓ Ride lasts 2 minutes
✓ Line moves slowly

This handmade, beautiful old carousel was built in 1917, when "handmade" really meant something. This ride can actually be romantic, especially at night.

QUITE GOOD, more fun and romantic than you might think
Tips: Almost always open for Surprise Mornings. Ask a cast member to snap a picture of you both.

Skyway to Tomorrowland

✓ Cable car ride
✓ Lasts 5 minutes
✓ Line moves quickly

This is a one-way aerial tram ride to Tomorrowland. It provides an interesting view as well as a relaxing, away-from-the-throngs escape. Handicapped visitors are allowed to leave their wheelchairs at one end and take a round trip.

QUITE GOOD
Tip: Try getting on in Tomorrowland—the line there is usually much shorter.

It's a Small World

✓ Boat ride
✓ Lasts 10 minutes
✓ Line moves quickly

This pleasant and upbeat musical boat ride was created for the 1965 New York World's Fair. The music is catchy and it will get you both in the mood for Fantasyland.

QUITE GOOD

Legend of the Lion King

✓ Live and animated show
✓ Lasts 25 minutes
✓ Line moves to fill theater

This stage show combines live action, animation, and impressive special effects to create a simply wonderful miniversion of the animated film. This one may require a wait; it is worth it.

EXCELLENT, do not miss
Tip: Try this early or any time that you see that the line is not huge.

Peter Pan's Flight, Snow White's Adventure, and Mr. Toad's Wild Ride

✓ Low-speed rides
✓ Each lasts about 2–3 minutes
✓ Lines move slowly

We put these three rides together because they are so much alike. Despite the fact that these are basically kiddie rides, you might find them fun. Snow White has been redesigned due to complaints that it was too frightening for younger children. It may still be too scary for some young children.

OK, especially if you have small children
Tips: The waits can be long. Any of these rides may be intense for very young children.

Dumbo

✓ Midway-type ride
✓ Lasts less than 2 minutes
✓ Line moves very slowly

Six new Dumbo cars have been added to this ride in an effort to shorten the typically long waits.

A MUST for young children
Tips: Catch this one early. It is usually open for Surprise Mornings. Waits may still be long.

The Mad Tea Party

✓ Midway-type ride (spins)
✓ Lasts 2 minutes
✓ Line moves slowly

The speed of rotation of these spinning teacups can be controlled by the riders. Usually, this is a rather mild ride, aimed mostly at younger children.

OK; can be fun, especially if you enjoy feeling dizzy
Tip: Usually open for Surprise Mornings.

The Restaurants of Fantasyland

King Stefan's Banquet Hall is a beautiful restaurant located inside the castle. For atmosphere and ambience, it is hard to beat. The food is not great, though, and you'll need reservations to get in. The other Fantasyland eateries offer fast food. The Pinocchio Village Haus is a large indoor restaurant that features burgers, bratwurst, sandwiches, and even a turkey burger. Lumiere's Kitchen has a good selection of kid foods: grilled cheese sandwiches and chicken nuggets. For snacks and beverages, there's Hook's Tavern, the Enchanted Grove, and Mrs. Pott's Cupboard.

The Shops of Fantasyland

The King's Gallery, inside Cinderella Castle, has an interesting assortment of trinkets created by old-world artisans. Pricey, but nice to look at. Mickey's Christmas Carol offers a selection of Disney Christmas ornaments. There is also a candy store and several novelty shops.

Tomorrowland

Tomorrowland used to resemble a 1950s shopping mall: lots of concrete and neon and very little of "tomorrow." We are happy to tell you that a total redesign has been completed and, with the help of creative geniuses such as George Lucas, this area has become imaginative and exciting. The theme is more like a Jules Verne science-fiction vision: a strange blend of the old and the new. Whatever you want to call it, it looks really neat. The tired old rides have been replaced with several outstanding attractions.

Alien Encounter
✓ Special-effects show (not a ride)
✓ Lasts 20 minutes
✓ Line moves quickly

This attraction got off to a bad start when Michael Eisner, the Disney CEO, rode it during a test run. "Not scary enough," he declared, and it was back to the drawing boards for Alien. We have ridden it before and after and were impressed both times. The plot, a botched attempt at teletransportation, is good. The show is an awesome display of new technology.

QUITE GOOD, kind of creepy
Tips: The lines here are usually long. If you do not like being in total darkness, skip it. Too intense for young children.

The Timekeeper

✓ Film and audio-animatronic show
✓ Lasts 15 minutes
✓ Line moves quickly

This show, which includes a CircleVision 360 (360-degree) film narrated by a Robin Williams robot, is exciting, clever, wild, and zany in a way that only Robin Williams could have made it.

EXCELLENT, not to be missed
Tips: This attraction is held in a large theater, which, if the lines aren't outrageous, will allow everyone in to see it. Ask the cast members at the door how long the wait will be.

Space Mountain

✓ High-speed roller coaster ride
✓ Lasts 3 minutes
✓ Line moves quickly

This is one of the World's most popular attractions. It is a roller coaster inside of a planetarium. It is fast and fairly rough. The waits in line here can be interminable.

EXCELLENT, if you like this type of ride
Tips: If you go for a Surprise Morning and this ride is not open, ask for the opening time and be there to get in line. It often opens later but before the park opens to the public.

Tomorrowland Transit Authority

✓ Gentle tram ride
✓ Lasts 10 minutes
✓ Line moves very quickly

This is the old WED-Way People Mover, renamed. It is a magnetically propelled car (called linear induction), the kind Japan is investing heavily in as a train system.

INTERESTING, but not memorable
Tip: If you want to see the inside of Space Mountain without riding it, this is the way to do it.

The Astro Orbiter
✓ Midway-type ride
✓ Lasts about 2 minutes
✓ Line moves very slowly

This is a recycled version of the old StarJets ride. It will give you a good view of Tomorrowland. Definitely mild.

OK, more interesting to look at

The Carousel of Progress
✓ Show with revolving stage
✓ Lasts 20 minutes
✓ Line moves quickly

This audio-animatronic show demonstrates how technology has impacted the home over the last three decades.

QUITE GOOD
Tip: Try this show when the other attractions are busy.

Grand Prix Raceway
✓ Miniature raceway
✓ Lasts about 5 minutes
✓ Line moves slowly

This is nothing more than a raceway with small, motorized go-karts. The pace is slow, and a runner-track restricts steering. This ride is very popular with children, especially those whose parents don't let them drive the family car.

OK, a kiddie ride

Take Flight
✓ Special-effects ride (very mild)
✓ Lasts 6 minutes
✓ Line moves very quickly

This ride travels slowly through the history of aviation. Not only interesting, it has one segment that is even exciting.

GOOD, not Splash Mountain, but worth it
Tip: Try it when the other rides begin getting too crowded.

Skyway to Fantasyland
✓ Cable car
✓ Lasts 5 minutes
✓ Line moves quickly

This is the one-way aerial tram ride back to Fantasyland.

Food in Tomorrowland

We hope that the future has better food to offer than this area. Cosmic Ray's Starlight Cafe is the Magic Kingdom's largest fast-food restaurant. Besides its usual fare of burgers and hot dogs, Ray's has recently added rotisserie chicken and tossed salad. Still, it is noisy and crowded. The Plaza Pavilion is another large, counter-service eatery and features pizzas, chicken, and sandwiches. Nearby, however, is a charming outdoor patio near the water's edge. Auntie Gravity's is a breath of fresh air with its frozen yogurt and natural foods, and the Lunching Pad offers turkey legs and chips.

Mickey's Toontown Fair

If you're coming to Disney World with small children, this is one place you won't want to miss. New in 1996, this area will make you feel like you are *in* a cartoon. It's really a small animated, three-dimensional village, complete with the homes of both Mickey and Minnie Mouse and a small country fair. There's even a kiddie roller coaster, the Barnstormer. This is a must for small children, as there's lots for them to see and do. Attractions include Goofy's Wiseacre Farm, Donald's Boat, and a meeting with the Mouse himself. There's also Toon Park, Pete's Garage, and Mickey's Hall of Fame. Toontown

Fair is also thriving with other Disney characters. The photo opportunities here are endless. On the downside, it gets very crowded. We suggest that you arrive early and if you are traveling without young ones, just simply take a quick look.

The Barnstormer at Goofy's Wiseacre Farm
✓ Kiddie roller coaster
✓ Short, lasts only a few minutes or less
✓ Line moves slowly

This short roller coaster is intended for young children. Still, it can be too exciting for some youngsters. The ride goes literally *through* Goofy's farm. Some very good sight gags.

OK, fun for kids

MAGIC KINGDOM ATTRACTIONS NOT TO MISS
✓ Big Thunder Mountain
✓ The Haunted Mansion
✓ The Jungle Cruise
✓ Legend of the Lion King
✓ Pirates of the Caribbean
✓ SpectroMagic Light Parade ♥♥♥ (see Chapter 5)
✓ Splash Mountain and Splash Mountain photo ♥
✓ The Timekeeper
✓ Fantasy in the Sky Fireworks ♥♥

Epcot

We love the fantasy of the Magic Kingdom: the rides, the shows, and the delightful and fanciful realities created there. MGM is a celebration of the cinema, and we do love the movies. But there is something more at Epcot. Educating while entertaining is something that Disney does better than anyone, and every area and every exhibit in Epcot is rich with information and fun. This is an exciting place for curious minds.

Epcot is nearly twice the size of the Magic Kingdom. It is divided into two areas: Future World and the World Showcase. Future World displays the triumphs of science and technology. Its themes are health,

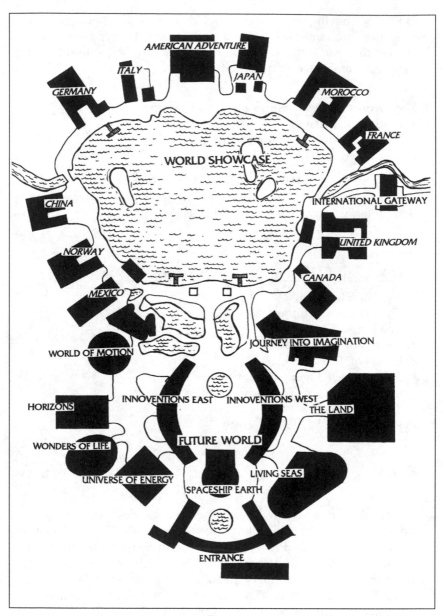

Epcot

energy, agriculture, the oceans, transportation, imagination, and communications. Each theme is featured in a different pavilion, and each pavilion has its unique attractions and exhibits. The eleven countries of the World Showcase encircle a sparkling, freshwater lagoon. Together they comprise a small world's fair.

ℰPCOT TIPS

- Each area of Epcot has different operating hours. Future World opens early and stays open until 7 or 8 P.M. The World Showcase opens at 11 A.M. and then closes after IllumiNations, at either 9 or 10 P.M., depending on the season. On the busiest days of the year, both areas may be open until 10 P.M.
- Surprise Mornings at Epcot are on Tuesday and Friday.
- Don't forget your guidemap. You will need it here. You can pick one up at one of the shops just inside either the main entrance or the International Gateway.
- The World Showcase is least crowded right after it opens.
- Future World is busiest in the morning after about 9:30 A.M. and into midafternoon. By late afternoon, the crowds begin to thin out as guests move on to the World Showcase. The hour or two before Future World closes is a good time to visit.
- Try splitting up your Epcot tour. Spend one morning at Future World, then do something fun at your resort. Another day, spend the morning around the pool and get to Epcot in time for the opening of the World Showcase.
- Don't miss the great live entertainment around the World Showcase. For more information, see Chapter 5.

Future World

This part of Epcot is a celebration of human triumphs. It is also the busiest part of Epcot. There's lots to do, much more than can be done in one day. If you want to see everything here, count on at least a few days.

Spaceship Earth
✓ Slow ride
✓ Lasts about 15 minutes
✓ Line moves quickly

This ride is inside the huge geosphere and will take you through the history of communication.

EXCELLENT, one of Epcot's best attractions—don't miss it
Tips: This ride is usually open for Surprise Mornings. After the park opens to the public, this is the first place where the entering crowds stop, and it very quickly becomes too busy. Save it for later if there is a long line.

Earth Station and the WorldKey Information Service

Located at the base of the geosphere and as you exit from Spaceship Earth, Earth Station is the place to go for information and dining reservations. The WorldKey terminal is a video display that will connect you to actual living people who will make your reservations. Be forewarned: they can see you.

Innoventions

Innoventions is one of the newer attractions at Future World. It is a showcase for the latest technologies. From automated home appliances to Personal Digital Assistants, you will find the most fascinating pieces of innovative electronics.

Detractors feel that it is little more than an advertisement for the high-tech companies that display their wares. Be that as it may, this place is neat. Innoventions offers hands-on displays, live demonstrations, and the latest in interactive media. Not just for computer nerds, this place is cool.

The Disney imagineers promise to keep Innoventions changing with the times and, from what we are able to see, they are making good on that pledge.

Tip: Innoventions gets very crowded. Either get there as soon as the park opens or try it late in the day.

The Fountain of Nations Water Ballet This delightful fountain, located at Innoventions Plaza, is a classic example of Disney imagination. The formula is simple: take one large fountain and add the genius of Disney. The result is simply wonderful. The columns of water are controlled by a computer and are timed perfectly to accompanying music. It is a symphony of motion. If you think that this is neat in the daylight, try dropping by after dark. Don't miss the other lighting effects around the plaza. For fountain "performance" times, consult the Epcot guidemap.

The Wonders of Life Pavilion

This pavilion is our favorite. It gets very busy, and we suggest that you come right after opening. Inside are shows, films, and dozens of hands-on displays. All of it is good.

Body Wars
✓ Simulated thrill ride
✓ Lasts 5 minutes
✓ Line moves quickly

Like Star Tours at Disney–MGM, this ride doesn't really go anywhere; it merely creates the illusion. The show is a journey into the human body aboard a miniaturized "inner-space ship." It's realistic and exciting. The motion of this ride is jerky.

EXCELLENT
Tip: Lines can get long, but they move quickly.

The Making of Me
✓ Film
✓ Lasts 15 minutes
✓ Line moves very slowly

This cute film ♥♥ features Martin Short, and it is both humorous and touching. If it starts in a few minutes, get in line.

EXCELLENT
Tips: The theater is small and the lines can get long. Make an effort to see it early, or wait until late in the day.

Cranium Command
✓ Show
✓ Lasts 20 minutes
✓ Line moves to fill theater

Another of our favorites, this show features audio-animatronics, animation, and special effects. Throw away your preconceptions about this attraction and see it. It is what Disney does best.

EXCELLENT, not to be missed

Tips: In all but the busiest of times, the wait for this show should not be much of a factor. Don't miss the preshow.

Goofy About Health
✓ Show
✓ Lasts 15 minutes

This low-key multiscreen show features Goofy getting wise about fitness and health.

OK, for children

Hands-on Activities
✓ Various displays and exhibits
✓ No set time limits
✓ Lines move slowly

The Wonders of Life Pavilion is full of exhibits that involve your participation. Have your golf swing analyzed, or hop onto a video exercycle and see the sights. There are lots of things to do that are fun and informative. Don't miss the Sensory Funhouse.

GOOD to VERY GOOD, don't pass by this area

The Universe of Energy Pavilion

Ellen's Energy Adventure
✓ Slow ride
✓ Lasts about 30 minutes
✓ Line moves slowly

In its last incarnation, this attraction was a real snoozer. No longer. Completely revamped, it now features comedian Ellen DeGeneres in a nightmare version of "Jeopardy," during which she appears with Jamie Lee Curtis, Bill Nye the Science Guy, and Alex Trebek. The show includes film, special effects, and audio-animatronic dinosaurs. It is clever and funny.

ENTERTAINING, with well-done special effects
Tips: This ride holds nearly 600 people at a time. The only movement of the line is when one show lets out and another goes in. The wait here looks worse than it is.

The Horizons Pavilion

Horizons
✓ Slow ride
✓ Lasts 15 minutes
✓ Line moves quickly

This ride takes you through a series of sets that re-create past and current visions of the future. The sets and effects are quite good, and the ride is interesting.

GOOD

The World of Motion Pavilion

Test Track
✓ High-speed thrill ride
✓ Preshow lasts 20 minutes, ride lasts 5 minutes

Due to open in spring of 1997, after this book goes to press, this attraction's speed of 65 mph will make it the fastest at Walt Disney World (Space Mountain is only 28 mph). Designed to give riders a "sneak peak" into the world of automotive testing, Test Track promises to be the next best thing to a proving grounds experience. After having seen it under construction and having experienced a computer simulation, we are ready for the real thing.

The Living Seas Pavilion

The centerpiece of this pavilion is its saltwater aquarium. Some 200 feet across, it is one of the largest fish tanks in the world. It's brimming with reef fish of every sort. The layout of the Living Seas is such that you're nearly surrounded by glass walls, water, and scores of tropical fish. Next to a reef dive, it doesn't get much better than this. The pavilion is divided into three areas, each with its own exhibits and theme.

The Caribbean Coral Reef Ride
✓ Slow ride
✓ Lasts 3 minutes
✓ Line moves slowly

This ride is only mildly interesting. It takes you "down" to the aquarium in a "hydrolator" and for a brief ride through an underwater tunnel.

OK

Sea Base Alpha   This part of the Living Seas is the real meat and potatoes of this pavilion. It is a prototype research facility and is chock-full of intriguing displays.

Sea Base Concourse   This part of the research facility is an interesting but quick walk-through.

The Land Pavilion

This is the largest of the pavilions in Future World, and its focus is agriculture. While this may not be on your top ten list of interests, this pavilion has a lot to offer both in entertainment and in food. Besides the ride, film, and show, it is home to the Sunshine Season Food Fair, which is the largest collection of eateries in Epcot.

Living with the Land
✓ Boat ride
✓ Lasts 10 minutes
✓ Line moves very quickly

This cool and pleasant boat ride takes you through the history of agriculture and into its future. It is scenic and fascinating. The sets and special effects are memorable.

EXCELLENT, not to be missed

Food Rocks
✓ Audio-animatronic show
✓ Lasts 10 minutes
✓ Line moves to fill theater

This show features a kitchen full of rockin' and rollin' fruits and vegetables. The music here is classic rock, with lyrics praising good nutrition.

GOOD and cute
Tip: Waits here never seem too long.

The Circle of Life
✓ Film
✓ Lasts 20 minutes
✓ Line moves to fill theater

This film replaces the tired and unexciting *Symbiosis*. The theme of this film is ecology, and the stars are Simba, Timon, and Pumbaa from *The Lion King*. The message is inspiring and upbeat.

GOOD
Tip: This theater seats more than 400. Check for times at the entrance and ask if you will make it into the next show.

The Greenhouse Tour
✓ Walking tour
✓ Lasts 45 minutes
✓ By reservation only, $6 per person

This fascinating tour goes through the greenhouses of the Land, where you will see the latest in agriculture techniques. The tours are conducted by real agriculturists.

QUITE GOOD
Tips: Make your reservations inside the pavilion, at the small kiosk near the entrance to Food Rocks. This is a popular tour.

Journey Into Imagination Pavilion

This wonderful pavilion is definitely one not to miss. There are lots of fun things to do here. After you have spent some time inside, don't miss the whimsical fountains outside.

Journey Into Imagination
✓ Slow ride
✓ Lasts 13 minutes
✓ Line moves quickly

This ride seems to lack the excitement typical of most Disney attractions. Cute, happy, and warmhearted, yes, but captivating and interesting, no.

OK

Honey, I Shrunk the Audience
✓ 3-D film
✓ Lasts 25 minutes
✓ Line moves to fill theater

Remember Professor Wayne Szalinski from Disney's feature film, *Honey, I Shrunk the Kids?* Well, he's back. This "movie experience" could easily be one of the most fun things here at Walt Disney World. We'll keep the details a surprise.

EXCELLENT, what you came here for—don't miss it!
Tips: Usually open for Surprise Mornings. Try this early or try it late. Whatever you do, be sure to catch this. Waits here can be long.

The Image Works   This area is a fascinating playground of hands-on devices that utilize touch, sound, and light in ways too unusual to even describe. There are no lines and, when it is crowded, you will have to wait to use some of the "games." Children, unfortunately, tend to monopolize them.

The Restaurants of Future World

There are only two table-service restaurants in Future World. The Coral Reef ♥♥ is located in the Living Seas Pavilion, and it combines a memorable atmosphere with good food. The Garden Grill at the Land Pavilion is set on a turning carousel. For our reviews and more details about them, see Chapter 6.

The Sunshine Season Food Fair in the Land Pavilion is a carnival of eateries. It features five or six "shops" and a large selection of foods: sandwiches, soups, barbecue, ice cream, and lots more. Go early, as it gets crowded and noisy. Other interesting eateries are Pure and Simple at the Wonders of Life Pavilion and Pasta Piazza and the Electric Umbrella at Innoventions. Drop by Fountain View Espresso and Bakery in the Innoventions Plaza for some rich pastries and good espresso. The Odyssey Restaurant is currently closed, and no plans have been announced.

The Shops of Future World

There are quite a few shops in Future World, although many of them seem to specialize in souvenir items. For more interesting stuff, check out Sea Base Alpha at the Living Seas Pavilion, the Green Thumb

Emporium at the Land, Field Trips at Innoventions West, and Well and Goods at the Wonders of Life.

FUTURE WORLD ATTRACTIONS NOT TO MISS

- Body Wars
- *Cranium Command*
- *Honey, I Shrunk the Audience*
- The Innoventions Plaza fountain
- The Living Seas aquarium
- Living with the Land
- *The Making of Me*
- Spaceship Earth
- Test Track
- Ellen's Energy Adventure

The World Showcase

The World Showcase is a pleasant stroll around a large freshwater lagoon. Each of the 11 areas in this grand walk is a "country," and each has been carefully created to present an architectural, cultural, and culinary taste of that land. Each nation has some sort of exhibit or show, and two even feature rides. All of the pavilions have shops with arts, crafts, and other products that represent each of the countries. Some of the pavilions feature outstanding films.

Don't expect to find the real Norway or the real Japan here. This is Walt Disney World, and these countries are merely interesting concoctions imagineered to provide a taste of Italy or the flavor of Morocco. But neither should you dismiss the World Showcase as totally fanciful. Exceptional care has been given to the landscaping and architecture of each country. From the well-tended version of Vancouver Island's Bouchart Gardens to the real olive trees of Italy, a serious effort has been made to present a horticultural sampling of each nation represented. The gardens and landscaping around the lagoon are a gardener's dream. With such attention paid to buildings and streets, it is easy to get the sense of a Japanese garden or a Bavarian village. To complete the travel experience, each pavilion offers a sampling of foods, and many of the cast members around the lagoon are native to the lands they represent. There is also some form of local entertainment at virtually every pavilion, and some are simply delightful.

At the end of each day here at the World Showcase, there is IllumiNations, a spectacular laser light fireworks show. Timed precisely to classical music, this dramatic display is the perfect end to an evening at Epcot. For more details, see Chapter 5, Live Entertainment and Nightlife.

The World Showcase Plaza is the gateway to the World Showcase. The two shops here, the Port of Entry and Disney Traders, offer the usual collection of Disney and Epcot logo merchandise and sundries.

Besides walking around the World Showcase, two *Friendship* launches make regular passages across the lagoon from the docks near the Showcase Plaza.

We'll take you clockwise around the lagoon, which is our favorite direction. We won't give you every detail about what you will see here; we'll give just enough information to help you make your own discoveries. Exploration is the operative word here. Spend time in each of the countries, sit awhile, and catch the entertainers. Check your guidemap for times. Look in every nook and alley. You never know what you'll find.

We'll briefly mention the table-service restaurants here. For details and our reviews, see Chapter 6.

Mexico

This pavilion resembles an Aztec pyramid and is surrounded by a lush, tropical jungle, complete with squawking parrots and colorful orchids. Inside, the world of old Mexico comes alive with the beat of mariachi music. Featured is a display of Meso-American artifacts of amazing beauty and workmanship. A plaza of colorful shops offer baskets, hats, piñatas, jewelry, and men's and women's fashions, all in great abundance.

Also inside is the stunning San Angel Inn, Mexico's restaurant ♥♥♥. Set on the banks of El Rio del Tiempo (River of Time), it enjoys an atmosphere unique even at Disney World. Under a dark sky and surrounded by jungle, you can enjoy Mexican cuisine while a volcano smoulders in the distance.

Outside the pavilion is Cantina San Angel, a counter-service restaurant that has a small but south-of-the-border menu. The Cantina features Mexican beer and is a good place to sit and listen to one of the musical groups that perform here throughout the day. Check for show times.

El Rio del Tiempo (The River of Time)

✓ Boat ride
✓ Lasts 9 minutes
✓ Line moves very quickly

This ride reminds us of It's a Small World except that it travels through the history of Mexico.

GOOD, try not to miss it

Norway

This quaint pavilion features a cobbled town square, a lovely Norwegian stave church, and a formidable replica of Akershus Castle. From the sod roof to the tiled cottages, the detail work in this "village" is impressive. Don't miss the Stav Kirke. For browsers, Puffin's Roost offers an array of Norwegian products (toys, clothes, jewelry, and hats), making this one of our favorite World Showcase stops.

Inside the miniature castle is the Akershus restaurant, whose menu comes straight from Norway. Kringlas Bakeri og Cafe offers an interesting selection of Scandinavian open-faced sandwiches and pastries as well as Norwegian Ringnes beer.

The Maelstrom

✓ Boat ride and film
✓ Lasts 15 minutes
✓ Line moves quickly

An exciting voyage aboard a Viking ship, this ride is fun and offers one brief thrill. There is lots to see during the trip, and we even recommend a second look. The film is outstanding and has inspired us to put Norway on our list of places to visit.

EXCELLENT, don't be afraid of the thrill and don't miss this ride and film

China

The centerpiece of this beautiful pavilion is the ornate Temple of Heaven, re-created here in intricate and colorful detail. Music and landscaping come together to make the courtyard an exceptionally restful retreat. We recommend that you sit awhile and wait for the entertainment.

Shopping is outstanding at the Yong Feng Shangdian shopping gallery. All things Chinese are found in this large bazaar. Set aside some time, as it is a unique browsing experience.

China features a sit-down restaurant, the Nine Dragons, and a counter-service eatery, the Lotus Blossom Cafe. The Lotus Blossom has a small and fairly uninspired menu that includes lo mein and sweet and sour pork. Food is acceptable and inexpensive.

The Wonders of China: Land of Beauty, Land of Time
✓ Film
✓ Lasts 20 minutes
✓ Line moves to fill theater

This beautiful and poetic 360-degree film delivers just what its title promises. Visitors stand against rails to watch. You'll be so entranced that you'll hardly notice you're standing.

EXCELLENT, not to be missed
Tips: Check at the door for the time of the next show and browse until a few minutes before it begins. The theater will almost always accommodate everyone waiting.

The Village Trader   Just beyond China and nearly to Germany is the Village Trader. This small shop features art, handcrafts, and clothing from Africa, India, and Australia. There's some interesting stuff.

Germany

Browse in the square here while the strolling accordion player is performing, and you'll feel as though you're in a travel documentary. The main attraction in this charming bit of Bavaria is the pavilion's restaurant, the Biergarten, which features a wild and zany rendition of German beer hall entertainment.

The quaint shops of this Bavarian village offer a large variety of handcrafted German merchandise: cuckoo clocks, glass and porcelain, authentic fashions, and even precision timepieces. There's even a European-style candy shop and a wine cellar with daily wine tastings.

Sommerfest is a counter-service German restaurant. Pick up a meal at the counter and find a nice place to sit in the square.

Italy

Some evening, we'd like to go for a ride in one of the gondolas parked out in front of Italy. It would be so romantic. Instead, we'll stroll in the shadow of the Doge's Palace and perhaps later will enjoy a dinner in the ristorante.

The shops in Italy offer the finest in Venetian glass and crystal, a colorful selection of Italian fashion wear, and a large choice of hand-crafted jewelry.

Culinary offerings here include a sidewalk vendor who sells pastries, desserts, and beverages from a small cart; there's also the large and boisterous Italian banquet hall, L'Originale Alfredo di Roma Ristorante.

The American Adventure

The American Gardens Theater is, perhaps, what makes this pavilion the centerpiece of the World Showcase (it certainly isn't this area's culinary offerings). The theater features a variety of performances, some with well-known entertainers. Others include high school and college groups from across the country and around the world. There is always something going on here, so check your guidemap.

The colonial-style building is home for both the pavilion's attraction, the American Adventure, and its eatery, the Liberty Inn Restaurant. Heritage Manor Gifts features an attractive assortment of crafts that are uniquely American. For collectors and gift givers, this is a place to browse.

We don't know what went wrong here with food at the American Adventure. It is a mystery to us why Disney opted to serve mediocre fast food.

The American Adventure Show
✓ Audio-animatronic show
✓ Lasts 30 minutes
✓ Line moves to fill theater

This patriotic journey through American history is narrated by "Mark Twain." It is interesting and even stirring.

QUITE GOOD

Japan

This lovely pavilion is marked by the torii gate on the shore of the lagoon. We always marvel at the Disney imagineers' attention to detail. The bases of this gate are covered with "oysters," as though the tide had fallen. From the towering pagoda to the Bijutsu-Kan Gallery, the rest of Japan has been just as meticulously created.

The Japanese garden should not be missed during your Epcot visit ♥. Try to get here before the crowds to enjoy its serene beauty. Visitors to Disney's Japan will enjoy a choice of three uniquely Japanese dining experiences as well as shopping in the fabulous Mitsukoshi department store. Kimonos, vases, lacquered bowls, and colorful masks are a few of the thousands of items offered in this large shop.

Tempura Kiku is Japan's tempura bar. The Teppanyaki Dining Room features grill-tables where performance chefs prepare your dinner with a sizzle and a flair. Japan is also home to the Yakitori House, a delightful and authentic Japanese fast-food restaurant that features a lovely garden dining area. The Matsu No Ma Lounge is a full-service bar, and its menu includes a variety of specialty drinks, sake, and a selection of Japanese finger foods including sushi and Kabuki beef. The view of the lagoon from here has no equal in Epcot. Try watching IllumiNations from the Matsu No Ma ♥♥♥.

Morocco

This pavilion, of all the countries, seems to best capture the feeling of being in a foreign land. Back among its winding, narrow streets and shops, you could almost forget that you are at Disney World. This exotic land even reaches out onto the sidewalk with a lively festival of musicians and dancers.

Tons of handcrafted tiles were imported to create the Chellah Minaret, the towering landmark of Epcot's Morocco. There is even an ancient waterwheel that "irrigates" the beautiful gardens along the lagoon. The shops here at Morocco are especially interesting. All things Moroccan are offered in this bazaar: jewelry, native clothing, brassware, leather goods, and more. Prices are fairly reasonable.

Morocco features one of our favorite Epcot restaurants, Marrakesh ♥♥. This exotic eatery boasts a menu of Moroccan cuisine and live entertainment at both lunch and dinner.

France

This pavilion enjoys a perfect location. Set where the waterway from nearby Crescent Lake enters the lagoon, Disney's France captures a sense of the lovely River Seine and the City of Lights. Small boats and artists' kiosks dot the river's edge. The Eiffel Tower rises beyond the mansard roofs. It is not quite Paris, but it is no doubt Gallic.

As you would expect, the emphasis here is on cuisine. This pavilion features two restaurants, a cafe, a pastry shop, and a winery. The shops are distinctly French, with offerings such as men's and women's fashions, original artwork, and the finest of perfumes.

The sidewalk cafe in this small piece of Paris is Au Petit Cafe ♥♥. It is quaint and picturesque. The two restaurants are the Bistro de Paris ♥♥♥ and Les Chefs de France ♥. French foods and wines are featured, and the settings and menus vary. Boulangerie Patisserie was a big hit with one of our mothers, who can sniff out good pastries at great distances. Croissants, brioches, tarts, and heavenly eclairs are just a few of the tempting treats here. Beverages are also served.

Impressions de France
✓ Film
✓ Lasts 20 minutes
✓ Line moves to fill theater

This film is beautiful, romantic, and unforgettable ♥♥. The theater is cool and offers each guest a seat. Need we say more?

EXCELLENT, not to be missed
Tips: Ask at the door for the next show time. If there is no crowd, browse until just before it begins.

Sidewalk Artisans de Paris Along the lagoon artists are at work. Some do sketches, some create chalk portraits, and yet others will snip your silhouette in black paper. The prices are all reasonable, and the work is good. One of these will make a much better souvenir than a photo taken in front of the geosphere.

The United Kingdom

Our favorite part of this pavilion is tucked away in a corner (which might be why we like it so much). The traditional English garden is the perfect spot for a rest after you've browsed the shops along the streets of London and visited Anne Hathaway's cottage. Pick a nice shady bench and enjoy this beautiful and relaxing hideaway.

We have always enjoyed shopping in Disney's Great Britain. There is something special about the Scottish woolens, fine English teas, and colorful assortment of wooden toys. A lot is here, and we suggest you give it a good looking over.

The U.K.'s restaurant is the Rose and Crown Pub and Dining Room. The pub has all the look and feel of the real thing as well as a selection of stouts and ales. The dining room features British cuisine and several different dining areas, one of which is outside overlooking the lagoon.

U.K. Food Carts   Two food carts are usually at each end of the pavilion. The cart nearest the International Gateway offers baked potatoes with a variety of toppings. After a potato, if you are still hungry, head over toward Canada and to the next cart. There you'll find a small assortment of desserts. (If you get there after one of our mothers, there may not be any eclairs left.)

Canada

We enjoy many things in Disney's Canada. The pavilion's 360-degree film is only part of the excitement. After the film, we like to take a walk through the mountain area, past its waterfall, and into the beautiful garden that re-creates the famous Bouchart Gardens of Vancouver Island, British Columbia. Colorful beds of flowers, willows, and maple trees make this a little slice of our neighbor to the north.

Back on the sidewalk along the lagoon, we listen for the Caledonia Bagpipes. In the shadow of the stone architecture of old Ottawa, this little musical group pipes away the folk tunes of Canada. Shopping here is good, too. The Northwest Mercantile has an intriguing selection of Canadian products. Maple syrup, Indian clothes and moccasins, and some real Innuit sculptures are only a few of the interesting items that you will find here. If you've ever wanted a Canadian Mounties hat, come and get it. La Boutique des Provinces, Canada's other shop, specializes in goods from the French province. Le Cellier is a moderately priced cafeteria-style restaurant.

O Canada!
✓ Film
✓ Lasts 20 minutes
✓ Line moves to fill theater

This is a CircleVision 360 (360-degree) film, like the one in China. All travel films should be this exciting.

VERY GOOD, no reason to miss this one
Tip: If it seems particularly crowded, ask one of the attendants if you'll make it into the next show.

ℛOMANCE AT THE WORLD SHOWCASE

- A meal or appetizers at San Angel Inn: ♥♥♥
- The garden of Japan: ♥
- A drink at Matsu No Ma Lounge during IllumiNations: ♥♥♥
- Lunch or dinner at Marrakesh: ♥♥
- Taking the *Breathless* Cruise from the marina at the Yacht Club (see Chapter 7 for details): ♥♥♥♥
- Having espresso and sharing a dessert in the evening at Au Petit Cafe: ♥♥
- Having a sketch done by a sidewalk artisan in France: ♥
- Dinner at the Bistro de Paris: ♥♥♥
- *Impressions de France:* ♥♥
- Spending a few quiet moments in the English garden: ♥

Disney–MGM Studios

This may be the smallest of the three theme parks, but it is a power-house of entertainment. With a modest amount of planning, you should be able to take in everything here in a few visits. Most of the attractions are geared to accommodate large numbers of visitors. The exception is Voyage of the Little Mermaid, and we will give you some tips for that show later.

𝒟ISNEY–MGM TIPS

- Disney–MGM Surprise Mornings are on Sunday and Wednesday.
- Check-out the tip board at Hollywood and Sunset.
- Attractions to hit early are Star Tours, Twilight Zone Tower of Terror, Voyage of the Little Mermaid, and the Great Movie Ride.

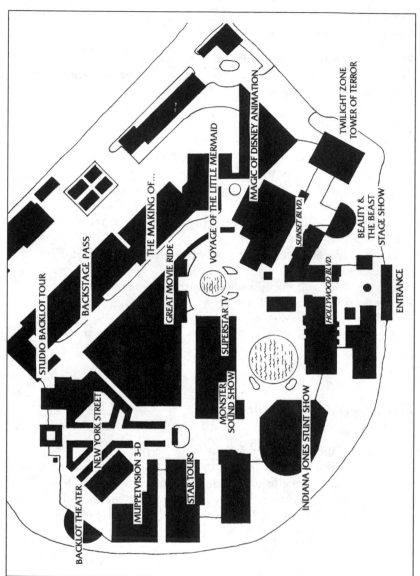

Disney–MGM Studios

- Some of the attractions ask for participants. Get involved. These are the moments that you will remember most fondly. Trust us on this. The attractions that feature guest participation are the Indiana Jones Epic Stunt Spectacular, the Monster Sound Show, and SuperStar Television.
- Take advantage of the roving photographers who will take your picture and then enhance it with Disney characters. These FotoToons make great memories.

The Boulevards

The Studio is Disney's zany vision of 1930s Hollywood and, like its real counterpart, the main thoroughfares here are Hollywood and Sunset. Along these palm-lined avenues are art deco storefronts, trolley cables, old bus benches, period billboards, fireplugs, vintage cars, and cast-iron street lamps. Evocative of the 1930s, the boulevards bring to life the delightful fantasy of a place that never was.

Along these streets are some interesting shops and more than just a few amusing sights. Watch for the Studios' wacky "streetmosphere" people, a crazy troupe of costumed characters that perform daily. Down Sunset, you'll see the "dilapidated and scorched" Hollywood Tower Hotel, home of the Twilight Zone Tower of Terror. There's lots to see and do along here, but we suggest that you try out some of the park's shows and attractions first, then come back later to explore.

The Attractions of Disney–MGM Studios

We really like this park. There is a lot of thought behind each attraction, and nothing except for the *Honey I Shrunk the Kids* Movie Adventure Set is aimed solely at children. Things here are intelligent and thoughtful, not to mention fun. We suggest that you give everything a chance. In particular, we encourage you to see the Backlot Studio Tour and the Magic of Disney Animation Tour. Both are excellent and seem, somehow, to be at the very core of the experience here. Disney–MGM Studios is more than a theme park—it is a working studio, and these attractions will bring you into these working areas to give you an intriguing look at the magic behind the movies.

Twilight Zone Tower of Terror
✓ Special-effects thrill ride
✓ Lasts 10 minutes
✓ Line moves slowly

If you don't mind being taken in an elevator to the top of a 13-story building and dropped several times to street level, then you're ready for this. The special effects along the way are some of the best we've ever seen, and the story line is good. The drops are over quickly and are not as bad as they sound (how many times have you heard *that* line?).

EXCELLENT, if the plunge doesn't frighten you off
Tips: This attraction is very popular and, since the line moves slowly, a long wait is likely. Usually open for Surprise Mornings.

Beauty and the Beast Stage Show
✓ Live show
✓ Lasts 30 minutes
✓ Line moves to fill theater

Real people perform this miniversion ♥♥ of the Disney classic film. The costumes, sets, and performances are all good, and the music is, we think, the best ever in a Disney animated feature.

EXCELLENT, do not miss
Tips: The 1500-seat Theater of the Stars will accommodate virtually everyone in line. The amphitheater is large, and all of the seats provide a reasonably good view of the stage. Seating begins 30 minutes prior to each show. Check for show times.

Star Tours
✓ Simulated thrill ride
✓ Lasts 10 minutes
✓ Line moves quickly

Based on the *Star Wars* films, this ride doesn't really go anywhere. It is a pod-like "ship" that merely simulates flight by coordinating film, sound, and a bit of rocking, tipping, and bucking. It is very convincing and very entertaining.

EXCELLENT, do not miss
Tip: Usually open for Surprise Mornings.

Voyage of the Little Mermaid
✓ Live musical show
✓ Lasts 20 minutes
✓ Line moves slowly to fill theater

This show combines live action and puppetry in a brief version of the Disney animated film. Everything about this show is excellent, especially the special effects.

EXCELLENT, do not miss
Tips: When you first get your guidemap, check for the time of the first show. Arrive 30 minutes before. Better a 30-minute wait early than a much lengthier one later. Only one theater-full of people is admitted at a time, and you may not be in line for the very next show; ask a cast member.

The Great Movie Ride
✓ Adventure "train" ride (slow)
✓ Lasts 20 minutes
✓ Line moves very quickly

This ride takes you through a series of movie scene re-creations. The sets, audio-animatronics, and special effects are all worth seeing again and again. There are even a couple of "live shows" staged along the way. (There are two different versions of the shows, shown to alternating cars.)

EXCELLENT, do not miss
Tips: This ride is usually open for Surprise Mornings. Parts of it may be too intense for very young children.

The Indiana Jones Epic Stunt Spectacular
✓ Live show
✓ Lasts 30 minutes
✓ Line moves quickly to fill large amphitheater

This is a live-action stunt show. The special effects and scenery are memorable. This is an attraction executed on a grand scale, and it is exciting and fun.

EXCELLENT, do not miss

Studio Backlot Tour
✓ Tram tour with some excitement
✓ Lasts 35 minutes
✓ Line moves quickly

This wonderful attraction will provide a behind-the-scenes look at parts of this working studio as well as a special effects adventure. On the tour, you'll see the costume department, prop yard, and experience "Catastrophe Canyon." There's more, too.

EXCELLENT, not to be missed

Backstage Pass
✓ Walking tour and film
✓ Lasts 25 minutes
✓ Line moves quickly

This used to be part of the Backlot Tour. It was, and still is, a look behind the scenes at how special effects are achieved. Now, this attraction shows how the effects in a particular film have been done, and in this case it is Disney's live-action film, *101 Dalmatians*. It features sound stages, actual sets and props, and a film. We expect the movie featured here will change from time to time.

VERY INTERESTING and quite entertaining

The Making Of...
✓ Walking tour and film
✓ Lasts 25 minutes
✓ Line moves quickly

This attraction features a behind-the-scenes look at how a recent Disney animated feature has been created. It begins with a quick walk-through of a sound studio into a theater for a film.

INTERESTING and enjoyable

The American Film Institute Showcase
✓ Walk-through
✓ No time limit

This interesting exhibit features costumes, props, and set pieces from numerous films and television productions, past and present. We've seen some neat stuff here and recommend dropping by if you have an interest.

GOOD

The Magic of Disney Animation Tour
✓ Film and walking tour
✓ Lasts about 35 minutes
✓ Line moves quickly

This tour begins with a film that you will not soon forget. Robin Williams and Walter Cronkite join forces in an introduction so hilarious that you will want to see it again. The tour then takes you through the Disney animators' actual working areas. It is interesting. The grand finale is a memorable film of animation clips from Disney classics.

EXCELLENT

Tips: The waiting area showcases cels, sketches, and artifacts from Disney's most recent animated features. Don't miss the Sorcerer's Apprentice topiary as you exit.

SuperStar Television
✓ Show with audience participation
✓ Lasts 30 minutes
✓ Line moves slowly to fill theater

This show puts costumed visitors on stage and right in popular television shows. It is especially memorable when one or both of you gets into the show. "Tryouts" are held 20 minutes prior to each show. Get involved in this fun.

EXCELLENT

The Monster Sound Show
✓ Film and show
✓ Lasts 15 minutes
✓ Line moves slowly

This is another wonderful audience-participation show. It demonstrates the art of creating sound effects. The show is wild and hilarious as well as interesting.

VERY GOOD

MuppetVision 3-D
✓ Film and more
✓ Lasts 20 minutes
✓ Line moves quickly to fill large preshow area, then theater

This 3-D film is a lot more than just a film. We'll leave the rest a surprise.

EXCELLENT, not to be missed
Tips: The line here seems to come and go with the flow of people from nearby attractions, such as Indiana Jones. Try it when there isn't much of a line at various times throughout the day. The preshow should not be missed.

"Honey, I Shrunk the Kids" Movie Set Adventure
✓ Playground for children
✓ No time limit
✓ Line moves very slowly

This is a playground where objects are much larger than usual. Much, much larger. Everything is "rubberized" for safety.

OK, for small children, otherwise avoid it
Tips: Lines here can be awful and awfully slow. If this is a must-see for your child, we suggest that you get here early.

"New York" Street Set
✓ Walk-through
✓ No time limit

Here on the backlot of the studio, Disney has created a huge facade of New York City. It presents some nifty photo opportunities. Parts of the set were used during the filming of Dick Tracy.

GOOD

Backlot Theater
✓ Live musical show
✓ Lasts about 30 minutes
✓ Line moves to fill theater

This amphitheater features a live "mini" rendition of a recent animated Disney feature. With splendid costumes, colorful sets, special effects, and memorable performances, this is a show not to miss. Currently featured is *The Hunchback of Notre Dame*. It is fun, dramatic, and even touching.

OUTSTANDING, do not miss
Tip: Arrive early. Seating begins 25 minutes before the show.

The Restaurants at Disney–MGM Studios

Dining at Disney–MGM is better than at the Magic Kingdom. Here you will find the fine as well as the fun. There are four interesting table-service restaurants. The Hollywood Brown Derby ♥ is fine dining in a charming re-creation of the famous Hollywood eatery. The 50's Prime Time Cafe offers American food and fun, and Mama Melrose's Ristorante Italiano is Disney's neighborhood Italian eatery. The Sci-Fi Dine-In Theater will put you in the back (or front) seat of a car at the drive-in. For our reviews and more information, see Chapter 6. Reservations for these restaurants are strongly recommended.

The Studios has a large selection of counter-service restaurants. Hollywood & Vine Cafeteria of the Stars serves breakfast, lunch, and dinner. Meals are acceptable and inexpensive. The Soundstage features a themed character buffet breakfast and lunch. The Commissary offers a modest variety of interesting sandwiches in a fairly standard fast-food setting and the new Toy Story Pizza Planet has a selection of not-so-great pizzas, salads, and pasta.

The Backlot Express, located near the Indiana Jones show, features grilled chicken, burgers, and hot dogs in a pleasant outside sitting area, while Min and Bill's specializes in tacos, fruit, soft-serve, and snacks. The Sunset Ranch Market is really a group of food outlets that are set in an outdoor farmer's market. From fresh fruits and salads to hot dogs and chili, there's a lot to choose from here. For snacks and desserts, you can go to Dinosaur Gertie's or Starring Rolls. Starring Rolls is a little bakery around the corner from the Brown Derby, and it offers hot cocoa and tea; it's a nice spot for a light breakfast. Ellen's Buy-the-Book is both a bookstore and coffee shop. It features espresso, cappuccino, and pastries.

The Lounges at Disney–MGM Studios

Because this theme park is geared more towards adults, there are lounges here at Disney–MGM Studios. So drop in for an afternoon cocktail or an evening sip of wine.

- The Catwalk Bar is located upstairs from the Soundstage restaurant. It is very colorful and full of movie props. Seating is equally interesting. Beers, wines, specialty drinks, and espresso are offered along with a pretty interesting assortment of appetizer-like foods. It's a nice escape.
- The Tune-In Lounge is part of the 50's Prime Time Cafe and has a good selection of beers and wines.
- Mama Melrose's Bar, located right alongside the kitchen, will give you a great view of the chefs at work as you quaff your beer or enjoy your wine. The selection here is small but interesting.

The Shops at Disney–MGM Studios

If you're into movie memorabilia, you've come to the right place. Sid Cahuenga's One-of-a-Kind is one of Disney's most unique shops. There are several other shops along the boulevards that feature movie stuff, from T-shirts to photo books. Much of it is quite good. You'll also find lots of Disney character merchandise. Keystone Clothiers even offers a mouse-ears umbrella. For books and such, check out the new Ellen's Buy-the-Book, which is also a nice coffee shop. There's baby stuff, Twilight Zone Tower of Terror fashions, *Star Wars* memorabilia, and much more. The Studios provide interesting shopping, so set aside some time to browse.

DISNEY–MGM ATTRACTIONS NOT TO MISS

- Studio Backlot Tour
- Beauty and the Beast Stage Show
- The Great Movie Ride

- The Indiana Jones Epic Stunt Spectacular
- The Magic of Disney Animation Tour
- MuppetVision 3-D
- Star Tours
- Twilight Zone Tower of Terror
- Voyage of the Little Mermaid
- Backlot Theater

ℛOMANCE AT DISNEY–MGM STUDIOS

- Beauty and the Beast Stage Show: ♥♥
- Sorcery in the Sky fireworks: ♥♥ (see Chapter 5)
- The Hollywood Brown Derby Restaurant: ♥

The Animal Kingdom

Rumored for many years, a fourth Disney theme park will finally become a reality in spring of 1998 with the opening of the Animal Kingdom. The largest of all Disney theme parks, the Animal Kingdom will cover 500 acres, making it five times as large as the Magic Kingdom. It will be a first for Disney, offering a fusion of thrill rides, exotic landscapes, and encounters with *live* animals. Open from dawn to dusk, this park promises to involve guests in creature adventures of every sort and to do it without the usual parades and fireworks.

Of course, we haven't been able to see this park, which is, as we write, in its early stages of construction. From models, renderings, and interviews, we attempt here to give you a picture of it. "Subject to change" was a phrase we often heard during our research, so we offer this as an approximate look.

Paradise Oasis

Guests enter the Animal Kingdom through lush Paradise Oasis. Here, small animals roam free amidst a stunning waterfall and dense rain forest. Small streams wind along walkways through this breathtaking landscape. Beyond the cascade, the real focus of the park comes into view. The towering Tree of Life is one of Disney's most amazing creations. Fifty feet wide at its base and 14-stories tall, this masterpiece

Animal Kingdom

towers above the surrounding landscape. Nearly the height of Epcot's Spaceship Earth, it has the wild creatures of the world carved intricately into its huge trunk and roots.

Safari Village

The Tree of Life is located on a jungle island in the center of the Animal Kingdom. Known as Safari Village, this area is home for shops and restaurants as well as a theater located in the trunk of the great tree. Featured here is a computer animated film by Pixar Animations, entitled *Bugs*. The waters surrounding this island feature river cruises that take passengers through harrowing adventures and along to the other areas of the park. Such perils as fiery dragons, steaming geysers, and ferocious dinosaurs furnish some of the excitement.

From Safari Village, guests can enter any one of the three areas of the park: the Beastly Kingdom, Dinoland, and the Asian and African Villages. Each represents one of the three themes of this park: mythical creatures, extinct beasts, and the real and living animals of the wild.

The Beastly Kingdom

The Beastly Kingdom features the mythical creatures of fairy tales and legends. Visitors experience face-to-face encounters with imaginary and magical creations in attractions that feature such fanciful creations as fire-breathing dragons and unicorns.

Dinoland

Dinoland is home to the park's dinosaur population. Countdown to Extinction is the feature attraction here, and it shatters the bounds of previous Disney thrill rides. This time-travel adventure takes explorers back to the brink of dinosaur extinction in a race against time to save them from a meteoric disaster. The latest audio-animatronics and state-of-the-art special effects deliver a new level of interactive theme park entertainment.

Also here in Dinoland is the Boneyard Playground. An adventure park for children and adults, this area resembles a paleontological excavation where participants dig for the remains of extinct creatures in an interactive learning experience. Nearby are an archeological food court and a shop that features the world's largest selection of plastic dinosaur souvenirs.

The Asian and African Villages

Beyond Safari Village and across the waters are the living creatures of the Animal Kingdom. The Asian Village showcases the culture of that continent in a perfectly re-created town. The attraction here is a white-water river adventure. The African Village of Harambi transports guests to the African wilderness. Beyond its gates lies the Kilimanjaro Safari. This, the Kingdom's centerpiece attraction, is an adventure safari onto the 120-acre wildlife preserve. The journey begins by jeep, but soon travelers are lost and out of sight of their vehicle. Here, amidst the wild creatures and exciting landscape, participants battle wits with unscrupulous poachers in a special effects adventure. Lions, gorillas, hippos, and rhinos are just a few of the creatures found in the Kilimanjaro Safari.

Once "safe" from the safari adventure, travelers enter Conservation Station. Here they learn about endangered species and threatened environments and what can and is being done to save them.

OUR IMPRESSIONS OF THE ANIMAL KINGDOM

- There's promise of much more, but it is still too early for Disney imagineers to discuss the other attractions under development for this park. From what we have seen, the Animal Kingdom looks to be Walt Disney World's most ambitious creation. Watch for us in line when the gates open.

Other Walt Disney World Attractions

The Disney Institute

It's true that one of us wasn't very excited about this place. The very name "Institute" and such marketing catchphrases as "challenge," "self-discovery," "learning activity," and "program" were a turnoff. So, we both went (one of us reluctantly) and discovered what, oddly, is one of the Institute's best kept secrets: this place is fun. A lot of fun.

The Institute offers what it calls "Discovery Vacations." Guests select from 40 or 50 programs (there's that word again!), which offer activities such as computer animation, sports, gardening, and culinary arts. A few days after we arrived, we began to see the Institute for what it really is: another theme park, one that allows guests to get their hands on the Disney magic, to play with it and to make a bit of it themselves.

If you visit the Institute, don't come expecting to sit in classrooms listening to lectures. We're talking hands-on stuff here, and everything has been imagineered to get your creative juices flowing. Ready for a little golf? Prepare for play on a championship PGA course in a learning experience designed by Gary Player. Interested in computer animation? A powerful computer awaits you, loaded with the latest in 3-D software. Looking to try your hand at some of Disney's culinary wizardry? Join the famous chefs of the Institute in their state-of-the-art kitchens, and slice, stir, and sauté to your heart's delight. There's more: wine tasting, canoe adventures, radio and broadcast production, and personal fitness. Let the Institute be your key to unlocking the mysteries and magic that have made Disney World the playground of the world.

The Institute also features an artist-in-residence program that delivers a mix of well-known performers from a variety of the arts. Most often, these artists appear in the evening at the Institute's performing arts center and are available during the day for interaction with guests. Some of the luminaries who have participated in this program are underwater photographer Jean-Michele Cousteau, commentator Paul Harvey, singer and environmentalist John Denver, actor Andy Garcia, and basketball star Bill Walton. Together, resident instructors, guest presenters, and artists-in-residence cover an exciting array of interests. At the Institute, you can get involved in aerobics, architecture, golf, tennis, cooking, broadcast production, music, and topiary, to mention only a few. The Institute even has its own cinema, which offers preview screenings of films.

The Spa at the Disney Institute

To balance all of this activity, there is the Spa at the Institute. With whirlpool tubs, steam rooms, and saunas, this luxurious and state-of-the-art spa offers an array of personal treatments and therapies that will get you both in a relaxed and sensual mood. Such temptations as aromatherapy and hydrotherapy, body wraps, facials, and massages of every sort are just a few of the spa's offerings. And the spa is not just for women. Our time here was sublime, and an afternoon of treatments left us *both* enjoying a sensuality that lasted our entire visit. For more information about the Spa at the Institute, see Chapter 7.

The Institute: Where and What

The Institute is located on 90 beautiful acres adjacent to the Buena Vista Golf Course and across the lake from Downtown Disney. Its studios, performance center, Amphitheater on the Green, cinema, and fitness center more resemble a small town than Disney World. Barns, mills, porches, and a town square all work to enhance this rural ambience. Dotted with lakes and landscaped in lush Disney fashion, the Institute offers a charm and sense of tranquillity simply not found elsewhere at Walt Disney World.

Besides atmosphere, the Institute features some impressive facilities. "State of the art" is pretty commonplace here and can describe any one of a dozen Institute areas: the performing arts or fitness centers, the closed-circuit television and radio stations, the 18-hole championship golf course, lighted clay tennis courts, six swimming pools, or full-service spa. All have been created to meet Team Disney's relentless pursuit of perfection.

The Institute is home to two eateries: Season's Dining Room and Reflections, a lakeside coffee and sandwich shop. Season's sunny and bright dining area is centrally located and features three meals daily. For more details about Season's, see Chapter 6. Reflections is located near the bungalows and features an interesting selection of gourmet coffees, quality baked goods and pastries, and sandwiches. The relaxing poolside patio is a place where you'll want to spend time.

Accommodations at the Disney Institute

As Institute guests, you'll stay in one of the accommodations that used to be the Disney Village Resort and is now known as the Villas at the Disney Institute. The two-story bungalows feature one-bedroom suites and are scattered along the shores of the central lake. Each features a bedroom with double queen beds, a living room with sitting area and wet bar, a small bathroom, and a patio or balcony. Nearby are the one- and two-bedroom, split-level townhouses set along the shore of adjacent Lake Buena Vista. Swimming pools and hot tubs are located throughout the areas, and footpaths connect all the Institute facilities. All accommodations are of the home away from home category, offering kitchens or wet bars. Institute lodgings are also available for non-Institute guests. For more details, see the section on the Villas at the Disney Institute in Chapter 2.

How It All Works

So you like the Institute and want to be part of the fun. What next? There are two basic ways to participate. You can be either a day guest or an Institute guest. For $79 per person, day visitors get up to two programs, access to the Sports and Fitness Center, and an evening performance. Anyone can be a day guest, and reservations can be made up to two weeks in advance.

Institute guests stay at the Institute and can choose from the Basic, Deluxe, or World Choice plans. The Basic plan includes accommodations at the Institute, a ticket for one day/one theme park, and Institute programs and entertainment for your length of stay.

1997 Basic Plan Rates (three nights, per person/double occupancy)

Accommodation	Regular Season	Value Season	Holiday Season
Bungalow	$539	$499	$566
One-bedroom Townhouse	$606	$573	$633
Two-bedroom Townhouse	$711	$678	$736
Additional person	$275	$275	$275
Additional nights:			
Bungalow	$166	$153	$175
One-bedroom Townhouse	$189	$177	$197
Two-bedroom Townhouse	$223	$212	$232
Additional guests	$78	$78	$78

The Deluxe plan adds three meals daily at Season's and costs another $51 per person, per night. For the World Choice plan, add $76 per person, per night to the Basic plan. This all-inclusive plan offers the features of the Basic plus unlimited admission to all Disney attractions for length of stay, daily breakfast at the Institute, lunch and dinner each day at a wide variety of restaurants throughout Disney World, plus use of bicycles and nonmotorized recreation. A minimum three-night stay is required for all plans, and a $200 deposit is due two weeks after booking.

When you've selected the dates for your Institute visit and made your reservations, a reservation kit will be mailed to you, detailing the programs available during your visit. After your deposit has been received, you may begin reserving programs, which can be done by telephone up to three months in advance. Institute reservationists are very knowledgeable and have actually participated in most of the activities.

Once you have made these arrangements, you have only to arrive. Last minute and day-to-day changes can be handled easily by the Institute's programming staff.

For Institute reservations, call (800) 282-9282.

OUR RECOMMENDATIONS FOR THE DISNEY INSTITUTE

- Give this place a chance. It's much more fun than you think.
- Check out the Institute's numerous children's programs.
- Make your arrangements as far ahead as possible in order to get the activities that most interest you both.
- Be sure to spend some time at the spa early in your visit. Book your treatments early.
- Rent or bring bikes for your Institute experience. It's the perfect mode of transportation for this lakeside enclave.
- Want just a taste of the Institute? Try the Dinner and Performance Package: Dinner at Season's followed by the evening's performance, for $27 per person. To see who is live and onstage, check the World Update you receive at your resort.
- During our visit, we particularly enjoyed both the Wine, Wonders, and Song, and Romantic Dinners.

ROMANCE AT THE INSTITUTE

- We find this place to be quite romantic. Treatments at the spa, special activities together, and unforgettable evening entertainment all add up to a blissful and relaxed vacation. Remember, Pleasure Island and the rest of Walt Disney World await just around the corner.

Discovery Island

This small island, located in Bay Lake, is unlike any of Disney's other attractions. The focus here is on wildlife. Real, live wildlife. There are no audio-animatronic birds and no robotic reptiles. This beautiful and densely tropical isle is Disney's own zoological park, certified and accredited by the American Association of Zoological Parks and Aquariums.

A short boat ride from the Magic Kingdom, Discovery Island seems a world away. This overlooked Disney gem offers a unique getaway from the hustle and bustle of the other attractions. Take a lazy stroll down a shady path. Watch hundreds of rare birds in one of America's largest walk-through aviaries. Come prepared to explore, and don't forget a picnic lunch from your favorite restaurant.

Discovery Island is an 11-acre sanctuary for more than 250 species of reptiles, mammals, and birds. While this may not be a place that you would wish to spend an entire day, you will find that there are plenty of things to fill a morning or afternoon. This is a small and quiet place, which is precisely what makes it so attractive. Not only is there no need to hurry here, but there is no temptation to.

What you will find are shady paths that wind lazily through bamboo thickets and under a dense canopy of trees. There are toucans, kookaburras, macaws, and dozens of other birds. In fact, there are whole flocks in natural aviaries. You may even be lucky enough to spy Discovery Island's resident bald eagle. The island also enjoys a small population of exotic mammals and reptiles. From the lumbering Galapagos tortoises to the miniature Asian muntjac deer, Discovery Island provides one delight after another. The three shows here are small and intimate, like the rest of the island. The Thirsty Perch, the island's store, offers a selection of beverages, snacks, and souvenirs. Several nice picnic areas are available.

One-day admission to Discovery Island is $11 for adults and $6 for children. Admission is included with the Length of Stay and World Hopper Passes.

OUR RECOMMENDATIONS FOR DISCOVERY ISLAND

- This place is especially nice and especially deserted during the fall months.
- Make arrangements with one of your favorite restaurants to prepare a picnic lunch ♥♥.
- Nesting season for the island's feathered inhabitants runs from February to early fall.
- Feeding time at Pelican Bay is 3:30 P.M.
- This attraction is closed annually from mid-February to mid-March.

The Disney Water Parks

So far, Disney has built three water parks, and each one seems to get better. River Country was the first, followed by Typhoon Lagoon. Just when you thought they couldn't get much grander, along comes

Blizzard Beach. Whether you're young or old, visiting with your family or as a couple, these parks will very likely provide a day's worth of excitement and entertainment. Each has kiddie pools, slides both tame and wild, raft rides, and wave pools.

Admission to all water parks is included in both the Length of Stay Pass and the World Hopper Pass. One-day admission to either Typhoon Lagoon or Blizzard Beach is $25 for adults and $19.50 for children. Admission to River Country is $16 ($12.50 for children).

All three parks suffer from the same problem: too many people. At peak times, you will find yourselves spending more time in line than having fun. Here are a few ways to avoid the crowds:

- Arrive early. Get there 30 minutes before the park opens, and use the first few hours for the slides and raft runs.
- Arrive late. During the summer months, the water parks stay open until 8 P.M. Arrive around 4 P.M., when the crowds are starting to thin out. Most offer a discounted afternoon rate. In the summer, the late afternoon is cooler and the sun is kinder.
- Try a water park when the weather is "less than ideal." The water is heated to 80 degrees at each and, in inclement weather, it may be brisk, but the park will be all but empty.
- Arrive right after an afternoon thundershower. The rain will have driven the crowds away.

More Water Park Tips

- The hours to the water parks vary with the seasons. Check with Guest Services or the "World Update" for the operating hours.
- Towels are available as rentals. Wear shoes or flip-flops. For women, one-piece bathing suits are best for the slides. There are changing rooms, but, if you like, you can wear your suit under your clothing to avoid having to change.
- Do not forget sunblock or sunscreen. The Florida sun is brutal, even on an overcast day. Besides being dangerous, a sunburn is uncomfortable. You don't want to spend your romantic Disney vacation being too sore to be touched. We usually wear light T-shirts to protect ourselves from the sun.
- The food at Disney aquatic theme parks is typical fast food. Have one of the restaurants in your resort pack a nice lunch.
- Leave jewelry and watches back in your room. This stuff tends to fall off while you're zooming down slides. No personal swim

gear is allowed in any of the parks, including masks, fins, rafts, and floats.

- As soon as the park opens, go stake out a place with lounge chairs. Some spots are in the shade, and some are not. Take your pick and deposit a few of your things on enough lounges to provide each of you with one. If you don't, someone else will.
- Rental lockers are available at all of the water parks. If you have valuables with you, such as a camera or a bag, you can't leave them lying around. This may be Disney World, but it is still planet Earth.
- Use the first few hours after opening to hit all of the fast-moving slides and raft rides. Save the lazy tubing, swimming, and surf-riding for later.

River Country

The first of Disney's water recreation parks, River Country is also its smallest. This is the "ol' swimmin' hole" a la Huck Finn, and while it's not executed on the grand scale of Typhoon Lagoon or Blizzard Beach, it has its charm.

Not far from Discovery Island, River Country is set perfectly on the shore of Bay Lake. The cool breezes from the lake make it particularly nice. There is more emphasis here on landscaping and beauty than on exciting slides. Huge man-made boulders, waterfalls, and lots of trees make this place seem less of an attraction and more like a natural occurrence. River Country consists of several areas. Bay Cove is the large swimming area and the heart of the attraction. It is actually an area of the lake that has been walled off. The water here is kept clean and circulating, making it a large, sand-bottomed swimming pool. There is a lot of fun to be had here, though mostly for the younger set. Rope swings and a large boom are several ways to enter the cove. There are also two pretty decent water slides, Hoop 'n Holler Hollow, and a gentle raft ride, oddly misnamed White Water Rapids. If you are looking for excitement, this may not be the place for you.

River Country also has a large swimming pool. Upstream Plunge is not far from Bay Cove. It features two steep slides. Cypress Point Nature Trail is a short and scenic stroll through the wetland area along the lake.

There are two counter-service restaurants. Pop's Place is the larger of the two, offering burgers, hot dogs, salads, and a variety of snacks. The Waterin' Hole, a snack bar, opens only during the busier seasons.

Picnicking is permitted at River Country, which may be the best way to get some good food.

River Country is located at Fort Wilderness. Buses make the trip from the Ticket and Transportation Center (TTC) throughout the day. The water park can also be reached by taking the Fort Wilderness boat from the Magic Kingdom dock.

Typhoon Lagoon

Typhoon Lagoon tells the story of a small fishing village hit by a typhoon. The storm has left the village in ruins—creating the perfect aquatic theme park. Mount Mayday is the most prominent feature of the crazy world of Typhoon Lagoon. Speared atop its peak is an old shrimp boat. Every half hour, a fifty-foot geyser of water spews from its smoke stack. Look around, and you can't help but notice that things are are way out-of-whack. The storm has left this place utterly askew. Buildings lean this way and that, seemingly about to topple.

These delightful effects are everywhere. Nothing has escaped the wrath of the typhoon or the notice of the Disney imagineers. There is more here than just a cute story and some nifty props, though. Typhoon Lagoon's 56-acres is jammed with slides, creeks, raft rides, and a rumbling surf pool.

Of all the attractions here, Humunga Cowabunga is the only one that we would hesitate to recommend for everyone. This steep, 50-foot, high-speed water slide is a bit too vertical. If this kind of speed is your thing, you'll love it. Six other slides here range from mild to exciting. None approaches the speed or height of Humunga Cowabunga, and we think that you'll like them all. Three of them are raft runs of varying lengths. The remaining slides are body slides: Rudder Buster, Stern Burner, and Jib Jammer are each exciting and fairly fast.

Castaway Creek winds lazily around the park, and you can hop aboard a tube almost anywhere and float to your heart's content. This little river takes you through some amusing effects: a tunnel, a waterfall, and under a leaky bamboo pipe.

Ketchakiddie Creek is a miniversion of this park, and it is just for kids (adults admitted only when accompanied by a child). Shark Reef offers a snorkeling experience through a lagoon of live fish. The water in this pool is much cooler than the rest of Typhoon Lagoon.

Typhoon Lagoon offers two counter-service restaurants, the Leaning Palms and Typhoon Tilly's. There are also two "beach shacks" that serve snacks, soft drinks, beer, and wine coolers. And of course, no theme park would be complete without shopping. Here at Typhoon Lagoon, you have Singapore Sal's, which carries souvenirs, Typhoon Lagoon merchandise, and a variety of sundries.

Blizzard Beach

Disney imagineers like to give every place a "spin," and this could be the tallest tale of all. Blizzard Beach, so the story goes, is the result of a freak winter storm that blasted this piece of Walt Disney World with snow and ice. It was too great an opportunity to pass up, so work was begun immediately on a ski resort. Before the resort was completed, however, the temperature returned to normal. Hopes for a Disney ski complex were dashed.

Ready to shut the whole thing down, the resort operators noticed an alligator frolicking in the water from the melting snow. The place would, they quickly realized, make for the perfect water adventure park. So, what had once been ski slopes, slalom courses, and bobsled runs were hastily converted into some of the wildest and tallest water slides anywhere. And so began Blizzard Beach.

We have told you more than once that Disney's creations continue to get better and better. Blizzard Beach is certainly proof of this. Words like wild, crazy, and zany only begin to describe it. The Disney imagineers must have had a lot of fun thinking up this one.

The cluster of buildings at the entrance to Blizzard Beach resembles alpine lodges. Here and there are banks of melting "snow." Icicles hang from the eaves, and racks of skis sit useless in the sun. The centerpiece of the park is Mount Gushmore. A real chairlift runs to the small chalet on its snow-covered summit. From there, a steep staircase leads up to the nearly vertical ski jump/water slide. Other slides and chutes run down the mountain, twisting and turning in all directions. Ice and snow glitter realistically in the bright sun. Comic details are everywhere: the Avalunch snack bar, a lone ski sticking out of a snow bank, and a potbellied stove.

Summit Plummet is the high-speed water slide that claims to be the tallest and fastest in the world. Or jump aboard a large raft at Teamboat Springs and zoom down the mountain. The six-passenger raft twists and turns along 1,200 feet of splashing waterfalls.

Runoff Rapids is a tube ride down a choice of three flumes. Slush Gusher is a slide nearly as high as Summit Plummet but nowhere near as steep. Snow Stormers runs through a zigzag slalom course, complete with banks of snow and flag gates. Toboggan Racer is a rather tame eight-lane slide down one of the gentler slopes on Mount Gushmore.

If the slides of Blizzard Beach get too crowded, head off to explore. It won't be hard to find Melt-Away Bay, a one-acre swimming area with a sand beach. Here in the shadow of Mount Gushmore, waders and swimmers splash away the day. The Blizzard Beach Ski Patrol Training Camp, about halfway up the slope, is an area designed for preteens. Here, a series of events such as Mogul Mania and the Ice Flow Walk present comical challenges at this goofy training camp. Or, as an alternative, hours can be spent drifting lazily around the park in tubes along the wonderful Cross-Country Creek.

Blizzard Beach has two snack bars, Avalunch and the Warming Hut, and one rather large counter-service restaurant called the Lottawatta Lodge. With seating either inside or in a pleasant courtyard, this Caribbean-style ski lodge is the place to take your appetite. Pizza, hot dogs, hamburgers, and other fast Disney foods are available at the many counter windows. (Even with a large opening week crowd, the wait was minimal.) The Beach Haus offers a large selection of Blizzard Beach memorabilia, Disney character merchandise, and even some interesting apparel.

$\mathcal{L}$ ive Entertainment and Nightlife

Don't ask us why Walt Disney World is not known for its live entertainment. By our reckoning, Disney could be the single largest employer of talent anywhere. While we enjoy the make-believe part of Disney, we also spend time seeking out the numerous and unusual forms of live entertainment. No matter how many times we visit, the World has something to offer that is new and exciting. Whether it is a French mime, a country and western band, or the orchestra in the lobby of the Grand Floridian, we are certain that you too will find much to enjoy.

In this chapter, we'll give you the scope of the performances available along with details about them. And of course, we'll tell you where and when to find them. And since the Disney imagineers are continually inventing new and exciting things, we'll give you some tips on how to keep abreast of anything special that may be happening during your trip.

Live Entertainment in the Theme Parks

There's a lot of live entertainment in the parks, and your ticket to finding it will be your theme park guidemap. Updated weekly, these will tell you what you'll need to know to find parades, fireworks, character encounters, life performances, and other unique events. As we've mentioned, you can get one of these nearly anywhere in each of the parks or at your resort's Guest Services. Since much of this live entertainment occurs at particular times and often only on certain days of the week, you'll want to pick up all three guidemaps early in your visit and use them to help you find what interests you both.

Live Entertainment in the Magic Kingdom

Main Street USA   The Walt Disney World Band performs every morning in Town Square on Main Street. During the busy summer months, they usually give several concerts.

One of our favorite Main Street groups is the Dapper Dans, Disney's tap-dancing barber shop quartet. They usually begin around 10 A.M. and wander Main Street, performing at unannounced times. It's just hit or miss; we recommend "hit."

Another group of musicians found here are the Rhythm Rascals, a zany washboard and banjo troupe that will have you laughing while you tap your feet. This gang reminds us of Spike Jones and his band (if you are old enough to remember them). At Casey's Corner, a ragtime pianist will bring the old days alive, and the Kids of the Kingdom offer musical shows at the stage in front of Cinderella Castle. They are particularly popular with children but are not among our favorite performers in the Magic Kingdom.

Adventureland   J. P. and the Silver Stars ♥ is a steel band that performs authentic Caribbean music at the Caribbean Plaza, near Pirates of the Caribbean. Check out the unique instruments used by this rhythmic group as they offer up a touch of the islands. If you've never heard this kind of music, don't miss it. And while you're in Adventureland, check out the "drum machine" in the plaza near the entrance to the Jungle Cruise.

Frontierland   There's zany fun throughout the day at the Diamond Horseshoe Jamboree. This saloon show features singers, comedians, magicians, and lots more. See your Magic Kingdom guidemap for show times.

Fantasyland   The Sword in the Stone Ceremony is scheduled throughout the day in the plaza near the castle. This reenactment of the King Arthur legend is performed with the participation of a young guest selected from the audience. It is cute and heartwarming, especially if the youngster is yours.

A variety of bands from all over the U.S. perform each week at the Fantasy Faire Stage. On special occasions, you are likely to catch the Walt Disney World Band here as well.

Tomorrowland   For out-of-this-world entertainment, try the Galaxy Palace in Tomorrowland. Imagineers have been beating the bushes for something a little, well, alien. Silly and largely for children.

Live Entertainment in Epcot

Epcot offers a large assortment of unique and talented performers from all over the world. Each country in the World Showcase has its own offering. Some performers seem to be permanent fixtures, others are guests. The guest artists come to Disney World for a year or two, usually in the "country" of their origin in the World Showcase. These are some of the most interesting performances at Walt Disney World, and we urge you to seek them out, not only to enjoy their performances but also to chat with the artists. It is a rare opportunity for cultural exchange.

Epcot also offers a variety of guest artisans that might include a Persian rugmaker or a French glassblower. Such craftsman can be found in the countries around the World Showcase and are usually mentioned in the guidemap. Here and there around Epcot, you'll also find high school and college bands and choruses from all over the U.S. and the world.

First we'll discuss entertainment at Future World, then we'll cover the World Showcase.

Future Corps   This drum and bugle group plays a variety of popular tunes. They are entertaining and, being professionals, are outstanding. Performances are usually at Innoventions Plaza.

The Anacomical Players   This impromptu theater group performs in the Wonders of Life Pavilion. Their sketches about health often involve the audience. Look for the Anacomical Players stage area on the main floor of the pavilion.

The JaMMitors   The JaMMitors are a wacky band of garbage can musicians. You'll have to see this to believe it. Look for them daily in the Innoventions breezeway.

The Kristos   The Kristos are android-like aliens that perform a hypnotic and acrobatic sort of dance at the Innoventions Logo Plaza. Try to catch them.

Following are the live entertainment shows available at the World Showcase.

Mexico   You're bound to find some good Mexican and Latin American musicians here each day. Try timing a performance to a snack at the sidewalk cantina ♥. Other performers include Huitzilin, a group of Mexican musician-storytellers.

Norway   Live entertainment here has been spotty of late, with none of the wonderful Norwegian folk music of previous years. Check your guidemap to see what's happening here; if they have Norwegian entertainment, don't miss it.

China   The performances are typically a solo musical performer and a small group of Chinese acrobats. We suggest that you stroll by to see where they will be and then return for a later show, finding a bench nearby. Arrive early enough to sit and enjoy the courtyard. The piped-in music in China is particularly pleasant. If you take the time, you will see a lot that a walk-through would miss. By the time the performers arrive, you'll feel as though you're in China.

Germany   There's some fine German music here, with the Oktoberfest Musikanten playing daily in the courtyard and the lively Alpine Trio appearing in the Biergarten restaurant. Strolling around the pavilion while the live musicians play will provide the perfect mood for your "visit to Germany." Check the guidemap for times, and make your entrance accordingly.

Italy   Several musical groups have been performing here. Both I Cantanapoli and Tzigantzi are worth the trip. Live entertainment is also part of dinner at L'Originale Alfredo di Roma Ristorante. This eatery is a little slice of Italy: gay, colorful, and noisy. It's a good choice for a fun and festive meal.

The American Adventure   Inside the rotunda are the Voices of Liberty, an a cappella choral group performing medleys of traditional American ballads. Arrive a few minutes early. It is a good show, especially if you have a place to sit down. In front of the pavilion, check out the Sons of Liberty, Disney's fife and drum corps, complete with traditional costumes.

The American Gardens Theater, a large stage near the pavilion, offers a selection of performing artists and groups. Often, you will find a high school band or chorus or a big-name performer. During the course of a Disney week, the variety of entertainment here is pretty impressive. Check your guidemap. If someone well known is performing, give yourselves plenty of time to get a seat.

Japan   With our favorite Epcot entertainer, the Fantasy DreamMaker, on a sabbatical, entertainment here in Japan now includes several traditional Japanese drum groups. Interesting yes, but not terribly exciting.

Morocco   There's almost always something exciting going on here: musicians, acrobats, dancers, and an exotic street show make Morocco one of Epcot's hottest showplaces. Check your Epcot guidemap so you can explore the marketplace during this colorful street festival.

Inside Marrakesh restaurant ♥♥ is a belly dance show during both lunch and dinner. In both cuisine and atmosphere, Marrakesh delivers a truly exotic restaurant experience.

France   Gypsy music, a clown, and even a French accordionist are part of the lively show here along the river Seine. If you're lucky, you might even catch the exceptional Nicolas, the mime in the bubble. Look for his performances in the Epcot guidemap.

The United Kingdom   Live entertainment here has recently undergone a rebirth. The music of the Beatles comes alive with British Invasion, a talented foursome of musicians who perform throughout the week. Other performers include Scottish bagpipes and, lately, some live entertainment in the Rose and Crown Pub. Look there for the magic of Jon Armstrong and a lively show by pianist Pam Brody.

Canada   The Caledonia Bagpipes also appear to be a permanent feature here in the Canadian Pavilion, and the Canadian Comedy Corps, often in the company of a kilted Goofy, performs its slapstick act at various times throughout the day.

Roaming Entertainment in Epcot

There's other entertainment, too, and much of it simply roams the World Showcase. The Cirikli is one of the most unusual troupes of live entertainers you'll ever see. These beautiful "stilt birds" wander the World Showcase daily, looking for a nesting place. Don't miss these extraordinary performers. Other roaming entertainers include the World Class Brass comic musicians and the Junkanoo Bus steel band. Other performers come and go. Check your Epcot guidemap for details.

Live Entertainment at Disney–MGM Studios

The Boulevards' "Streetmosphere"   Along both Hollywood and Sunset Boulevards, you'll find a wacky band of street performers, all in outrageous costumes. These zany "streetmosphere" characters almost always involve unwary onlookers in their comic routines. These are the denizens of Disney's 1930s Hollywood, and we urge you to catch their performances. It is easy to rush through the boulevards heading to rides and attractions elsewhere, never realizing what you're missing. Don't forget to come back here later to catch the shows.

The Studio's Soundstage   This theme park is also a working studio. During the year, television programs are produced in its three large sound stages. Often, they involve audiences. Check at the Production Information Window just inside the front gate for ticket availability and show times.

Street Musicians   A variety of bands play at various places throughout the park. The Tubafours Quartet, Toon Town Trio, and Hollywood Hitmen offer their own brand of musical entertainment and street comedy.

Muppet Characters   The Muppets can be found around the back of the Muppet Theater. Always fun, these characters are especially entertaining for young children.

Beauty and the Beast Stage Show ♥♥   This lavish stage production takes place in a large theater on Sunset Boulevard. Beautifully costumed performers dance and sing to the memorable music of the animated Disney classic.

Backlot Theater   This amphitheater features live performances of one of Disney's animated feature films. The current offering is *The Hunchback of Notre Dame*. Sets, costumes, and performances are all memorable, and we advise that you not miss it.

Disney Parades

The Magic Kingdom is famous for its parades, and for 1997, the Remember the Magic Parade will be featured. With floats, costumes, characters, and music, this parade celebrates 25 years of Disney magic. Also featured every evening during the anniversary year will be the SpectroMagic Light Parade (see the section on nightlife at Walt Disney World later in this chapter). Both are worth seeing.

Disney–MGM Studios also features a daily parade, and this year it is The Toy Story Parade. We expect Hercules sometime late in 1997.

Check your theme park guidemaps for details and the times of these parades.

Live Entertainment at Downtown Disney

This new area also includes Pleasure Island and the Village Marketplace, and, with a dozen nightclubs and plans for a performing arts center and a Cirque du Soleil Theater, it will be a powerhouse of live entertainment. Live bands will run the gamut from jazz to country. For more details, see the section on nightlife at Downtown Disney later in this chapter.

Live Entertainment at the Disney Institute

Each evening, the performing arts center at the Disney Institute features a guest artist. The Dinner and Performance Package features dinner at Season's followed by the evening's performance, for $27 per person. To see who is live and onstage, check the World Update.

Live Entertainment in the Disney Resorts

The Grand Floridian

Each day from 3 to 6 P.M., a pianist plays in the grand lobby. In the evenings, from 9 to 11 P.M., a small orchestra performs on the landing outside of Mizner's Lounge on the second floor. The music is pleasant and can be heard from anywhere below. Either entertainment is reason enough to drop by to see this elegant place ♥.

The Polynesian

Another form of live entertainment to consider is one of the three dinner shows at the Poly. The Luau ♥, Mickey's Tropical Revue, and 'Ohana each have something interesting to offer. For details, see Chapter 6.

Fort Wilderness

Both the Hoop-Dee-Doo Musical Revue and the All-American Backyard Barbecue are popular events here. Hoop-Dee-Doo is an old-fashioned saloon show, and the Barbecue features a good country band. While not exactly a performance, the Campfire Singalong is definitely entertainment. This nightly event is held near the Meadow Trading Post and is free to all Disney resort guests. It features Disney movies on an outdoor screen, a marshmallow roast, a campfire singalong, and a visit by Chip and Dale.

Port Orleans and Dixie Landings

Both resorts feature entertainment in the lounges of their central areas. The Cotton Co-Op and Scat Cat's Club each usually have a singer/ entertainer in the evenings. Performances usually beginning after 9 P.M. Drop in for a drink and enjoy.

The Swan and the Dolphin

Juan and Only's Cantina and Bar, at the Dolphin, frequently features a Flamenco guitarist in the evenings, and the Lobby Court Lounge at the Swan has its own pianist in the evenings, Thursdays through Saturdays. Gulliver's Grill at the Swan has been offering a magic show during dinner.

ℛOMANTIC LIVE ENTERTAINMENT

- Have a drink at Mexico's sidewalk cafe during a Mariachi performance: ♥
- The belly dance show during a meal at Morocco's Marrakesh restaurant: ♥♥
- The Beauty and the Beast Stage Show at Disney–MGM Studios: ♥♥
- Musical entertainment at the Grand Floridian: ♥
- The Polynesian Luau at the Polynesian Resort: ♥

Nightlife at Walt Disney World

During your romantic getaway at Walt Disney World, you'll most certainly want to get out in the evening and have some fun. This is the Vacation Capital of the World, and that means there'll be lots to do. During the busy times of years, the parks are all open late and Disney World is running at full-throttle. Finding something to do in the evening will be a matter of choice. Whether you want to follow dinner with SpectroMagic or the Twilight Zone Tower of Terror, or whether you wish to take a dip in the pool or go out dancing, you'll find plenty to do after dark.

During the off season, there is not quite so much going on. The theme parks and attractions all close relatively early. The Magic Kingdom and Disney–MGM Studios usually close at 6 P.M. and the World Showcase at Epcot closes at 9 P.M. While Epcot features

IllumiNations every night, the other parks stay open late with nighttime parades and fireworks only on weekends.

We like the off season because it fits our pace. With fewer people in the parks during the days, we have plenty of time for theme park excitement. We then use the evening to ease back, spend some time together, and to get out in search of that something special. Whether it's the busy season or not, you'll both find lots of nightlife at Walt Disney World. Besides dining out, you will be able to enjoy Pleasure Island, Board-Walk, dinner shows, the movies, great shopping, hot tubbing, special and seasonal events, and "resort hopping."

Fireworks Over Disney

Disney offers a fireworks show in each theme park to choose from.

IllumiNations   IllumiNations ♥♥ is a spectacular fireworks and laser light show staged each evening over the Epcot's World Showcase Lagoon. Featuring the perfect orchestration of music, blazing rockets, and colored fountains, this is an event simply too outstanding to miss. IllumiNations 25, a special version of this show created for Disney's 25th Anniversary Celebration, will be featured for 1997. There are numerous spots along the lagoon from which to watch the show, and we suggest that you arrive early to get one. One of our favorites is from the bridge between the United Kingdom and France or in the garden area right below it. Be sure that you can see the large sphere in the center of the lagoon and do your best to avoid being downwind of the show, unless you enjoy the smell of gunpowder.

Fantasy in the Sky   Featured in the Magic Kingdom, Fantasy in the Sky ♥♥ is another great fireworks show set to music. Catching this during 1997 should be easy, as it will be offered every night of the year. The most symmetrical view of the show is from Main Street. A less-crowded view can be had from Mickey's Toontown Fair, where, at the end of the show, you can hop aboard the train waiting at the station and ride around to the Main Street Depot for an easy exit.

Sorcery in the Sky   At MGM, Sorcery in the Sky ♥♥ is considered by many to be the finest pyrotechnic display at Disney. Set to the most memorable of Hollywood's film scores, this show occurs only when the park is open late, during the busier months, or on holidays. If it is scheduled during your visit, don't miss it. Viewing is best from Hollywood Boulevard.

The SpectroMagic Light Parade

The SpectroMagic Light Parade ♥♥♥ is another event not to miss, and it too will be featured every night during the year of the 25th Anniversary Celebration. After 1997, we expect to see something else in its place. This musical parade features floats and Disney characters all aglow with fiber-optics, lights, and special effects of every sort. After this show, parades will never be the same. We promise. Check the Magic Kingdom guidemap for the route of SpectroMagic, and arrive early to stake out a good place along it.

Disney's BoardWalk

More than a resort, Disney's BoardWalk features a 1930s "seaside" promenade of nighttime entertainment: shops, restaurants, clubs, amusements, a dance hall, and sidewalk entertainers. One of Disney's newest hot spots, we suggest you set aside an evening to spend here. Have dinner, catch some entertainment, take a stroll along the BoardWalk, and dance the night away. There is simply too much to do here to miss this exciting place.

Begin your evening at the BoardWalk with dinner reservations. For fine and innovative dining, the Flying Fish is one of our favorites. Spoodle's Mediterranean cuisine is another fine choice, and both ESPN Club and the Big River Grille and Brewing Works feature good food. For details, see Chapter 6.

After dinner, stroll the BoardWalk Promenade and nosh a dessert at BoardWalk Bakery or enjoy a gelato at Seashore Sweets, an old-fashioned soda fountain. There are sidewalk vendors, too, offering a selection of treats that range from hot dogs and crepes to coffees and pastries.

Then there's browsing along the Promenade. Wyland Gallery features the marine artistry of Peter Wyland as well as the work of other internationally renowned painters and sculptors. Thimbles and Threads offers shoppers a look at some of the latest Disney designer fashions, while the Screen Door General Store has an assortment of groceries, snacks, Disney stationery, and decorative items.

The BoardWalk's strong suit, though, is entertainment, and there's enough here to keep you busy into the wee hours. Happening along the Promenade are magicians, portrait artists, jugglers, fire-eaters, a small arcade of carnival games, and "surrey" rentals. Riding around the lake on one of these four-wheel bicycle/carriages is more fun than we can describe.

Also along the BoardWalk are several of Disney's newest and most interesting nightspots.

Atlantic Dance   This stylish 1930s dance hall features a 10-piece orchestra with vocalists and a large dance floor. Put them together, and you have a night of romantic dancing. Often, the music is played a bit loud and there is a tendency to play more current hits late in the night, but we have really enjoyed our time together here. We just hope they stay truer to the 1930s theme. There's a selection of light foods, too, such as California rolls and pizza as well as the bar's five signature martinis. French doors open onto a splendid outdoor balcony ♥♥ that offers an outstanding view of IllumiNations.

Atlantic Dance is open from 8 P.M. to 2 A.M. nightly for those 21 and older. Cover charge is $5.

Jellyroll's   The main attraction at this neighborhood-style bar is the music and antics of its dueling pianists who match wits here each evening from 7 P.M. to 2 A.M. There's singing, playing, and lots of rowdy fun. Jelly's has a full bar, and we suggest that you give this place a try. It's a surprisingly good time.

ESPN Club   Besides a good eatery and bar, this club is heaven for sports lovers. There's more than 70 video monitors here, with satellite feeds covering sporting events worldwide. Select what interests you with your own controls. There are scoreboards, live interviews, Internet terminals, state-of-the-art video games, pep rallies, and more than you can think of when it comes to sports input. There's also a theater-size video array featuring special sporting events. It is *the* place to go for the big game or championship boxing match (cover charges may apply to special events).

Big River Grille and Brewing Works   Besides its pub menu, this place makes its own beers and ales. Drop in here and get a sampler of the day's brewing. The atmosphere is interesting, and the brews and food are quite good.

The BelleVue Room   Located in the BoardWalk Inn, this quaint lounge features a full-service bar with a variety of tempting sweets. Furnishings here will take you back to the 1920s and 30s; vintage radios play old-time shows. It is a comfortable and quiet escape, and it even has a beautiful outside balcony overlooking the BoardWalk green.

Downtown Disney

Sometimes a place grows so much that it simply becomes something new. Such is the case for Pleasure Island and the Village Marketplace. The year 1997 will be a time of rebirth for this area, as it more than doubles in size to add a host of theaters, restaurants, shops and stores, a performing arts center, and several nightclubs. Renamed Downtown Disney, it will envelope both Pleasure Island and the Village Marketplace, making it nothing less than one superstar attraction; the West Side Esplanade will open summer of 1997. Downtown Disney is the largest expansion of its kind in Disney history, and it is sure to become one of the brightest stars of nighttime entertainment.

Getting to Downtown Disney   Buses run nearly all day from Disney resorts to the east side of Downtown Disney (the Village Marketplace) and in the evening to both Pleasure Island and the new West Side Esplanade. Driving is easy too, but parking becomes more of a problem as the evening progresses. For $5, there's valet parking at Pleasure Island.

Dining at Downtown Disney   You'll find a wide selection of eateries here, from fast food to fine dining. Table-service restaurants on the new West Side Esplanade will include Wolfgang Puck's Cafe, House of Blues, and Bongo's Cuban Cafe. On the east side, there's Rainforest Cafe, Fireworks Factory, Fulton's Crab House, Portobello Yacht Club, Cap'n Jack's Oyster Bar, and Planet Hollywood. For details, see Chapter 6.

Fast-food offerings are many and include street vendors, D-Zerts, Missing Link Sausage Company, and Minnie Mia's Italian Eatery. There are more, and you'll find food in nearly all of the clubs on Pleasure Island, too.

The New West Side Esplanade (opens summer 1997)   Attractions along the West Side Esplanade will include a Virgin Records Megastore with an outdoor stage for live performances, a host of boutiques and shops, and some serious additions to Disney nightlife.

- House of Blues: This restaurant and nightclub, co-owned by Blues Brother Dan Aykroyd, will feature live music seven nights a week:

blues, R&B, jazz, and country. Set to open the summer of 1997, it will feature a Delta-inspired menu of jambalayas, etouffees, and other Creole favorites. For more details, see Chapter 6.

- Bongo's Cuban Cafe: Owned by superstar Gloria Estefan, this stylish dance club and restaurant will bring to Disney all of the excitement of Miami's South Beach. Opening in the summer of 1997, Bongo's will feature the exotic cuisine and Latin rhythms of South America.

- Cirque du Soleil: Premiering in winter of 1998 will be this amazing international troupe of dancers and acrobats, performing in one of Downtown Disney's most celebrated architectural achievements. The avant-garde, tent-like Cirque du Soleil Theater will feature a cast of more than 70 in a high-energy mix of music, magical lighting, incredible costumes, and acrobatics and dance. It will be the stunning showcase for a truly unique performance. This world-renowned Montreal-based troupe will perform twice daily, five days a week.

Pleasure Island at Downtown Disney

Really a small theme park, the "theme" here is adult, nighttime entertainment. Street entertainers, dancers, and live bands are the big draw. Every night, Pleasure Island celebrates New Year's Eve with an exciting fireworks show. Be forewarned that the music in the dance clubs is quite loud. Admission to this island of clubs, shops, and restaurants is $18 per person and is included in both the Length of Stay Pass and the World Hopper Pass.

The Neon Armadillo   The Neon Armadillo is a country and western club featuring line dancing and a Southwest decor. Not even lovers of this style of music, we are always drawn to the 'Dillo. The songs are singable and danceable and, before long, the small dance floor comes alive. There is a full-service bar and small menu of nachos, wings, and burgers.

The Pleasure Island Jazz Club   This is our kind of place. A cozy club with small tables in front of the stage, this is a place we like to go for good music and a light meal. Appetizer-size dishes, such as crab cakes, quesadillas, salads, and rich desserts, and some good jazz make this one of our favorites at Pleasure Island.

The Rock 'n Roll Beach Club   This is the place where we go to dance. With hundreds of lights and special effects, the music more reflects our times: the Beatles, Rolling Stones, and other familiar sounds. The bands here are always good, both instrumentally and vocally, and it won't take long for you to get into the dancing and singing. The full-service bar also offers pizza, subs, and a small selection of sandwiches.

The Comedy Warehouse   It is one of the Island's most popular clubs and features a handful of improvisational and stand-up comics. The humor is clean and harmless; vulgarities are not part of this or any other Disney show. Occasionally, a well-known comic may appear, in which case an additional admission will be charged. Five shows are offered nightly, and lines here are a regular occurrence.

8TRAX   This dance club plays the recorded music of the seventies. We're not sure what we were listening to back then, but it wasn't this stuff. Still, the sound system is impressive, and the ambience, multi-level dance floor, and special effects are futuristic. Offered here are a full-service bar and burgers, fries, and sandwiches.

Mannequins Dance Palace   Mannequins was once voted the number one contemporary dance club in the Southeast U.S. It is the only club on the Island that requires patrons to be 21 years of age or older. The main dance floor is a huge turntable, and the decorative mannequins are garbed in strange leather costumes. All this and the contemporary music make this *the* place for the younger crowd.

The Adventurer's Club   Here you have something both unique and uniquely "Disney." Pretending to be one of those stuffy, British gentleman's clubs of the 1920s, the club offers a wacky group of actors who perform and interact with guests throughout the evening. The club itself is worth a good look, and if you pick up a program card at the door, you'll know where and when the next zany show takes place. We wandered in here on our first visit and stayed until 1:30 A.M.

The Shops of Pleasure Island   The Island offers a lot of stuff simply not available elsewhere. Among our favorites are Suspended Animation, which features original Disney animation cels, lithographs, and art, and Avigator's Supply, with its nice selection of clothing and leather goods. Other shops feature music and movie memorabilia, amusing T-shirts, and Pleasure Island logo merchandise.

The Pleasure Island West End Stage   This show features nightly live bands. The music is good and people dance in the street. This is the place to be for the nightly New Year's Eve Celebration, which includes dancers, special effects, fireworks, and confetti cannons. It alone is nearly worth the price of admission. Be sure to find out what time this will happen, because "midnight" here is not always midnight.

The AMC Pleasure Island Theaters   Adjacent to the Island, this complex currently features 10 state-of-the-art cinemas that show the very latest feature films. Sometime in the summer of 1997, it will become a *24*-screen complex. Maybe a nice romantic comedy would be just the thing on one of your evenings out.

Seasonal Nightlife

During the course of each year, Walt Disney World offers a variety of special events. Many of these happen during the evening hours, further spicing Disney nightlife. From the Jolly Holidays Dinner Show to the Walt Disney World Wine Festival, there's almost always something interesting going on. Other seasonal events include the Pleasure Island Mardi Gras Celebration, Mickey's Very Merry Christmas Party, Mickey's Not-So-Scary Halloween Party, the Annual Jazz Festival, Chinese New Year, and Epcot Swingin' Summer Nights. New events are added each season, so check to see what's going on during your visit.

Resort Hopping

Any visit to Disney World is not complete unless you get the chance to check out the Disney resorts. If you have never seen the Grand Floridian, the Polynesian, or the Contemporary, take a monorail ride and do some exploring. There is plenty to see, and you can look these places over for your next visit. Don't leave out the Wilderness Lodge and its award-winning lobby.

While you're out in the evening at any of the Magic Kingdom resorts, don't forget to look for the Electric Water Pageant on the Seven Seas Lagoon. This display of electrical and musical magic passes by each resort on the lagoon around 9 P.M. Check at any resort for the exact time. There are good viewing places all along the beach areas of the Polynesian, the Grand Floridian, the Contemporary, the Wilderness

Lodge, and Fort Wilderness. Try the fourth-floor lake overlook at the Lodge for something especially nice.

Resort hopping is especially fun during the weeks between Thanksgiving and Christmas, when the World is decked out in its Christmas finery. Nearly every resort has a beautifully decorated tree in its lobby, and there are tree lighting ceremonies each night. Disney characters and free refreshments are almost always part of the entertainment. Last year, we caught a chorus of bell ringers playing Christmas carols at the Wilderness Lodge.

Even if it's not the holiday season, many of Walt Disney World's lounges are quiet and romantic places and offer interesting selections of appetizers and hors d'oeuvres. Try skipping dinner and traveling around the World in search of tasty treats. Some of our favorite spots are Martha's Vineyard at the Beach Club, the Territory Lounge at the Wilderness Lodge, Scat Cat's at Port Orleans, and the California Grill bar at the Contemporary. There are lots of others, and we'll leave them for you to discover.

THE ROMANCE OF DISNEY NIGHTLIFE

- A night of slow dancing at Atlantic Dance: ♥♥♥♥
- Relax in the afternoon before your Disney evening out: ♥♥
- Have a nice hot tub before you go out for the evening: ♥♥
- SpectroMagic Light Parade at the Magic Kingdom: ♥♥♥
- Watch the Magic Kingdom fireworks or the Electric Water Pageant from one of the swings on the beach at the Grand Floridian or the Polynesian: ♥♥♥♥
- Dine at Portobello and have an evening out at Pleasure Island: ♥♥
- A light dinner at Pleasure Island's Jazz Company: ♥♥
- "Resort Hopping" at Christmastime to see the decorations and tree lighting ceremonies: ♥♥
- Have a wine flight at the Beach Club's Martha's Vineyard lounge: ♥♥♥
- IllumiNations from second-floor outside balcony of Atlantic Dance: ♥♥

CHAPTER 6

$\mathscr{D}$ining at Walt Disney World

Several years ago, Disney Food and Beverage director Dieter Hannig promised to make Walt Disney World a dining destination. We are happy to report that his project, which began with the celebrated California Grill, is having its effect on nearly every eatery at Disney. From fast food to fine dining, menus are being upgraded with fresher, better-prepared, and more interesting foods. For us, it has meant many more memorable meals and a few extra pounds to work off. For you, it will mean more fine dining as well as improved food across the whole spectrum of Disney dining. And what a spectrum it is. With more than 200 places serving food, the chefs of Disney have conjured a magical diversity of eating experiences. From a hot dog on Main Street to the gourmet elegance of Victoria and Albert's, there's a taste for every palate and purse, and we have tried them all. (Did we mention those few extra pounds?)

Making "Reservations"

Dinner reservations at Walt Disney World are now known as "Priority Seating Arrangements." What this means is that you will make the usual "reservations." When you arrive at the restaurant, you will check in with the maitre d' and be given the next available table.

- We suggest that you do make priority arrangements and that you arrive 10 minutes early. Simply, there are places you just won't get into without them.
- Priority arrangements may be made up to 60 days in advance by phoning (407) WDW-DINE (939-3463).

- Same-day, theme park dining reservations by phone are available only to Disney resort guests. Touch 55 on your room phone.
- Guest Services at your resort has a variety of restaurant menus. Look them over, make your choice, and then let Guest Services make the call.
- Reservations are most necessary after 7 P.M., for character meals, dinner shows, and theme park table-service restaurants.
- For character breakfasts, King Stefan's will take reservations only up to seven days ahead, and both Olivia's and the Soundstage at Disney–MGM Studios, 30 days ahead. All others will allow reservations up to 60 days in advance.
- Make arrangements for dinner shows when you reserve your room.
- Theme park eateries will take same-day reservations at the door beginning in the morning. Stroll by and make yours.

Dining Tricks and Budget Tips

Over the years, we have learned to be imaginative with our approach to the pleasures of dining at Walt Disney World. Here are some of our ideas.

OUR TIPS FOR BREAKFAST

- Virtually all table-service restaurants and room services will fix anything that you desire. To get what you usually eat for breakfast, all you have to do is ask.
- For luxury and convenience, try room service and breakfast in bed ♥♥♥♥. It's only a little more expensive and will leave you feeling as pampered as you should feel.
- Try sharing a breakfast. The portions at most table-service restaurants and room service are large enough for all but the hardiest of eaters.
- Enjoy a poolside breakfast ♥. Pick up your breakfast at the food court and find a nice table on a patio or out by the pool.
- Fix your own breakfasts. Get a refrigerator from housekeeping ($5 a day or free, depending on your resort), and make a simple breakfast right in your room. Ingredients and supplies can be found either at the Gourmet Pantry at the Village Marketplace or nearby at Gooding's at the Crossroads Plaza.
- Watch out for food courts if you are in a hurry for breakfast. The usual hours for breakfast are very crowded, and you can find yourself

standing in line for pancakes instead of Splash Mountain. Try having breakfast earlier or later. Food courts usually open at 6 A.M.

OUR TIPS FOR LUNCH

- Eat dinner for lunch. One bonus is that the same food served at dinner is cheaper at lunchtime.
- Have some appetizers for lunch. Pick a fancy, expensive restaurant and share a salad and an appetizer ♥.
- Room Service ♥♥♥. Need we say more?
- Avoid the crowds and have an early lunch, as soon as places begin to serve, usually 11:30 A.M.
- Have a breakfast buffet for an early brunch. These are usually character meals and offer many foods appropriate for midday dining. Most usually serve until 11:30 A.M.
- Plan a picnic ♥♥. Have your favorite restaurant pack a lunch and head off to Discovery Island, Typhoon Lagoon, or some other outdoor Disney attraction.

OUR TIPS FOR DINNER

- Share a meal at one of the pricier dining spots. Try sharing a salad, a couple of appetizers, an entree, and a dessert.
- Pull out all the stops at least once during your vacation. Dress up and go someplace extravagant ♥♥♥.
- At the deluxe resorts, try in-room dining ♥♥♥. Hint: You can order anything from *any* restaurant at your resort, even if it's not on the room service menu.

Dining in a Lounge

Many of the lounges around Disney feature appetizers and finger foods from the restaurants adjacent to them. Lounges at Walt Disney World are not what you find in the outside world. Usually, they are quiet, comfortable, and often quite intimate. For a light meal or simply a large variety, dining in a lounge will likely be quite pleasing. Some even feature live entertainment. Martha's Vineyard at the Beach Club, the Matsu No Ma Lounge in Epcot, the Crew's Cup at the Yacht Club, and the California Grill bar are just a few of the many interesting choices.

Special Dietary Needs

In recent years, we have witnessed a "World"-wide change in menus all across the spectrum of Disney eating establishments. Menus have been revamped to include foods that more reflect what people are eating today. It is a simple matter to find low-fat meals, vegetarian entrees, and a host of healthier and lighter meals. Such foods can be found virtually everywhere, from counter-service eateries to the most elegant of gourmet dining spots. Fast-food outlets are even offering fruit as an option to French fries. Walt Disney World has become committed to satisfying the dietary needs of virtually every guest.

To test this commitment, we brought Aunt June and Uncle Jake to Walt Disney World. These folks are on a no fat, vegetarian diet. No fat, no nuts, no olives, no cheese, no fish. If you are wondering what that leaves, we can tell you how surprised even we were at what the chefs of Disney created. By notifying the kitchens when we made our reservations, Jake and June enjoyed dinners created especially for them. From cold melon soup to grilled vegetables and couscous, each entree was handcrafted. After a few meals, we were saying, "We'll have whatever they're having."

For kosher requirements, 24-hour notice is needed. Note that kosher foods arrive at Walt Disney World prepared and frozen.

Disney Character Meals

These delightful experiences are usually buffets. Disney characters make the rounds during mealtime, visiting each table. Not just for kids, character meals can be fun and provide some great photo opportunities, too.

WHERE TO HAVE CHARACTER BREAKFASTS

- Artist Point, the Wilderness Lodge, with Pocahontas and friends
- Baskerville's, the Grosvenor (Tuesday, Thursday, and Saturday)
- Cape May Cafe, the Beach Club, with Admiral Goofy and crew
- Chef Mickey's, the Contemporary, with Mickey and Minnie
- County Fair, the Hilton (Sunday)
- Crystal Palace, Magic Kingdom, with Winnie the Pooh and friends
- Fulton's Crab House, Pleasure Island, with Mickey and crew
- Garden Grill, The Land, Epcot, with Farmer Mickey and Minnie
- Garden Grove Cafe, the Swan (weekend days)

- Harry's Safari Bar and Grill, the Dolphin (Sunday brunch)
- King Stefan's Banquet Hall, Fantasyland, with Cinderella and friends
- 1900 Park Fare, the Grand Floridian, with Mary Poppins and friends
- 'Ohana at Papeete Bay, the Polynesian, with Minnie and friends
- Olivia's, Old Key West (Sunday and Wednesday), with Winnie the Pooh and friends
- Soundstage, Disney–MGM Studios, with classic Disney film characters

WHERE TO HAVE CHARACTER LUNCHES

- Crystal Palace, Magic Kingdom, with Winnie the Pooh and Friends
- Garden Grill, The Land, Epcot, with Farmer Mickey and Minnie
- Soundstage, Disney–MGM Studios, with classic Disney film characters

WHERE TO HAVE CHARACTER DINNERS

- Baskerville's, the Grosvenor (Wednesday)
- Chef Mickey's, the Contemporary, with Mickey and Minnie
- Crystal Palace, Magic Kingdom, with Winnie the Pooh and friends
- Garden Grill, The Land, Epcot, with Farmer Mickey and Minnie
- Gulliver's Grill, the Swan (Monday, Thursday, Friday)
- Liberty Tree Tavern, Magic Kingdom, with Mickey and friends
- 1900 Park Fare, the Grand Floridian, with Mickey, Minnie, and Goofy

Dinner Shows

For an evening of fun and food, try one of Disney's dinner shows. We suggest that you set aside some time for one and make a reservation when you book your room.

The Polynesian Luau

Unlike many of the cute and typical Disney productions, this one features authentic South Pacific entertainment. The colorful show features performers from a variety of South Sea islands. There is hula dancing, fire dancing, and the authentic music of the South Seas. This is just the kind of thing that we like best: authentic and exotic entertainment.

You'll be seated at long tables and fed endless amounts of chicken, ribs, and seafood. Tropical drinks (alcoholic or nonalcoholic) are included in the price. The food is good, though not memorable.

Adults, $37; children (ages 3 to 11), $20; children under 3, no charge. Gratuity is not included. There are two shows, at 6:45 and 9:30 P.M. A 10% discount is available with a Magic Kingdom Club or American Express card.

This show is a lot of fun. It's even romantic ♥♥.

Mickey's Tropical Revue

This is a late-afternoon children's version of the Polynesian Luau, featuring a mix of South Sea performers and Disney characters. It is fun if you have small children. At the end of the show, the performers bring the kids onto the stage to teach them Polynesian dancing. The food is the same as the Luau. Don't forget your camera.

Adults, $31; children (3–11), $15. Gratuity is not included. One show at 4:30 P.M. 10% discount is available with Magic Kingdom Club or American Express card.

The Hoop-Dee-Doo Musical Revue

This saloon-style show has been a regular feature at Fort Wilderness for many years. It is very popular, and tickets to it do not come easily. Pioneer Hall, the setting for the Hoop-Dee-Doo, is an amusing recreation of an Old West dance hall, complete with velvet curtains, rough-hewn beams, and saloon-like tables and chairs.

The cuisine is country cooking: barbecued ribs, fried chicken, salad, bread, corn on the cob, baked beans, and strawberry shortcake. Beverages include beer and wine. The show is memorable—a delight of song, dance, and corny laughs—and the food is good. The performers are obviously talented, and their timing is flawless. This is not sophisticated entertainment, mind you, but it is good, wholesome Disney fun.

Adults, $37; children (3–11), $20. 10% discount for American Express and Magic Kingdom Club.

Tip: Transportation to this show is tricky. Check with your Guest Services.

The All-American Backyard Barbecue

Offered only during the summer and the first few months of fall, this picnic-table feast features live country music, Disney character fun, and a hearty selection of backyard favorites: chicken, burgers, hot dogs, ribs, corn bread, barbecue beans, and lots more. There's even beer and wine, and it's all surprisingly good. If you enjoy this kind of thing (or especially if you've never tried anything like it), we recommend you give it a go. Reservations are required and can be arranged through Disney dining reservations at (407) WDW-DINE (939-3463). Adults, $35; children (3–11), $25. Pricing includes tax and gratuity.

The Jolly Holidays Dinner Show

This seasonal show is one of our favorite Disney events. We rarely miss it. It is always offered during the weeks between Thanksgiving and Christmas. Part of a package including accommodations, tickets to this dinner show are usually available to the public. The feast is a traditional Christmas dinner of turkey, ham, and all of the accompaniments.

The show features nearly 200 costumed performers in a Christmas tale. The music, song, and dance are all memorable, and the costumes are magnificent. Given that the Jolly Holidays package also features some of the year's most outstanding resort discounts, this is one event not to miss.

The price is included in the package. If tickets are sold separately, the prices should be about $60 for adults and $40 for children.

MurderWatch Mystery Theater

Presented on Saturday nights at the Grosvenor, this show features music and drama during a prime rib buffet. Guests participate in two nightly shows. Adults, $34; children, $19. For reservations, call (800) 624-4109.

A Bit of Dinner Entertainment

If you are looking for a bit of entertainment during dinner instead of a production, you can choose from among a number of restaurants that feature live dinner music.

- Flagler's at the Grand Floridian ♥♥: strolling musicians and singer waiters and waitresses
- Gulliver's Grill at the Swan: magician on Tuesday, Saturday, and Sunday nights.
- Hollywood Brown Derby at Disney–MGM ♥: a pianist

- L'Originale Alfredo di Roma Ristorante at Epcot: a group of musicians and singers
- Palio at the Swan ♥♥♥: strolling violinist or guitarist (or both), Tuesday through Saturday only
- Marrakesh restaurant at Epcot ♥♥: Moroccan musicians and belly dancer, for lunch and dinner
- Victoria and Albert's at the Grand Floridian ♥♥♥♥: a harpist
- The Biergarten at Epcot: shows during lunch and dinner

Not Your Unusual Dinner Shows

The following restaurants do not feature song or dance during dinner. What they do offer, however, are talented performing artists.

- Both the California Grill and the Flying Fish feature "performance kitchens" with counter seating. At either, chat with the chefs and enjoy the show. At the Grill, try our regular seats at Yoshi's sushi bar.
- Victoria and Albert's Chef's Table is much more than a fine show. Here in the kitchen of Chef Scott Hunnel, you will be wined and dined to *your* tastes and whims by a world-class culinary team. We promise you an unforgettable gastronomic event. With wine pairing, prix fixe dinner is $160 per person.

Restaurants of Walt Disney World

We didn't take any surveys to come up with the following reviews. We didn't poll other diners, and we didn't consult other restaurant reviews. Simply, we just ate everywhere—many places more than once, and some places many times. These are not all of Disney's eateries, simply those we felt were worthy of mention.

We expect that menus will change from time to time. Such is the way of good restaurants. Some of our favorite dishes may no longer be available. Quality and service may vary too, one of the unfortunate realities when it comes to restaurants. However, the following should give you a pretty good idea of what each restaurant is like and just how good the food is.

THE RATINGS

$ Inexpensive, less than $15 per meal
$$ Moderately priced, $15 to $25 per meal
$$$ Expensive, more than $25 per meal

We have also included the price range for dinner entrees. Remember, many of these restaurants serve pretty much the same food at lunchtime for about 25% less. For the quality of the food, we have used the following guidelines:

★ Acceptable means simply OK. This is our lowest rating.

★★ Good food means tasty but not memorable. This is the kind of meal that leaves you satisfied but that you won't go home talking about.

★★★ Very good food is memorable, well prepared, even creatively conceived. A find, indeed, if it is moderately priced.

★★★★ Outstanding food is the stuff of memories: imaginative, perfectly prepared, and artfully presented, the creation of a world-class chef and a first-rate kitchen. A culinary experience.

AKERSHUS
$$ ★★★
✓ Norway Pavilion, Epcot
✓ Table-service buffet: lunch and dinner
✓ Norwegian beer, wine, and full-service bar
✓ Priority seating advised
✓ Atmosphere is quaint and medieval. One of the best lunching places around the World Showcase Lagoon.

This is Norway's charming re-creation of a medieval fortress, and this year we've noticed a real improvement in the food. The buffet is a Norwegian "koldtbordt" and featured foods include the outstanding breads and cheeses of Norway and an assortment of hot and cold dishes. Herring, smoked salmon, stuffed pork loin, vegetable salad, and a daily chef's special are just a few of the 40 tasty items offered here. One of the more exotic eateries along the World Showcase, we think this is worth a meal. Akershus also serves Norway's Ringnes beer on draught. It's very good.

This restaurant is just what you'd expect if you were to dine in a castle: high, beamed ceilings; arched, cut-glass windows; and sturdy wooden furnishings. Cast members are young Norwegians dressed in traditional peasant garb.

ARIEL'S
$$$ ★★★ ♥
✓ The Beach Club
✓ Table service, dinner only

✓ Full-service bar, an award-winning wine list
✓ Priority seating advised
✓ Atmosphere is pleasant, especially by the aquarium
✓ Tip: Diners here get free child care while dining at the Beach Club's children's center. For arrangements, call the Sandcastle Club at (407) 934-3750.

This year will bring some big changes to Ariel's: a new menu and a new decor. Just what it will be has not yet been determined, but we can tell you that the menu will feature seafood from the Northeast and will be a bit less pricey. We suspect too, that the "Under the Sea" theme will remain intact and that Ariel's will not lose its charm and ambience. What we can tell you is that chef Richard Blanke has already impressed us with his current Ariel fare. Under his careful supervision, the current food at Ariel's is delicious, imaginative, stylishly served, and much better than it has been in past visits. We await, with great interest, Ariel's new incarnation.

ARTHUR'S 27
$$$ ★★★★   ♥♥♥♥
✓ The Buena Vista Palace
✓ Table service, dinner only
✓ Full-service bar, award-winning wine list
✓ Reservations required
✓ Atmosphere is sublime and unforgettable
✓ Tips: Valet parking is complimentary for patrons of Arthur's. This restaurant is worth the trip. Evening attire is appropriate.

Arthur's is an elegant and award-winning gourmet restaurant. Located high atop the 27-story Buena Vista Palace at Hotel Plaza, this modern restaurant manages to feature large expanses of glass and crystal chandeliers without sacrificing warmth and comfort. Diners are seated at private tables that each enjoy amazing vistas of Walt Disney World. A dining experience here during fireworks will be unforgettable.

The food is well prepared and imaginative. Service is flawless. Arthur's 27 is a first-class dining experience with all of the accoutrements. The menu is large and intriguing, and the wine list is exceptional. Truffle ravioli with veal and mushrooms, baked salmon in strudel leaves, and herb-crusted tuna are typical of the many fine offerings.

One of the nicest things about this restaurant is that it offers three prix fixe dinners. For a set price, you can create your own gourmet meal. Prices range from $50 per person for the four-course Excitement Dinner to $60 for the six-course Gourmet Dinner. Expensive, yes, but really a value if you compare it to the a la carte prices.

ARTIST POINT
$$ ★★★ ♥♥
- ✓ The Wilderness Lodge
- ✓ Table service, breakfast and dinner
- ✓ Full-service bar, good wine list from the Pacific Northwest
- ✓ Reservations suggested
- ✓ Atmosphere is woodsy and very pleasant
- ✓ Tip: This eatery excels at grilled fish.

This handsome restaurant is set amidst the splendor of one of Disney's grandest creations, the Wilderness Lodge. Inlaid wooden tables and huge canvases of western vistas make this a very pleasant place. Large windows overlook the courtyard and geyser, giving it a high-timber ambience.

The Artist Point features the fare of the Pacific Northwest. The emphasis here is on fresh and natural, and the Artist Point has managed it well. A superb Caesar salad and a Northwest Salmon Sampler would be the perfect beginnings to any meal. The menu varies to accommodate the season. During our visits, dishes such as smoked prime rib, maple-glazed king salmon, and an unforgettable Dungeness crab filet were just a few of the interesting choices. Servers seem willing, but the food comes slowly, which is acceptable if you're not in a hurry. The Artist Point offers an all-you-can-eat character breakfast.

AU PETIT CAFE
$$ ★★★ ♥♥
- ✓ France Pavilion, Epcot
- ✓ Table-service sidewalk cafe, lunch and dinner
- ✓ Full-service bar, French wines
- ✓ Reservations not accepted
- ✓ Pleasant, even romantic atmosphere if not too crowded
- ✓ Tip: A nice place for a shared dessert and espresso in the evening before the park closes.

The menu here is basically the same as that of Les Chefs de France, with a few additions such as quiche. The setting for this delightful cafe is along the lagoon promenade, and in the evening it is memorable indeed. It is shaded and quite comfortable in all but the hottest of weather. Service can be brusque, and this place can be too crowded.

BEACHES AND CREAM
$ ★★
✓ The Beach Club
✓ Table service with take-out, breakfast, lunch, snacks
✓ Reservations not accepted

This fifties-style soda shop is one of our regular haunts when we are at the Beach or the Yacht. For us, a stay at either of these resorts is simply not complete without a swim and a great double-chocolate ice cream soda. Hamburgers and turkey burgers are very good, and the hot dogs are easily Disney's finest. Also a terrific assortment of soda-fountain concoctions. Beaches even has an egg cream. Nothing elaborate here, just good old American fare and someplace fun to enjoy it. Breakfasts here are fairly ordinary fast food or continental-style.

BIERGARTEN
$$ ★★
✓ Germany Pavilion, Epcot
✓ Table-service buffet: lunch and dinner
✓ Beck's beer and German wines
✓ Priority seating advised
✓ Atmosphere is well themed, quaint, and fun

The inside of this restaurant feels like an Alpine village square, complete with building facades, waterwheel, and tree. Servers are costumed in Austrian peasant garb, and you'll find yourselves sitting beer hall–style at large tables with other guests. It's all quite pleasant, and the dinner show features a trio of musicians who will entertain you with music and zany antics. It is a fun taste of Germany.

The food here though, has suffered some since the Biergarten has become a buffet. Still, some of it is good. The large buffet includes sauerbraten, rotisserie chicken, sausages, wurst salad, and spaetzle, to mention just a few items. The apple strudel is memorable and the German beer comes in large steins. Overall, the restaurant is a pleasant experience.

BIG RIVER GRILLE AND BREWING WORKS

$$ ★★★
✓ The BoardWalk
✓ Table-service lunch and dinner
✓ Full-service bar and fresh-brewed beers and ales
✓ Priority seating not required
✓ Atmosphere is an eclectic blend of wood and metal

Yes, Disney is making beer. This pub-style restaurant features such home brews as Rocket Red, Wowzer's Wheat, and Tilt Pale Ale. And good it is! Try a sample tray of small glasses of each plus the day's special. The pub-style menu offerings include Lobster Pot Pie, sirloin steak, Rocket Red Ale Chicken, catch of the day, and a selection of good sandwiches and salads. Good food, good drink, and a nice place.

BISTRO DE PARIS

$$$ ★★★★   ♥♥♥
✓ France Pavilion, Epcot
✓ Table service, dinner only
✓ Full-service bar with a good selection of French wines
✓ Reservations required
✓ Atmosphere is intimate, romantic, and very Gallic
✓ Tip: Ask for a table for two by a window.

This is definitely classic French fare, and it is served in an intimate and romantic bistro setting. The menu here, as well as in the other two restaurants of Epcot's France, has been designed by three well-known Gallic chefs: Roger Verdé, Paul Bocuse, and Gaston LeNôtre. Appetizers run the course from foie gras to salmon tartare. Seafood casserole, grilled tenderloin of beef with mushrooms and green peppercorn sauce, breast of duck with cherries and red wine sauce, and rack of lamb for two make up this small but interesting menu. The Bistro is the "upstairs place," located above Les Chefs de France.

BOATWRIGHT'S DINING HALL

$$ ★★★
✓ Dixie Landings
✓ Table service, breakfast and dinner
✓ Bar features a variety of regional beers

✓ Reservations recommended only during peak mealtimes
✓ Atmosphere is themed but not unforgettable

This is Dixie Landings' only table-service eatery, and it is surprisingly good. This is not fine dining, but it is good, hearty fare for a reasonable price. The setting is a large, warehouse-like boat factory. The walls are covered with real antique boatwright gear, from giant augers to chisels and mallets. Overhead, you see a partially completed keel and framed-out vessel. Boatwright's is decorative and comfortable.

The cuisine has a definite bayou flair. Servings for both breakfast and dinner are large. If you are inclined to share an entree, this is a place to do it. Tin Pan Breakfasts are complete and hearty breakfasts served in a large pan. Dinners range from burgers and fried catfish to ribs and grilled pork loin. There are even more elaborately prepared Cajun specialties, such as Bayou Bouillabaisse and pirogue of pasta and seafood.

BONFAMILLE'S CAFE

$$ ★★★ ♥♥
✓ Port Orleans
✓ Table service, breakfast and dinner
✓ Full-service bar, regional specialty beers
✓ Reservations suggested during peak mealtimes
✓ Atmosphere near the garden is quite nice
✓ Tip: Order the Shrimp Orleans appetizer as an entree. It is outstanding.

The first time we visited Bonfamille's, it took us by surprise. The restaurant features a glassed-in garden area, and sitting by it was quite romantic. We were really expecting bland, manufactured food—wrong again. We were delighted to find a menu that features a mix of American and Creole entrees, even an intriguing variety of inexpensive sandwiches. Breakfasts feature a wide array of standards plus Skillet Combos, which are gigantic meals featuring eggs, potatoes, and ham, chicken, or Andouille sausage. Dinners run the gamut from T-bone steak and tortellini with vegetables to jambalaya. We loved the Dixie Blackened Voodoo lager and the Bourbon Street bread pudding. Not the finest dining at Disney, but good dining at a reasonable price.

BONGO'S CUBAN CAFE
✓ Downtown Disney

We haven't been able to find out much about this place, which is scheduled to open in the summer of 1997. Owned by Latin superstar Gloria Estefan and her husband, Emilio, this cafe/dance club will bring to Walt Disney World both the cuisine and rhythms of Cuba and South America. It will feature a restaurant and live music and will almost certainly be an exciting place.

CALIFORNIA GRILL

$$$ ★★★★ ♥♥

✓ The Contemporary
✓ Table service: lunches of appetizers and pizza; dinner
✓ Full-service bar; outstanding wine list
✓ Priority seating necessary
✓ Atmosphere is stylish and modern with a stunning panorama
✓ Tips: Have dinner here during the Magic Kingdom's fireworks show or have late-night sushi in the quiet and comfortable lounge overlooking the park.

Set high atop the Contemporary, this wonderful restaurant occupies an equally lofty place on our list of favorites. Stylishly designed and casually elegant, the Grill offers an unsurpassed view of Disney World as well as an exciting performance kitchen. But the real show here is the food. Chef Cliff Pleau and his staff provide an ever-changing menu driven by what is freshest and finest in the marketplace. Much of what is served here is airfreighted in from California, and this no-compromise approach can be savored in every dish that leaves the kitchen. From the opening basket of focaccia, baked in the grill's Tom Chandly oven, to the heavenly citrus soufflé, the voyage here is memorable indeed. Openers of alderwood-smoked salmon, sushi, and goat cheese ravioli are sublime beginnings for an unforgettable dining experience.

For us, selecting what to eat is the only dilemma. The grilled pork tenderloin with polenta and balsamic-smothered mushrooms or the pan-seared yellowfin tuna with Asian slaw and blackbean cake? There's so much great food here that everything seems like the best thing on the menu. Add to this a solid wine list from the best California vineyards and the Grill's knowledgeable and faultless service, and what you have is a dining experience not to be missed.

CAPE MAY CAFE

$$ ★★

✓ The Beach Club
✓ Table-service buffet, breakfast and dinner
✓ Full-service bar
✓ Reservations suggested
✓ Atmosphere is pleasant, though hardly memorable
✓ Tip: To make the Clambake a memorable meal, add a lobster. It's the most reasonably priced one at Disney, too.

A character breakfast with Admiral Goofy and friends is featured here each morning. The spread is large, and the quality is quite good. If you can't find something here, they'll be glad to fix it for you.

We wish that the Clambake Dinner were as good as it sounds. Promising a buffet of New England-style seafood, Cape May delivers instead a large selection of food that is simply adequate. As good an idea as a seafood buffet may sound, this kind of delicate food just doesn't stand up well to large batches and steam tables. Still, while this is not seafood dining at its best, Cape May offers a moderately priced, all-you-can-eat buffet that includes chicken, shrimp, fish, clams, and much more.

CAP'N JACK'S OYSTER BAR

$ ★★ ♥

✓ The Village Marketplace
✓ Table service, lunch and dinner
✓ Full-service bar
✓ Reservations not accepted
✓ Atmosphere is charming, especially if you sit by a window overlooking the water.

Cap'n Jack's is almost more of a bar than a restaurant. Almost. Overlooking the lake and Pleasure Island, this cozy little eatery is immersed in nautical decor. Fish nets, polished brass, leather, and the usual seaside amenities make this place rather inviting.

The menu isn't large, and most entrees tend to be on the small side, so this is not a good place to share. Jack's Shrimp Ziti, Zesty Crab Cakes, and shrimp or clams from the steamer are some of the offerings. There are also chowders and salads. The food is well prepared and tasty. This is a nice place for a light meal.

CAPTAIN'S TAVERN

$$ ★★
- ✓ Old Port Royale, the Caribbean Beach
- ✓ Table service, dinner only
- ✓ Beer, wine, and specialty drinks
- ✓ Priority seating suggested during peak hours
- ✓ Atmosphere is comfortable, woody, and nautical

The only table-service restaurant at the Caribbean Beach, Captain's Tavern offers a modest menu of seafood, poultry, and meats. Quality and value are both good here, due to a recent adjustment of cuisine. We particularly enjoyed the chicken wings and found our other choices to be tasty and competently prepared.

CHEF MICKEY'S

$$ ★
- ✓ The Contemporary
- ✓ Table-service character buffet: breakfast and dinner
- ✓ Wine and beer
- ✓ Priority seating a must
- ✓ Atmosphere is noisy and fun

Both meals here are the usual Disney buffets. Breakfasts feature a spread of egg dishes, pancakes and French toast, breakfast meats, and fruits and cereals. Dinners offer an interesting selection of poultry, fish, pastas, and roast beef as well as numerous side dishes and desserts. The food is fair, but you'd be missing the point if you visited Chef Mickey's for that. This is a place for Disney character fun, and it is one of the most popular character meals in the land.

CONCOURSE STEAKHOUSE

$$ (dinner $$$) ★★★
- ✓ The Contemporary
- ✓ Table service, breakfast, lunch, and dinner
- ✓ Full-service bar, good wine list
- ✓ Priority seating recommended for dinner
- ✓ Atmosphere is noisy and modern
- ✓ Tip: Get here early and beat the crowds.

For breakfast and lunch, the Concourse Steakhouse offers a well-prepared selection of a la carte standards. Lunches include salads, sandwiches, and a very good burger. While this would not be considered fine dining, it is most certainly good eating.

Dinners here enter yet another realm. With an upscale menu of seafood, poultry, and good cuts of meat, this restaurant features dishes that are well prepared, well conceived, and handsomely presented. The creamed spinach is memorable. But for the clamor of the Contemporary's noisy Concourse, we would not hesitate to recommend it.

CORAL CAFE
$$ ★★
- ✓ The Dolphin
- ✓ Table-service buffet, open 6 A.M. to midnight
- ✓ Beer and wine
- ✓ Reservations not required
- ✓ Atmosphere is not memorable

"All-day dining" is this restaurant's claim, and it offers both buffet and a la carte standards for breakfast, a salad bar and sandwiches for lunch, and a themed buffet each evening. Monday and Friday feature seafood specialties; American classics are the Tuesday, Thursday, and Saturday fare; and Mama Mia's Italian cuisine is featured on Sunday and Wednesday. Occasionally, special buffets highlight such regions as Mexico and the Caribbean.

CORAL ISLE CAFE
$$ ★★
- ✓ Great Ceremonial Building, the Polynesian
- ✓ Table service, breakfast, lunch, and dinner
- ✓ A few wines
- ✓ Reservations suggested during the peak mealtimes
- ✓ Atmosphere is pleasant

As we have said, the premium resorts each have an all-purpose restaurant that serves all three meals without a lot of fuss. This is the Polynesian's, and it is a pleasant place to enjoy a meal. This is not fine dining, and it makes no pretense to be.

The house specialty for breakfast is Auntie Kaui's Tonga Toast, a banana-stuffed French toast. From cereal and pancakes to omelettes, you will likely find something here. Lunches include some specialty sandwiches and salads, each with a Polynesian flair. Dinners include everything from sandwiches to fairly expensive entrees such as New York strip steak. Most entrees are priced moderately, and sandwiches are inexpensive. The Coral Isle features a selection of ice cream desserts. All in all, this is a pretty good value when eating at Walt Disney World. The Coral Isle is scheduled for refurbishing this year.

CORAL REEF
$$$ ★★★   ♥♥
✓ The Living Seas Pavilion, Future World, Epcot
✓ Table service, lunch and dinner
✓ Reservations required
✓ Atmosphere is especially nice by the aquarium

The Coral Reef is a beautiful and romantic place to dine. This is not the finest seafood at Disney, but the atmosphere more than makes up for it. The restaurant is adjacent to the Living Seas aquarium, and diners can enjoy a thrilling view. Entrees include Dover sole, grilled tuna, Maine lobster, beef tenderloin, and grilled chicken.

CRYSTAL PALACE
$$ ★★★
✓ Main Street USA, Magic Kingdom
✓ Table-service character buffet: breakfast, lunch, and dinner
✓ Priority seating strongly suggested

We've always loved the look of this restaurant but have never cared for the its cafeteria-style cuisine. Things have changed. Now with a marvelous buffet, the Palace features a surprising array of imaginative and well-prepared dishes. We expect the menu will change over time, but during our meal we enjoyed a wonderful variety of quality fresh salads and both hot and cold entrees, including made-to-order fajitas. Breakfast is a fairly standard Disney breakfast buffet, and dinner adds a variety of carved meats and fish filets. For our money, this is easily the best place to eat in the Magic Kingdom.

DOLPHIN FOUNTAIN
$ ★★★
✓ The Dolphin
✓ Table service, fifties soda shop, open 11 A.M. to 11 P.M.
✓ Atmosphere is loud, bright, and fun
✓ Tip: Good fries. Also serves espresso and cappuccino.

"The Golden Oldies" here refer more to the fried foods than to the fifties rock 'n roll background music. Hot dogs, hamburgers, grilled chicken sandwich, and BLT about sum it up. Toss in a salad, some nachos and fries, and a large selection of soda fountain sweets, and you've pretty much described this fun place. This is the Beaches and Cream of the Dolphin. Every resort should have one!

ESPN CLUB
$$ ★★★
✓ The BoardWalk
✓ Table service, lunch and dinner
✓ Full-service bar
✓ Atmosphere is noisy, like being at a sports event

This full-service restaurant is also a sports/entertainment club. With a 220-seat arena and wall of video monitors showing the most popular sporting events, this is definitely *the* place to go for the big fight or the playoff game. With more than 70 video monitors and tableside audio controls, a bank of Internet terminals, and state-of-the-art computer games, this is a sports lover's nirvana.

Not just the ultimate in sports entertainment, this place also has an interesting menu of well-prepared standards. Salads, pasta, and a selection of large and tasty sandwiches makes ESPN an eating place too: try the grilled chicken, BBQ pork, or the club sandwich. The burger here is outstanding (not to mention huge). Lots of good finger foods too, to go with the sporting events and drinks.

EVERGREEN'S
$ ★★
✓ Poolside at Shades of Green
✓ Table service, lunch and dinner
✓ Full-service bar, including draught beer

✓ No reservations
✓ Atmosphere is pleasant
✓ Tip: Try the Angus Beef Burger.

This is basically a lunch place, but it is a good one. The menu is small, including pizza, rotisserie chicken, a very good hamburger, and a variety of sandwiches and salads. The atmosphere is pleasant and restaurant-like except for the upside-down tennis court (with players) on the ceiling. Antique golf and tennis equipment adorn the walls. This is a popular lunching place for golfers.

50's PRIME TIME CAFE
$$ ★★
✓ Disney–MGM Studios
✓ Table service, lunch and dinner
✓ Full-service bar
✓ Reservations suggested
✓ Atmosphere, though not romantic, is really Disney and a riot

There is more about this place that is standard Americana than simply the menu. Prime Time looks like the average American kitchen of the 1950s. Each table has its own TV that plays snippets of *I Love Lucy, I Married Joan,* and other 50s sitcoms. There are old appliances, cupboards, and decorations that are the authentic stuff. Walters and waitresses are Mom and Pop, and you'd better finish your food if you expect to get dessert. The food is good, but the experience, especially if you lived through this period, is worth the price. (It is a bit disconcerting to see that things from our youth are now antiques.)

The menu features burgers, meat loaf, grilled chicken, salads, soups, and other American classics.

FIREWORKS FACTORY
$$ ★★
✓ Pleasure Island (admission not required)
✓ Table service, lunch and dinner
✓ Full-service bar, outstanding selection of brew
✓ Reservations not required
✓ Atmosphere is interesting, colorful, and fun. Can be noisy.
✓ Tip: A good place to have dinner before a night out at Pleasure Island.

The Fireworks Factory is run by Levy's Restaurants of Chicago. It is basically a barbecue place with above-average barbecue. It offers a large menu for both lunch and dinner as well as one of the biggest selections of beers at Disney. The food is quite good, and we frequently dine here on appetizers. Entrees include mesquite-smoked chicken, shrimp quesadillas, applewood-smoked baby back ribs, and barbecued shrimp. The bread basket features cornbread, and the barbecued beans are the best that we've ever had out.

The "story" of this restaurant is that it was once a fireworks factory, *before* the explosion. You can just imagine the decor. A sort of post-incendiary motif, with lots of fun details. The bases of the tables look like manhole covers.

FLAGLER'S
$$$ ★★★ ♥♥♥
- ✓ The Grand Floridian
- ✓ Table service, dinner only
- ✓ Full-service bar
- ✓ Priority seating advised
- ✓ Atmosphere is elegant and romantic

Flagler's has long been one of the standards of Grand Floridian dining. Its fine Italian cuisine and singing waiters lend more than just a touch of romance to an outstanding dining experience. Word is that Flagler's is about to enjoy something of a face-lift and that the menu will soon feature regional U.S. cuisines with an emphasis on the fresh and innovative. Knowing the management and the culinary staff of the Grand, both of whom are committed to being the best in all they do, we feel confident in recommending whatever new face this fine eatery puts on. In fact, we're already anxious to try it.

FLYING FISH
$$$ ★★★★ ♥♥
- ✓ The BoardWalk
- ✓ Table service, dinner only, from 6 P.M.
- ✓ Full-service bar, outstanding wine list
- ✓ Priority seating a must
- ✓ The atmosphere is 1930s and stylish; a beautiful restaurant with beautiful appointments

✓ Tip: For excitement, try the counter by the kitchen. There's a "back room" if you are in more of a quiet mood.

Another of our very favorites, the Flying Fish is something of a sister to the California Grill. Whether because the Fish's chef, John State, was once sous chef at the Grill or because the two offer both stylish and innovative dining, we sense a relationship here. We even caught the Grill's chef, Cliff Pleau, dining here one evening. We weren't surprised at his good taste.

What makes these two eateries so wonderful is that as much as they seem alike, they offer *very* different dining experiences. Chef State's specialty is long-simmered stocks and aromatic reductions. This is *not* California cuisine, simply an extraordinarily conceived and perfectly prepared interpretation of the classics. The Flying Fish's oak-fired strip steak, served over browned and quartered potatoes and sugar snap peas, is the quintessential grilled steak. We suspect that the sautéed snapper, wrapped in thinly sliced potatoes and served on a bed of sautéed leeks with Cabernet reduction, will become this restaurant's signature dish (on the other hand, there is so much great food here that it could be said of almost anything on the menu). From opening wine to after-dinner port, from starters to desserts, there is so much to savor here that we have only just begun to get to know this place.

FULTON'S CRAB HOUSE
$$$ ★★★
✓ On the riverboat at Pleasure Island (admission not required)
✓ Buffet character breakfast; table-service dinner
✓ Full-service bar with a very good wine list
✓ Priority seating strongly suggested
✓ Atmosphere is fairly busy and noisy, with nice views from quarterdeck
✓ Tips: Shellfish is this restaurant's specialty. Try eating on the outside deck.

If you have an appetite for the freshest of shellfish and crabs without the fanfare of nouvelle cuisine, head over to Fulton's. Simply, this is an outstanding seafood eatery that specializes in seafood standards. What amazes us about this place is not just its incredible assortment of fish and shellfish but how it manages to get it here with that fresh-off-the-boat taste (check out the day's airfare receipts posted in the hallway for the answer). Fanny Bay oysters, Alaskan king crab, and

Penn Cove mussels are but a few of the memorable offerings on Fulton's large menu. Be sure to ask the wine steward to suggest one of the fine West Coast vintages, something ideally suited to your entree. We heartily recommend one of the crab sampler platters. Mornings here at Fulton's feature a Disney character breakfast with Mickey and friends.

GARDEN GRILL
$$ ★★
✓ The Land Pavilion, Future World, Epcot
✓ Table service, family-style: breakfast, lunch, and dinner
✓ Beer and wine
✓ Priority seating a must
✓ Atmosphere is pleasant, although part of the trip is noisy

Built on a revolving deck, this restaurant transports diners through a scenic part of this pavilion's attraction. Character meals are featured here throughout the day with Farmer Mickey and Minnie. Service is family-style, and the food will keep coming as long as you are willing. On a recent visit here, we found the food to be quite good. Hardly fine dining, the lunch and dinner menus included rotisserie chicken, steak, fried fish, and several side dishes. Breakfast is the usual Disney morning buffet. All in all, a very good value.

GARDEN GROVE CAFE/GULLIVER'S GRILL
$$ ★★ (lunch) / $$$ ★★★ (dinner)   ♥
✓ The Swan
✓ Table service, breakfast, lunch, and dinner
✓ Full-service bar with modest wine list
✓ Priority seating suggested for dinner
✓ Atmosphere tells a story; pleasant and comfortable

Not really two restaurants, this eatery changes its name for dinner to become Gulliver's Grill. As the Garden Grove Cafe, breakfast offerings include a large buffet of American standards. Lunches feature a la carte salads, sandwiches, and daily specials.

Dinner at Gulliver's Grill is much more upscale. Utilizing the story of *Gulliver's Travels,* dinner begins here with a bit of wine poured into cup-size thimbles. It's not long before you realize that the entire restaurant resembles a large birdcage and, like Gulliver, you are inside.

The menu is fairly imaginative with a large selection of steaks, poultry, and seafood. Service is outstanding, the food is very well prepared, and all in all it's a very pleasant restaurant experience. The Caesar salad is the best we can remember having.

GRAND FLORIDIAN CAFE
$$ ★★★ ♥♥
✓ The Grand Floridian
✓ Table service, breakfast, lunch, and dinner
✓ Full-service bar
✓ Reservations suggested during peak hours

This is the Grand Floridian's all-purpose restaurant, and as you might expect it is an outstanding place to eat. It is also a very good value. The menus for each meal are large and interesting. While the Grand Floridian Cafe is not fine dining, it is an excellent place to get a very good meal. Beautiful table service and a splendid view make this a good choice for any meal. The Grand Floridian Cafe is beautiful and pleasant.

Breakfasts include everything from a muffin to Mexican-style eggs served on a tortilla. Lunches include an impressive array of sandwiches, salads, and a few entrees. For dinner, the Cafe offers everything from an outstanding burger to prime rib. There is also chicken pot pie, Maine lobster, and meat loaf. This is one of those restaurants that has something for everyone.

HARRY'S SAFARI BAR AND GRILL
$$$ ★★★ ♥♥
✓ The Dolphin
✓ Table service, dinner only
✓ Full-service bar, excellent wine list, many imported beers
✓ Reservations recommended

Harry's is a fun place to dine, especially if you have your children with you. You and your kids will arrive at your table to find a giant stuffed gorilla already seated and waiting for you. The restaurant is safari-themed and memorable. Service is outstanding and the food is wonderful. In short, Harry's is worth the trip. Lots of great appetizers and outstanding entrees are offered, such as prime beef, shrimp and crab cakes, and a vegetable feast.

A variety of fresh fish comes prepared in one of four delectable ways: hickory-smoked; pan-grilled with pistachios, pecans, and citrus; key lime barbecued served with black bean salsa; or jerk-blackened with plantains and tropical salsa. It's your choice. Portions are not overly large.

Harry's is beautiful, well-themed, and fun.

HOLLYWOOD BROWN DERBY
$$$$ ★★★ ♥
✓ Disney–MGM Studios
✓ Table service, lunch and dinner
✓ Full-service bar, good wine list
✓ Priority seating suggested
✓ Tip: In good weather, ask for a table on the patio

This elegant re-creation of the famous Brown Derby of Hollywood features white linen service, potted palms, and a handsome sunken dining area. We are happy to report that recent changes here have greatly improved both cuisine and quality. Lunches at the Derby feature seafood, pastas, roast chicken, and a chef's special. Dinners are more elaborate with a variety of the imaginative and the traditional. Our recent visit was an experience in fine dining. The Pacific Rim Tuna was memorable, as were appetizers and desserts. The remarkably unique and wonderfully fresh Cobb salad is one of this eatery's signature dishes. Add to all of this the live piano performance, and the Brown Derby ranks as one of only a few in-park restaurants at Walt Disney World worthy of praise.

HOUSE OF BLUES
✓ Downtown Disney
✓ Table service, lunch and dinner
✓ Full-service bar

Opening sometime in 1997 will be this monster hit of a theme-restaurant and nightclub. The House of Blues (HOB) is currently playing in five other locations around the U.S. and serving up a combination of soulful blues and Southern home cookin'. Looking ramshackle and dilapidated on the outside, HOB more resembles a museum of African American folk art on the inside.

Looking over the Los Angeles HOB menu simply made our mouths water: Creole fettucini, crawfish pizza, Tennessee-style ribs, a mesquite veggie sandwich, and Bayou Voodoo Chicken are only a few of the offerings that appealed to us. There was much more.

House of Blues isn't just a theme-restaurant. Behind its weathered, roadhouse exterior and beyond its tantalizing menu, HOB has managed to be a concert hall for all of the biggest names in blues, R&B, and country music. Expect this place to be sensational, and expect it to be very, very successful.

JUAN AND ONLY'S CANTINA AND BAR
$$ ★★★
✓ The Dolphin
✓ Table service, dinner only
✓ Full-service bar
✓ Reservations not required
✓ Tip: Try a light meal of appetizers in the bar.

We think that Juan's offers Disney's best Mexican food. Granted, the romantic atmosphere of Epcot's San Angel Inn is hard to beat, but the food at Juan's is simply better. Entrees here run the gamut from the usual to the gourmet. Entrees include fajitas, excellent chili rellenos, Red Snapper Vera Cruz, Roast Pork Adobado, and a large selection of combination platters.

The atmosphere is cute and south-of-the-border. This place has a story, and the decor (the bar is actually a jail) and menu tell the tale. This is a nice, colorful place to eat and frequently offers live entertainment.

KIMONOS
$$$ ★★★ ♥♥
✓ The Swan
✓ Table service and sushi bar, dinner only
✓ Full-service bar
✓ Priority seating recommended
✓ Atmosphere is beautiful and romantic

If you are looking for a place to enjoy sushi and feel like something stunning, quiet, and out of the way, Kimonos is it. This handsome eatery features Japanese lanterns, black-enameled bamboo, plush leather chairs, and hanging kimonos. Offerings of sushi, sashimi, and tempura are excellent. Karaoke is featured later in the evening, and we would suggest that you arrive and depart accordingly.

KING STEFAN'S BANQUET HALL
$$$ ♥♥♥
✓ Fantasyland, Magic Kingdom
✓ Table service, breakfast, lunch, and dinner
✓ No bar (this is the Magic Kingdom!)
✓ Atmosphere is beautiful and memorable.
✓ Tip: Drop in for a dessert and a cappuccino.

By the time this book goes to press, King Stefan's will have a new incarnation as "Cinderella's Royal Table." Located inside Cinderella Castle, this newly named eatery promises a new and improved menu. We have been waiting a long time for this charming restaurant to have a cuisine equal to its ambiance. We hope the wait is over.

Whatever happens here, we would expect to see it begin each day with a popular character breakfast. Priority seating arrangements have always been a must for those wishing to dine in this princely, medieval dining hall.

L'ORIGINALE ALFREDO DI ROMA RISTORANTE
$$ ★★
✓ Italy Pavilion, Epcot
✓ Table service, lunch and dinner
✓ Beer and Italian wines only
✓ Reservations suggested during mealtimes
✓ Restaurant is attractive but crowded and noisy

With a band of entertainers singing and playing during dinner, Alfredo's can be a fun place to eat if you don't mind the noise. Featured dishes here are the standards that have become known as Italian cuisine. Fettucini Alfredo, of course, is the signature dish. Pasta is made fresh.

LE CELLIER
$$ ★
✓ Canada Pavilion, Epcot
✓ Cafeteria, lunch and dinner
✓ Beer and wine
✓ Reservations not accepted
✓ Atmosphere is not memorable

Pork pie, seafood stew, and fried chicken are featured here, and none of it is memorable. With a number of other choices nearby (including the restaurants at the nearby Yacht and Beach Clubs), we see no reason to eat here.

LES CHEFS DE FRANCE

$$$ ★★★   ♥

✓ France Pavilion, Epcot
✓ Table service, lunch and dinner
✓ Full-service bar with French wines
✓ Reservations are a must, unless you arrive before 12:30 P.M. for lunch and 6 P.M. for dinner
✓ Atmosphere is pleasant, especially in the evening

The kitchen and menu at Les Chefs are supervised by three of France's most famous chefs: Roger Verdé, Paul Bocuse, and Gaston LeNôtre. The restaurant itself is fancy, with paneled walls, exquisite fixtures, and works of French impressionist art. Service is impeccable, and tables are dressed with white linens. It is a delightful re-creation of a Parisian restaurant.

We like the food here. It is well prepared and imaginative, though a bit rich and creamy for our tastes. Still, Chefs de France does have its light offerings: a vegetable plate and a salmon tartare. Menus for lunch and dinner differ greatly, with only a few shared entrees. Dinner, naturally, is considerably more expensive. Some of the lunch entrees: brochettes of prawns with rice and basil butter, chicken breast in puff pastry with cream sauce, and braised beef in Burgundy with pasta. Dinner entrees include beef tenderloin with brandy sauce, broiled salmon with sorrel cream sauce and fresh vegetables, and filet of snapper and spinach baked in puff pastry. Both menus include an ample wine list as well as a good selection of soups, salads, and desserts.

LIBERTY TREE TAVERN

$$ ★★

✓ Liberty Square, Magic Kingdom
✓ Table service, lunch and buffet dinner
✓ Reservations strongly suggested
✓ Atmosphere is pleasant and comfortable
✓ Tips: Try the Liberty Tree for lunch. If you are looking for a light meal, try splitting one of the large sandwiches.

Decor here is Colonial American and it is done quite well, down to the "hand-hewn" ceiling of the waiting area. The Liberty Tree Tavern is a pleasant and restful place to eat. The food is well prepared but not great. The lunch menu offers a variety of large sandwiches and such entrees as fresh fish, turkey dinner, pot roast, and shrimp and vegetable pasta. The strawberry vinaigrette salad dressing is quite good. The Liberty Tree Tavern is sponsored by Stouffers.

The Character dinner buffet features roasted chicken, flank steak, and several accompaniments.

MAMA MELROSE'S RISTORANTE ITALIANO
$$ ★★
✓ Disney–MGM Studios
✓ Table service, lunch and dinner
✓ Full-service bar
✓ Reservations strongly suggested
✓ Atmosphere is cute and interesting

This neighborhood-style Italian eatery features a pleasant atmosphere that is crammed with an eclectic collection of entertaining props. Where else but at Disney World could you eat under a stuffed swordfish wearing sunglasses? Mama Melrose's is comfortable and fun.

The pizzas outshine any of those sold at the counter-service restaurants. Such entrees as vegetable lasagna, breaded chicken breasts, and an assortment of pasta dishes are all well prepared. This is by no means fine dining, but, at these prices, you get good food. The Mega Deal pasta entree features all-you-can-eat pasta served four different ways. Try them all. Other entrees include chicken Marsala, seafood pasta, and veal piccata. Mama's is popular. Even with reservations, we had to wait a few minutes.

MARRAKESH
$$ ★★★ ♥♥
✓ Morocco Pavilion, Epcot
✓ Table service, lunch and dinner
✓ Full-service bar
✓ Reservations suggested
✓ The atmosphere here is exotic

✓ Tips: The Moroccan Diffa for Two provides a real assortment of tastes. There are other combination platters, too.

Marrakesh is one of Epcot's most exotic restaurants. Featuring a live belly dancer and musicians at both lunch and dinner, it is one of our favorites here. From a selection of couscous dishes to tagine of chicken, shish kebab, and Cornish Hen Emrouzia, Marrakesh delivers what so many other World Showcase restaurants merely promise: the exotic and the unique. If you are looking for a dining adventure beyond the usual, don't miss it.

MINNIE MIA'S ITALIAN EATERY
$ ★★
✓ The Village Marketplace
✓ Counter service, lunch and dinner
✓ No reservations

If you are looking for a quick bite while you're shopping at the Village Marketplace, this little place may be just the thing. The pizza is more like real pizza than that served at any fast-food outlet at WDW. There is also a selection of salads and other Italian entrees. Nothing great, but the food is inexpensive and fairly good.

NARCOOSSEE'S
$$$ ★★
✓ The Grand Floridian
✓ Table service, lunch and dinner
✓ Full-service bar
✓ Priority seating recommended
✓ Atmosphere is exceedingly noisy with a pleasant view
✓ Tip: Try this place for lunch. It's much more quiet.

Narcoossee's features a pricey selection of seafood and steaks, all competently prepared and well presented. Service is outstanding too, but the noise level here is hard to live with. Conversation for us was difficult in the extreme. While everything *tasted* good, it seemed that too much butter had been dolloped over everything. Even the swordfish seemed to be swimming in it.

Still, this is a very popular restaurant. Its classic offerings of steaks and seafood, Maine lobster and prime rib, continue to attract throngs of diners. Perhaps it simply isn't to our taste. It does, however, offer a pleasant selection of sandwiches and entrees for lunch. Add to this a yard of good ale, and Narcoossee's makes for one of our favorite lunchtime retreats from the Magic Kingdom.

NINE DRAGONS

$$ ★★ ♥
- ✓ China Pavilion, Epcot
- ✓ Table service, lunch and dinner
- ✓ Full-service bar
- ✓ Reservations suggested
- ✓ A beautiful dining room. Quiet and pleasant.
- ✓ Tip: Try snacking here on dumplings, if you wish to enjoy the atmosphere.

With all of its carved furnishings and beautiful Chinese artwork, Nine Dragons is a lovely place to dine. The food is well prepared but just not exciting enough for our tastes. Offerings include Mu Shu Pork and Kung Pao Chicken. Dinners here are served as entrees, not the usual family-style Chinese. Add the high cost, and we have a hard time recommending it. We have stopped here for hors d'oeuvres, however, and have enjoyed them.

1900 PARK FARE

$$ ★★★
- ✓ The Grand Floridian
- ✓ Table service, character buffets, breakfast, and dinner
- ✓ Reservations recommended (this place is popular)
- ✓ Atmosphere is noisy and gay.
- ✓ Tip: Bring your camera for some terrific pictures. Ask your server to snap a photo of the two of you with some of the Disney characters.

We think that this is Disney's best buffet. Offerings for both breakfast and dinner are large and the quality is surprisingly good. The only drawback is that Park Fare is noisy. First there's all of the children and characters and then there is the giant mechanical organ. If you are looking for peace and quiet, this isn't it. If you are looking for fun and a character meal, we doubt that you'll find a better one than this.

'OHANA AT PAPEETE BAY

$$ ★★ ♥

✓ Great Ceremonial House, the Polynesian
✓ Table-service buffet, breakfast, and dinner
✓ Full-service bar, Polynesian specialty drinks
✓ Reservations required for the King's Table
✓ Atmosphere is tropical, sometimes noisy

'Ohana at Papeete Bay is beautiful, and everything here is steeped in the flavor of the South Seas. From the "thatched roof" and stone floor to the fire-pit grill, 'Ohana has the feel of a Polynesian longhouse. Costumed servers bring you course after course of roasted meats and seafood on sword-like skewers. It is a South Seas feast, fit for a Polynesian king.

There is entertainment throughout the evening. Most of it is fun and games for kids, and it can get quite noisy. The food here is good. Grilled shrimp, chicken, and sausage as well as a wonderful vegetable lo mein make 'Ohana a good choice for fun dining entertainment.

OLIVIA'S CAFÉ

$$ ★★

✓ Old Key West
✓ Table service, breakfast, lunch, and dinner
✓ Full-service bar
✓ Reservations suggested for character breakfasts

Key West is the theme here, and Olivia's ambience is airy and casual. This is a very pleasant place to dine. The menus for each meal are large, and the food is fresh and tasty. The conch fritters are some of the best we've ever had (and that includes the Bahamas). Breakfasts run the course from fresh fruit to steak and eggs. You can also choose muffins, bagels, and some interesting egg dishes, such as the Sounds of Sunset Omelette. For lunches and dinners, enjoy a great assortment of munchies, sandwiches, and even a turkey pot pie. Other specialties include Blackened Gator, Boot Key Chicken and Rib Platter, and grilled shrimp. Olivia's is also home to an outstanding meatless burger.

The only drawback to Olivia's is getting there. You'll need a car or some fancy busing. Try busing from the Village Marketplace or one of the theme parks.

PALIO
$$ ★★★★   ♥♥♥
- ✓ The Swan
- ✓ Table service, dinner only
- ✓ Full-service bar
- ✓ Reservations suggested
- ✓ Tips: If you want to make a budget meal out of it, order one pizza and one of the more moderately priced entrees. Drop by later in the evening for an espresso or cappuccino and your choice of desserts.

Your meal at Palio will begin with a Boccalino, the traditional "little jug" of wine. This restaurant is easily Disney World's finest in Italian cuisine. It is, we think, one of the very best places to dine at Walt Disney World. If you are dining as a couple, let us suggest one of the comfortable booths where you may sit next to each other. Once the strolling violinist (or guitarist) begins, you'll begin to see why we rate this place as an outstanding romantic dining experience. Musicians play Tuesday through Saturday.

Palio is not a spaghetti-and-meatballs Italian restaurant. It is not difficult to eat here for about the same price as most of the Epcot restaurants. The food at Palio is incomparably superior. Entrees include seafood and spaghetti baked in parchment, ragout of lobster and tortellini, and pork alla Milanese. The osso buco was extraordinary, and we still long for the Risotto con Vongole. The specialty pizzas are small but exceptional. The dessert counter at Palio is Disney's finest, featurings about 20 incredible creations. The best of Disney.

PLANET HOLLYWOOD
$$ ★★
- ✓ Pleasure Island (admission not required)
- ✓ Table service, lunch and dinner
- ✓ Full-service bar
- ✓ No reservations accepted
- ✓ Atmosphere is very interesting, not at all romantic

✓ Tips: Ask for seating on the third floor. To avoid waiting in long lines at the door, try eating during the off-hours.

If this isn't the world's most outrageous Planet Hollywood, we would like to see the one that is. Built in a planet-shaped sphere, this restaurant is crammed full of real movie props and costumes. Loud and nightclub-like, it is also interesting and fun. Some of the food is quite good, but some is average. In our quest for the best burger of Disney, this one was a real disappointment. The Thai shrimp, however, was excellent.

PLAZA RESTAURANT
$ ★★
✓ Main Street USA, Magic Kingdom
✓ Table service, lunch and dinner
✓ Priority seating suggested
✓ Atmosphere is quaint and a pleasant escape

This turn-of-the-century, art nouveau eatery offers a fairly standard menu of well-prepared sandwiches including a Reuben, double-decker roast beef, and grilled turkey. Other tasty offerings include a Southwest chicken salad and a variety of burgers. Most are under $10. This is a nice place for lunch.

PORTOBELLO YACHT CLUB
$$ ★★★★ ♥
✓ Pleasure Island (admission not required)
✓ Table service, lunch and dinner
✓ Full-service bar, good wine list
✓ No reservations accepted
✓ Atmosphere is casual. Can be noisy at peak hours.
✓ Tips: If the weather is pleasant, try sitting in the beautiful garden area outside.

Portobello is one of our favorite places to eat at Walt Disney World. The menu features a large array of Northern Italian foods, all elegantly prepared. We've never had anything here that we didn't like a lot. One of our very favorites is Paglia e Fino con Salmone Affumicato (smoked salmon pasta). We have too many other favorites to list them all. However, the gelato cappuccino is one of our very favorite desserts, here or anywhere.

Don't miss eating here. For a moderately priced restaurant at Disney World, this place is one of the best. We like to share an entree along with several appetizers.

RAINFOREST CAFE
$$ ★★★ ♥♥ (eating on porch outside)
✓ The Village Marketplace
✓ Table service, lunch and dinner
✓ Full-service bar
✓ Priority seating strongly suggested
✓ Atmosphere is fun, exciting, and very noisy
✓ Tips: Avoid mealtimes; try eating at 4:30 P.M.

In last year's edition, we predicted that this would "out-Disney" Disney. We were right. Our recent visit to this fantastic eatery has confirmed what we had guessed: this is one *very* fun place to eat. The smoldering volcano exterior of this restaurant towers above the rest of the Marketplace. Inside, it is a dense "rain forest," complete with canopy of trees, periodic thunderstorms, and a host of robotic wildlife that all occasionally come to life. It has much of the detail and excitement of a theme park attraction. It's a wild place to eat!

What surprised us about the Rainforest was its food. Expecting the unremarkable cuisine common to theme-restaurants, we found instead a large and imaginative menu of well-prepared appetizers, entrees, sandwiches, and desserts. Even the collection of specialty drinks (alcoholic, if you like) was refreshing and delicious. We happily rate this place as a "not to miss" lunch or dinner. We'd suggest, however, that you steer away from the meat-type dishes, such as steak or pork chops. Everything else is simply wonderful. Don't miss the "Pieces of Ate" or the Coconut Bread Pudding. Have fun!

ROSE AND CROWN PUB AND DINING ROOM
$$ ★★ ♥
✓ United Kingdom, Epcot
✓ Table service, lunch and dinner
✓ Full-service bar with English ales and beers

✓ Reservations suggested
✓ Atmosphere in the patio is memorable, especially during pleasant weather or during IllumiNations

A pleasant enough place to eat, especially if the weather is cool enough to dine on the patio overlooking the lagoon. The food here is well prepared and tasty, although nothing here seems particularly memorable (much like real British cuisine).

Fish and chips, roast lamb, steak and kidney pie, and a chicken and leek pie are among the many offerings. The restaurant is divided into three sections; each has a distinctly different decor, and each is comfortable and quiet.

SAN ANGEL INN
$$ ★ ♥♥♥
✓ Mexico Pavilion, Epcot
✓ Table service, lunch and dinner
✓ Full-service bar with Mexican beer
✓ Reservations suggested during busy mealtimes
✓ Tip: Try having a cold Mexican beer and some nachos or other appetizer. This way, you'll get to enjoy the atmosphere without having to eat an entire meal.

What a beautiful place this is. It's always nighttime at the San Angel Inn, which is set amidst the facade of a quaint Mexican village. The restaurant overlooks the most scenic part of the pavilion's boat ride, where the River of Time passes through a dense and mountainous jungle. Enjoy your meal on the lovely plaza at the river's edge, while a volcano smolders in the distance. It is truly memorable; a charming and romantic spot.

While the food claims to be authentic Mexican, we do not find it to our liking. It is no match for the lovely surroundings.

THE SAND TRAP
$ ★★
✓ The Bonnet Creek Golf Club at Osprey Ridge and Eagle Pines courses
✓ Table service, breakfast and lunch
✓ Full-service bar

✓ Reservations not accepted
✓ Atmosphere is pleasant

This pleasant restaurant enjoys a country club setting. It would be just the place after a round on one of the Bonnet Creek courses. The menu includes the usual breakfast offerings and a selection of sandwiches, salads, and soups. The Sand Trap even makes its own potato chips.

SCI-FI DINE-IN THEATER
$$ ★★
✓ Disney–MGM Studios
✓ Table service, lunch and dinner
✓ Beer and wine
✓ Priority seating a must
✓ Atmosphere is cute and entertaining

At this popular restaurant, you'll eat in a "convertible" at a drive-in theater that shows nonstop 1950s sci-fi movie previews. Servers arrive on roller skates, and the menu features American standards jazzed up with such names as "The Thing They Call Seafood" (shrimp and scallop penne pasta) and "Attack of the Killer Sandwich." Sci-Fi's other offerings include a porterhouse steak, Caesar salad, and seasoned breast of chicken. It's all a lot of campy fun, and the food lately has gotten fairly good.

SEASON'S DINING ROOM
$$ ★★★
✓ The Disney Institute
✓ Table service, breakfast, lunch, and dinner
✓ Beer and wines
✓ Priority seating not required
✓ Atmosphere is sunny and pleasant

This is the Institute's restaurant, and we have heard some really mixed things about it. During our week at the Institute, however, we enjoyed the food here with only one or two exceptions. Not a bad record for almost any restaurant.

Breakfasts here include a variety of omelet-like dishes called Season's Skillets. There are also the usual eggs, pancakes and French toast, and lighter a la carte offerings. Lunches feature an outstanding variety of soups, salads, and sandwiches, all of it imaginative and well prepared. Dinners expand the menu without limiting your options. Additions are a reasonably priced variety of entrees that include seafood, pastas, and some interesting vegetarian fare. All in all, we wouldn't hesitate to return.

SPOODLE'S
$$ ★★★
✓ The BoardWalk
✓ Table service, breakfast, lunch, and dinner
✓ Beer and Mediterranean wines
✓ Atmosphere is interesting but noisy
✓ Priority seating for dinner suggested

Each of the day's meals at Spoodle's is a delight. In short, this is one of the best new, family-style restaurants at Disney. Not fine dining, Spoodle's offers instead an assortment of foods that range from the well prepared and interesting to the delicious and exotic. We think that Spoodle's breakfast menu is the best on-property. Both lunches and dinners feature an inspiring selection of wood-fired pizzas and Mediterranean "tapas," an interesting assortment of appetizer-type dishes. There's something at Spoodle's for every taste, and in our visits here, we have never been disappointed.

TEMPURA KIKU
$$ ★★★
✓ Japan Pavilion, Epcot
✓ Table service, lunch and dinner
✓ Full-service bar
✓ Reservations suggested
✓ Atmosphere is unusual and interesting

Not really a restaurant, Tempura Kiku is a fairly authentic tempura bar. With a few exceptions, most items on the menu are lightly battered and deep-fried, known in Japan as tempura. These include seafood, vegetables, and meats. There are tasty dipping sauces and a small selection of sushi and sashimi. The atmosphere is very Japanese: crowded yet comfortable. The quality of the tempura is very good.

Reservations are suggested, as there fewer than 30 seats at Tempura Kiku.

TEPPANYAKI DINING ROOM
$$ ★★★
✓ Japan Pavilion, Epcot
✓ Table service, lunch and dinner
✓ Full-service bar, Kirin beer and sake
✓ Reservations suggested during mealtimes
✓ Atmosphere is Japanese: pleasant and themed

If you have ever eaten at a Benihana's restaurant, then you will know what this experience is all about. Here at Teppanyaki, you sit at tables with other Disney guests. The center of each table is actually a cooking surface, where a Japanese chef will "perform." The chef's deft chopping and slicing skills and some knife-acrobatics are quite impressive. Entrees include shrimp, chicken, beef, and lobster, each sliced or cubed and grilled right in front of you. There are also grilled vegetables and several dipping sauces. The food is quite good, and the show is fairly entertaining.

TONY'S TOWN SQUARE
$$ ★
✓ Main Street USA, Magic Kingdom
✓ Table service, breakfast, lunch, and dinner
✓ Reservations a must
✓ Atmosphere is pleasant, though noisy when crowded (nearly always)

The theme here is from Lady and the Tramp, Disney's classic animated film. Cuisine is Italian with few surprises. The atmosphere is pleasant, especially in the glassed-in garden area. The breakfast menu offers several good frittatas, but we would suggest having them serve the tomato sauce on the side. Lunches and dinners include the usual spaghetti, lasagna, and Joe's Fettucini. Pleasant enough, but Tony's simply doesn't excel at anything.

VICTORIA AND ALBERT'S
$$$$ ★★★★ ♥♥♥♥
✓ The Grand Floridian
✓ Table service, dinner only, two seatings: 6 P.M. and 9 P.M.
✓ Full-service bar, outstanding wine list

✓ Priority seating only: make them when you book your room
✓ Victorian charm and elegance come to life. A real romantic experience.

If you are celebrating something special at Walt Disney World, whether a honeymoon, an anniversary, or simply being in love, and you are looking for a romantic dining experience that you will remember for years to come, let us suggest the award-winning Victoria and Albert's. The ambience here is unforgettably romantic, the service is white-glove and impeccable, and the cuisine of chef Scott Hunnel is a carefully practiced art. Serving a limited number of guests each evening, Hunnel and his staff meticulously prepare imaginative and innovative dishes using only the finest of ingredients from the international marketplace. Hunnel himself picks herbs each day from his own garden on the grounds of the Grand Floridian. Each dish, which is served by "butler and maid" serving team Victoria and Albert, is an individually prepared work of art.

The menu changes daily to accommodate what is freshest and finest, and there are offerings enough to appeal to any sensibility. Victoria and Albert's features three menus: the Standard, the Elite Premium, and the Vegetarian. Royal Wine Pairing may be added to each and provides a variety of outstanding vintages carefully selected by maitre d' John Blazon to enhance each of the six courses. Guests are served on Royal Doulton china, with Sambonet silver from Italy and Schott-Zwiesel crystal from Germany. During dinner, the live music of a harpist gently fills the air. Quite literally, we have experienced nothing like this restaurant. It is not your everyday *extraordinary* dining experience. We still gush about our experiences here.

If you are celebrating something *really* special at Walt Disney World, and you are looking for a dining experience that you will *never* forget, let us suggest Victoria and Albert's "Chef's Table." This beautifully appointed table, located right in the kitchen, offers a unique gastronomic experience. Chef Hunnel will create a menu based on your desires; while he works, you can take part in all of the excitement as you interact with this Grand culinary team. The most sought-after dining table in Florida, the Chef's Table seats only once during the course of the evening, and it is a once-in-a-lifetime experience.

Make no mistake about it, Victoria and Albert's is an unforgettable and sublime experience. Expensive, no doubt, but worth the price. What better thing can lovers do than to gather such memories?

Reservations for Victoria and Albert's are a must, and we urge you to make yours when you book your room. Evening attire is required.

WHISPERING CANYON CAFE
$$ ★★
✓ The Wilderness Lodge
✓ Table service, buffet and a la carte, breakfast, lunch, and dinner
✓ Full-service bar and specialty brews
✓ Priority seating recommended
✓ Wild West atmosphere is charming and entertaining
✓ Tip: There's a cozy little room in the back by the fireplace.

Whispering Canyon's real specialty is meals served family-style. Food arrives in large pans, and it's all-you-care-to-eat. "Sunrise Samplins'" include breakfast skillets of eggs, pan-fried potatoes, breakfast meats, biscuits, waffles, and more. A la carte offerings include fresh fruit platters or light continental fare. "Lunch Grub" is a barbecue served family-style: chicken, ribs, fried fish, baked beans, and corn on the cob. Other choices are available a la carte and include chili, salads, smoked prime rib, burgers, grilled chicken, and a sautéed vegetable platter. Whispering Canyon's fire-roasted dinner is a big spread, much of it smoked in the restaurant's outdoor smoker: ribs, beef, chicken, turkey leg, trail sausage, and a host of accompaniments too. Dinner a la carte offerings include a vegetable platter and a catch of the day. All in all, you get good hearty fare for a reasonable price.

WOLFGANG PUCK'S CAFE
✓ Downtown Disney

One of the chefs credited with creating California cuisine, Puck is the chef/owner of the celebrated Los Angeles eatery, Spago. Wood-fired pizzas, barbecue duck quesadillas, and four-cheese raviolis are among the specialties there. Other Puck dishes include penne pasta with prosciutto and goat cheese, wild mushroom tortellini, and Chinois chicken salad.

Since this restaurant isn't set to open until sometime late in 1997, we aren't able to tell you much about it or about its menu. Puck is considered to be one of America's great chefs, though, and with this being his first Florida establishment, we look forward to giving it a try.

YACHT CLUB GALLEY

$$ ★★★

✓ The Yacht Club
✓ Table service, breakfast, lunch, and dinner
✓ Full-service bar
✓ Reservations not required
✓ Atmosphere is themed and pleasant
✓ Tip: A nice place for lunch if you are over at Epcot. Simply stroll over from the International Gateway.

As we have mentioned, most of the premium resorts feature one all-purpose restaurant, which offers an assortment of dishes for each of the day's meals. We usually find ourselves comparing them all to the Yacht Club Galley. This is one of the best eating places around. Not a fine dining spot, the Galley serves food that is well prepared, tasty, and reasonably priced. Breakfasts are either a la carte or buffet. Lunches feature a large selection of soups, salads, and sandwiches, and dinner adds a number of New England–style entrees. In our many stays at the Yacht or the Beach, we have never been disappointed here.

Decor is yachty, with framed displays of knots and glass-encased models of the beautiful old J-Boats of last century's America's Cup races. Salt and pepper shakers resemble small lighthouses. This is a pleasant place to eat—not particularly memorable, but simply nice.

YACHTSMAN STEAKHOUSE

$$$ ★★★★ ♥♥

✓ The Yacht Club
✓ Table service, dinner only
✓ Full-service bar
✓ Reservations suggested after 6:30 P.M.
✓ Atmosphere is simple and beautiful
✓ Tip: Try the Chateaubriand for Two at less than $40.

If you are looking for the best steak at Walt Disney World, look no further. The Yachtsman Steakhouse features the finest in aged, grain-fed cuts of beef. The variety is large. From Kansas City strips to Chateaubriand, there is the perfect cut for every taste. And if steak is not your thing, the Yachtsman offers a full menu of lamb, pork chops, poultry, and a seafood steak of the day. All of it is excellent.

The Yachtsman Steakhouse is a charming, quiet, and woody restaurant. Like the menu itself, the decor here is simple yet elegant. We highly recommend this restaurant.

YAKITORI HOUSE

$ ★★
✓ Japan Pavilion, Epcot
✓ Counter service, lunch and dinner
✓ Kirin beer
✓ No reservations
✓ Garden atmosphere is charming and restful

When we eat in a foreign country, we always like to find restaurants where the locals eat. We guess that this same principle applies to Disney World. The first time we peeked in the Yakitori House, we were surprised to see that nearly every patron was Japanese. That it attracts so many visitors from Japan attests to its authenticity.

The menu here includes teriyaki sandwiches and Kushi-Yaki: skewered chicken, shrimp, or beef that has been basted in soy sauce and sesame oil. Yakitori also features a selection of Japanese sweets and beverages.

The restaurant itself is a bamboo-like structure. In good weather, we suggest eating outside in the lovely garden area.

CHAPTER 7

Recreation and Other Pastimes

There is so much to do at Walt Disney World that it would probably still be the Vacation Capital of the World even without its themed attractions. Boating, biking, tennis, golf, horseback riding, fishing, waterskiing, and parasailing are just a few possibilities when it comes to recreational activities. And Walt Disney World is also home to a number of world-class fitness centers that offer massage therapy, saunas, spas, and personal training. To round out your activities, the World also features a village of unique and interesting shops, just the place to browse away a lazy afternoon.

Mixing your theme park adventures with plenty of recreation and relaxation will make for a leisurely and more memorable romance holiday. These activities will get the two of you out of the mobs and into more intimate settings. So, open yourselves up to a delightfully different kind of Disney experience. Take a sail or a cruise. Ride a bike or ride a horse. Get massaged or get out and go shopping. Be adventurous: go waterskiing or parasailing. Or both. Take advantage of a World of fun together.

Golf

No matter how you slice it, Walt Disney World is a golfer's paradise. With 99 holes of championship PGA-level golf and over 20,000 resort rooms, Disney World is the largest golf resort in the world. The six courses each present unique challenges to both the amateur and the professional. There are five, 18-hole championship courses and one, 9-hole executive course. All are open to the public and, as Disney resort guests, you'll get discounted green fees and preferential tee times. Green fees are $100–$125 per round at each of the regular courses, cart included, and $24 at Oak Trail, the executive course. If this sounds a bit expensive, there is always play after 3 P.M. for around $60 per round. If you are planning a Disney golf vacation, you might wish to pick up a Disney Golf Season Badge. This badge costs $50 and gives you unlimited play after 10 A.M. on any of the five 18-hole Disney courses, for only $35 a round ($50 weekends). Good for a year and available at any of the Disney pro shops, this badge is a great deal if you plan to play even twice.

The six courses are located at three different locations around Walt Disney World. Both Osprey Ridge and Eagle Pines can be found at the Bonnet Creek Golf Club while the Palm and the Magnolia are located at Shades of Green. Oak Trail and the Lake Buena Vista courses are both near the Disney Institute. Here are the links, rated in order of difficulty by pros of the PGA:

- Osprey Ridge (6,680 yards, designed by Tom Fazio): Rated by the Pros as the toughest course here at Disney, this course has elevations that are not at all typical of central Florida. Osprey Ridge does not double-back on itself. It just takes off into the woods. Tom Fazio himself considers this one of his best courses.
- The Palm (6,461 yards, designed by Joe Lee): The eighteenth hole here has been rated the fourth toughest on the PGA Tour.
- The Magnolia (6,642 yards, designed by Joe Lee): This course has the Disney signature "Mousetrap" on its sixth hole. The final round of the Oldsmobile Classic is played here.
- Eagle Pines (6,309 yards, designed by Pete Dye): This low-profile course features dished instead of crowned fairways. Relatively flat, this course has no grass for rough.
- Lake Buena Vista (6,268 yards, designed by Joe Lee): This is a fairly short, wide-open course. Hole 16 is called the "Intimidator."
- Oak Trail (executive course, 2,913 yards, designed by Joe Lee): Green fees are $24 for nine holes, $32 for two rounds. No electric carts are allowed on this course, and golfers are allowed to carry their own bags.

Logistics

Tee times may be reserved up to 60 days in advance by Disney resort guests and 30 days ahead by day guests. These courses are busy during the peak seasons, and we strongly suggest that you arrange your tee times if you want to play early in the day. For tee times at any of the six courses, call (407) 939-4653.

Club and shoe rentals are available at all six courses and are $22 per round for men's or women's clubs and $6 a round for shoes. Rental clubs here are Titleist.

Transportation

Complimentary transportation to any of the Disney golf courses is furnished at any of the Disney resorts. This does not include the Swan, the Dolphin, and all of the hotels at Hotel Plaza. To arrange your transportation at a Disney resort, notify Bell Services of your tee times. Try to give them a day's notice.

Fantasia Gardens and Fantasia Fairways

These are Disney's entry into the mini-golf arena, and as you might expect, they are fanciful and fun. The theme of Fantasia Gardens is the animated classic *Fantasia*. With an amusing mix of music, dancing hippos, waterfalls, pirouetting alligators, and other such "hazards," this course specializes in the quirky and the absurd. Fantasia Fairways is something else altogether. This innovative putting course is designed to challenge even the advanced golfer. Sand traps, water hazards, and diabolically terraced greens make this both fun and good practice.

Both courses are located next door to the Swan. Open from 10 A.M. to midnight every day, green fees are around $8 for adults and $7 for children. The Starter Shack features a snack bar and video arcade.

OUR RECOMMENDATIONS FOR GOLF

- The Disney/Oldsmobile Classic takes place in October. Guests are advised not to schedule play during this week.
- Shirts with collars are required at all Disney courses.

Tennis

There are so many tennis courts around Walt Disney World that you might think it's a tennis resort. Located in a variety of places, you'll have little trouble finding a convenient court. Most feature full-service pro shops.

- The Contemporary features six lighted, hydrogrid clay courts. Open 8 A.M. to 8 P.M., reservations are recommended. The cost is $12 per hour or $40 for length of stay. Ball machines, practice lanes, and a pro shop are available. For reservations, call (407) 824-3578.
- The Grand Floridian has two clay courts. Open 8 A.M. to 8 P.M. Play costs $12 per hour or $35 to play against the pro. Ball machines and pro shop are available. Reservations are recommended. Call (407) 824-2433.
- The Yacht and the Beach Clubs have two lighted courts, use of which is complimentary to all guests of these resorts. The courts are adjacent to the Beach Club. Open 7 A.M. to 10 P.M. No pro shop, no reservations. Equipment is available at the resort's health club at no charge.
- Fort Wilderness has two lighted courts. Open 8 A.M. to 6 P.M., there is no charge for their use. Open to all Disney resort guests. Rental racquets are available at the Bike Barn. No reservations.
- Old Key West has two lighted courts, open 7 A.M. to 11 P.M. Use is complimentary for registered guests of Old Key West on a first-come, first-serve basis. Rental equipment is available at Hank's.
- The Swan and the Dolphin share four lighted tennis courts. Open from 8 A.M. to 11 P.M., cost is $12 per hour and is complimentary after 7 P.M. A full-service tennis club and pro shop are adjacent to the courts. Reservations only from 8 A.M. to 7 P.M.
- Shades of Green has two lighted tennis courts. Open from dawn until 10 P.M., use is complimentary for guests of the resort. No reservations.
- The Institute has four hydrogrid courts, which are available to Institute guests and as part of the $15 daily fee for the Institute Fitness Center. Hours are 8 A.M. to 8 P.M. For arrangements, call (407) 827-4455.
- The BoardWalk has two lighted, clay courts. Use is free to all BoardWalk guests. Equipment rentals are available.

OUR RECOMMENDATIONS FOR TENNIS

- Disney resort guests may make tennis reservations up to 30 days in advance. Call (407) W-DISNEY (934-7639).
- Tennis attire is required at all courts. Rental equipment is available everywhere.

Boating Around the World

One of our favorite things to do at Walt Disney World is to go boating. Despite the fact that we live on our own sailboat and have our own little fleet, we simply love boating around Disney. It is fun and gives an interesting perspective on this fabulous place.

A variety of craft are available nearly anywhere there's a body of water. Most marina rental areas open at 10 A.M. and stay open until dusk, usually 6 P.M.

Marina rental locations are listed following.

- The Seven Seas Lagoon and Bay Lake
    The Contemporary
    The Polynesian
    The Grand Floridian
    The Wilderness Lodge
    Fort Wilderness
- Lake Buena Vista and the Village Waterways
    The Village Marketplace
    Old Key West
    Port Orleans
    Dixie Landings
- Crescent Lake
    The Yacht and the Beach Clubs
    The Swan and the Dolphin
    Disney's BoardWalk
- Barefoot Bay at the Caribbean Beach
- Coronado Springs

Watercraft

All boats are not available at all locations. While prices and hourly minimums vary a little from marina to marina, the following should give you a good idea of what you will spend to rent a watercraft:

- Pedal boats, rowboats, and canoes: about $5 per half-hour
- Sailboats: most about $6 per half-hour
- Sunfish: $11 hourly
- Capri sailboats: $12 hourly
- Hobie Cats (for experienced sailors only): $19 hourly
- Aqua Cats, Aqua Fins: $10–14 hourly

- Water sprites (two-person mini "speed" boats): $17 per half-hour
- Canopy boats: $19 per half-hour
- Pontoon boats (Flote boats), 20 or 24 feet: $40 or $50 hourly
    - 20-foot pontoon boats can accommodate a maximum of 10 people.
    - 24-foot pontoon boats come with a driver.
- SeaRayder speedboats (the Contemporary only): $35 per half-hour

OUR RECOMMENDATIONS FOR BOAT RENTALS

- The Seven Seas Lagoon and Bay Lake are the best places to rent a boat. Since these two bodies of water connect, this makes for the largest area to explore. There is more to see, as well. If you are not staying in one of the resorts here, simply go and rent the boat of your choice at any of the marinas listed at the Seven Seas Lagoon or Bay Lake.
- The best selection of sailboats is at the Polynesian. We think that the Seven Seas Lagoon makes for the best sailing, too.

Other Boating Adventures

There are a few really special things that you can do on the waters of Disney. The most enchanting is to take a ride aboard *Breathless*, Disney's 1934 vintage, Chris Craft speedboat. Located at the Yacht and the Beach, this handsome wooden craft is a boat lover's dream. With perfect varnish-work and shiny chrome fittings, *Breathless* is available only with a driver. A half-hour cruise will cost $50 with up to five passengers.

For $140, this elegant yacht ♥♥♥♥ will take the two of you over to Epcot to watch IllumiNations. Truly romantic and unforgettable, this is the perfect experience for a special occasion.

For $85, up to eight persons can make the same IllumiNations cruise in one of the Yacht Club's pontoon boats. Also available are Magic Kingdom Fantasy in the Sky fireworks cruises (pontoon boat) at the Polynesian, Grand Floridian, and Contemporary (summer only). Cost is $85 for up to 10 passengers. Arrangements should be made through the marina at each resort.

Waterskiing is also available at Walt Disney World. The ski boats are all located at Fort Wilderness, and the cost for waterskiing is $82 per hour. You can be picked up for free, by boat, at any of the Magic

Kingdom resorts. Reservations with deposit are required and can be made up to two weeks in advance by calling (407) 824-2621. If water-skiing isn't enough of a kick for you, there's always parasailing. This is available only at the Contemporary. For 8 to 10 minutes of flight time, the cost is $40 per rider.

Biking

Rentals can be found at Fort Wilderness, the Wilderness Lodge, Old Key West, Dixie Landings, Port Orleans, the BoardWalk, Caribbean Beach, and Coronado Springs. Rates are pretty much the same every-where, around $3 per hour or $10 a day, and the variety includes men's, women's, children's, tandems, and bikes with child carriers. Most rental shops open around 10 A.M. and close around sunset.

The BoardWalk, Caribbean Beach, and Old Key West offer some really unique biking with their "surreys." These four-wheeled, carriage-like cycles are some of the most fun we've ever had pedaling. Available for two, four, or six persons, rentals are $12 per hour. Surrey rentals at the BoardWalk continue late into the evening.

OUR RECOMMENDATIONS FOR CYCLING

* Try one of the surreys at the BoardWalk. They're simply too much fun!
* Try renting your bikes at the Wilderness Lodge and riding around the lake to Fort Wilderness. There's also the Fort Wilderness Swamp Trail Nature Path for some real scenery.

Fishing Excursions

Over the years, the lakes and waterways of Walt Disney World have been stocked with thousands of fingerling bass. Fishing throughout central Florida is world famous, and guided fishing trips are available in a number of places at Disney World. Trips on Bay Lake, Lake Buena Vista, and on Crescent Lake all last two hours, accommodate up to five persons, and cost around $140. Trips include guide, gear, and refresh-ments. Reservations must be made in advance; trips may be canceled due to inclement weather. For reservations at Bay Lake, call (407) 824-2621; for Lake Buena Vista's Village Marketplace Marina, call

(407) 828-2204; and for Crescent Lake, call the BoardWalk at (407) 939-6486 or the Yacht Club at (407) 934-3256.

For something less extravagant, there's the Dixie Landings two-hour fishing adventure along the Sassagoula Waterway, for $50 per person. The boat can take up to five people; guide, equipment, bait, and soft drinks are included. Reservations for the 6:30 A.M. departure should be made in advance by calling (407) 934-5409. For something even simpler, try the Ol' Fishin' Hole at Dixie Landings for $3.50 or head out to the Fort Wilderness Bike Barn, rent a pole for about $4 a day, and fish the many waterways there. You can even rent a canoe and make a day of it.

Jogging and Walking

Nearly every resort offers a jogging or walking path. Check with the Guest Services at your resort for a map. Some of our favorite paths include the ones in the Yacht and the Beach/the Swan and the Dolphin area, the Wilderness Lodge to Fort Wilderness area, Dixie Landings and Port Orleans, and a long circuit around the Polynesian and the Grand Floridian. There are also especially nice paths at Old Key West, the Villas at the Institute, and the Caribbean Beach, as well. Walking and jogging have become national pastimes, and the folks at Disney have been paying attention.

Nature Walks

There are two pleasant nature walks at Walt Disney World. One is Discovery Island, Disney's own wildlife preserve. Admission is charged, but there is much more here than simply a walk. The other walk is on the north end of Fort Wilderness, which is open to anyone interested. The Wilderness Swamp trail runs for nearly two miles along the shores of Bay Lake and through some heavily forested areas. It is beautiful and quiet. This trail can be most easily reached by taking a boat to Fort Wilderness from the dock at the front of the Magic Kingdom. Pick up a map of the trail at Guest Services in nearby Pioneer Hall.

Horseback Riding

The Fort Wilderness Trail Ride departs daily from the Tri-Circle-D Ranch Livery and Trail Blaze Corral, located near the parking area to

Fort Wilderness. The horses are good ones (Arabians and Appaloosas), and the pace is very slow. It is more of a horseback walk. No galloping is allowed. If you are not an experienced rider, you may find this to be something special. It is scenic and fun.

Cost is about $17 per person. Children under 9 years of age are not permitted, and there is a 250-pound weight limit. Reservations are a good idea here, as this is a popular pursuit. For reservations up to five days in advance, call (407) 824-2621.

HORSEBACK RIDING TIPS

- Wear long pants and don't bring along a lot of stuff such as cameras and pocketbooks. Horses don't have back seats or glove compartments.
- Trips begin at 9 A.M., 10:30 A.M., 12 P.M., and 2 P.M. The ride lasts about 45 minutes.
- For experienced riders, this isn't much of a ride. But novices will enjoy it, perhaps even catching a glimpse of the Fort Wilderness wildlife population: deer, wild birds, and maybe even a gator.

The Spas of Walt Disney World

Spas are like sushi. If you've never eaten it, you might be a bit reluctant to try it ("What do I order? Will I like it? How do I eat it?"). These are not too different than the questions most people have when considering their first spa visit. As a couple that has recently discovered spas, let us set your minds at ease. Spa treatments are soothing and sublime. Whether partaking in aroma hydrotherapy or a facial, a seaweed wrap or a sports massage, we have discovered that these pampering treatments not only *feel* great but they leave us both with an enhanced sense of relaxation and sensuality. We simply can't think of a better way to spend the first afternoon of a vacation than in a spa. From our own experience, we can tell you that just a few treatments will get you both in the perfect mood for your romantic escape.

Walt Disney World is home to three new spas, and each has its specialties and character. All are designed to enrapture guests with a soothing blend of colors, music, and mood, and all three feature steam rooms, whirlpool baths, plush locker rooms, and comfortable lounges. Spa treatments fall loosely into several categories: massage therapies, skin and body treatments, and water therapies. There are many massage techniques: Swedish, Shiatsu, reflexology, and sports massage are the most common. Water therapies might mean a hydrotherapy massage, a mineral bath, or an exotic soak. Skin treatments include facials, body masques, seaweed wraps, aromatherapies, and body polishing. There's even hand and foot treatments. These things sound unusual, we know, but any of them will relieve tension, leave you feeling utterly pampered, and will bring your senses wonderfully to life. Spa treatments are *not* just for women. All of the Disney World spas feature treatments designed for men and we must tell you that *both* of us have really enjoyed these sensual experiences.

Another feature of spas is that they are expensive. Treatments usually cost $60 to $80 per hour. We think this kind of pampering is what vacations are all about. More than merely self-indulgent, the spa experience is about relieving stress, soothing sore muscles, and promoting well-being. We warn you: once you start, you won't want to stop. This stuff is deliciously habit-forming.

Each of the spas also has a health and fitness center with the latest in equipment. Also, all three feature a "spa cuisine" of fresh juices, soups, sandwiches, smoothies, and salads. Each of the spas offers a variety of a la carte treatments and day or half-day packages. Each also features gift certificates, and all have knowledgeable staffs of reservationists waiting to help you plan your spa experiences.

The Grand Floridian Spa and Health Club

Florida is the theme of this elegant place, and simply walking in the door here will immerse you in the heavenly smells of its custom-formulated, citrus-based spa and skin products. We are already hooked on the ruby-red grapefruit bath gel. Comfortable treatment rooms and spacious and luxurious lounges, complete with plush robes and slippers, herbal teas, and world-class amenities, make this the perfect addition to the exquisite Grand Floridian resort. Facilities and service here are first-class.

Offerings include a couple's treatment room, a 70-jet French hydrotherapy tub, "My First Facial" for young guests, a gentleman's facial, a Secret Garden Bath, soothing tired-legs treatment, and much, much more. We could spend a whole vacation here.

"We hope," says manager Deborah Evans, "that our guests will leave with peace of mind, a sense of calmness, and an understanding of the importance of time out and self-care."

To reserve your Grand Floridian spa experience, call (407) 824-2332.

The Spa at the Disney Institute

No expenses were spared in creating this place. From aerobics pool, gymnasium, and Cybex fitness center to the spacious and well-appointed lounges and treatment rooms, this spa is the very definition of "state of the art." Offering Phytomer beauty products, Sothys skin treatments, and the Judith Jackson line of aromatherapies, the Spa at the Disney Institute knows what it takes to please.

The wonderful "menu" here has such treatments as a half-day men's program, deluxe seaweed program, after-sports body therapy, European facials, French body polish, and aromatherapy hydromassage.

To get the treatment that you desire, we suggest reserving well in advance. For arrangements, call the Spa at the Disney Institute at (407) 827-4455.

The Spa and Fitness Center at the Buena Vista Palace

It only follows that this elegant and luxurious hotel, located on Hotel Plaza Boulevard, would offer a full-service spa to its guests. This spa offers not only a line of extraordinary treatments and a modern fitness center but also a first-class hair salon. This whole package is located in a separate part of the resort and features a private lap pool, outdoor whirlpools, and specialized treatment rooms. Spa cuisine here is served poolside or on a lovely and private patio.

Whether you are looking for herbal body wraps, relaxing massages, soothing aromatherapies, or rejuvenating facials, you'll find it all here. With an emphasis on the natural, the Spa at the Buena Vista Palace offers the full line of luxurious and natural Pevonia Botanical products. To arrange your blissful time here, call (800) 981-1472.

OUR RECOMMENDATIONS FOR THE SPAS OF DISNEY

- Be sure to arrive at least 30 minutes early to get yourselves relaxed in the spa's steam rooms and whirlpool baths.
- A single treatment will give you a day's use of the spa's fitness center.
- Get "His and Hers" massages, together in the couple's treatment room at the Grand Floridian Spa.

- The aromatherapy massage and seaweed facial at the Spa at the Disney Institute are particularly outstanding.
- The Spa at the Buena Vista Palace offers some very well-priced packages. Check them out.
- By the way, if you've never tried sushi, it *is* like a spa treatment: once you try it, you'll be hooked.

Health and Fitness Clubs

Many of the resorts at Walt Disney World feature health and fitness centers. These range from simple exercise rooms to the Disney Institute Health and Fitness Center, which is a virtual proving ground for the latest techno-equipment from Cybex.

- The health and fitness center at the Disney Institute *is* in a class by itself. Along with the luxurious facilities of the spa, guests here are treated to Cybex equipment that is still being developed: video exercise games, computerized training gear, and lots of other neat stuff. There's also a weight room and aerobics pool. The Health and Fitness Center at the Disney Institute is available without additional cost to Institute guests. Day guests and Disney resort guests pay $8 per visit. It's a bargain.
- The Buena Vista Palace Spa and Fitness Center is another superb facility. Life Fitness and Reebok equipment, one-on-one training, a full range of cardiovascular equipment, and the spa's private lap pool, steam room, sauna, and outdoor whirlpool tub are this club's offerings. Afterwards, enjoy a soak or a massage. Highlights here are Reebok Sky Walkers and Life Fitness Entertainment Cycles. Palace guests may use the facilities for $5 per day or $15 for multi-day use. Non-Palace guests pay $15 daily.
- The Grand Floridian Spa and Health Club offers the very latest in Cybex equipment and the superb facilities of the spa: sauna, steam room, whirlpool tub, and luxurious lounges and locker rooms. When you're finished exercising, enjoy one of the spa's treatments. Spa guests are entitled to use of these facilities and they are available for $10 per day for Disney resort guests.
- Body by Jake is the Dolphin's health club. With a complete selection of Polaris equipment, a coed Jacuzzi, saunas, an array of personal training, massages, and aerobics, Jake's is a complete fitness center. Jake's is available for $5 per day per room for all guests of

the Dolphin; for other Disney resort guests, it's $10 per day. Hours vary seasonally.

- The Ship Shape Health Club is shared by both the Beach and Yacht Clubs. This club features a large indoor, coed whirlpool, an array of Nautilus machines, sauna, and limited massage therapy. It is available to Yacht and Beach Club guests for $8 per visit or $12 for length of stay. Family passes are $20. Rates are considerably higher for guests of other Disney resorts.
- The Contemporary's Olympiad Health Club has recently enjoyed a face-lift. It is open to all Disney resort guests for $8.50 per visit or $16 for length of stay per individual, $20 for a family. This facility features the only tanning salon on-property ($8.50 for 20 minutes), as well as limited massages, aerobics, Nautilus and Lifecycle equipment, and sauna. Personal training is by appointment.
- Muscles and Bustles at the BoardWalk features sauna, steam room, and a host of Cybex equipment. For BoardWalk guests, cost is $8 per visit or $12 for individual and $20 for family length of stay. Rates are considerably higher for guests of other Disney resorts.
- The Swan Health Club is a modern facility with exercise equipment, Sprint weight systems, and a sauna. Use of this facility is complimentary with a stay at the Swan.
- R.E.S.T. Fitness Center at Old Key West offers a fairly complete exercise room, and use of it is complimentary to guests and club members. Facilities include a coed steam room, whirlpool bath, and Nautilus equipment.
- Disney's Coronado Springs, Shades of Green, and all of the hotels along Hotel Plaza (except the Travelodge) have fitness rooms with exercise equipment. All are available to resort guests.

Miscellaneous Sports

Some of the Disney resorts feature special sports that are not found elsewhere. Here is a brief list of them.

- Basketball: Old Key West
- Croquet: the Yacht and Beach Clubs, Disney's BoardWalk, Port Orleans
- Volleyball: the Beach Club, the Contemporary
- Bocci ball (lawn bowling): the Yacht and Beach Clubs

Shopping at Downtown Disney

While we don't expect shopping to be one of your main pursuits, we are sure that you'll want to get out and at least browse for a few mementos of your time together here. Know that there's more to shopping at Disney World than character merchandise. In fact, some of our favorite clothing is from the shops at the various Disney resorts. As we've mentioned earlier, you'll find some interesting shopping throughout the theme parks; you simply have to keep an eye out for it.

The Disney Village Marketplace is an area devoted almost exclusively to shopping. This year and next, it is expanding so much that it has been renamed Downtown Disney. Along with the shops of the Marketplace will be a lakeside esplanade of boutiques and stores. Except for a Virgin Records Megastore, it is too early to know what will be there, but we suspect it will be interesting.

The 18 shops of the Village Marketplace are open from 9:30 A.M. to 11 P.M. and are all located on the shore of Lake Buena Vista, adjacent to Pleasure Island. This area features a beautiful marina, restaurants, and some very amusing fountains. While these shops are hardly known for bargains, they do offer some unique and interesting wares.

Here are some of our favorite shops at the Marketplace:

- The World of Disney is the largest Disney character shop in the world. In fact, it is a Disney department store, complete with kitchen department, sleepware area, and so forth. It is decorated with life-size, whimsical flying machines and Disney characters piloting them. A lot of the stuff here is quite nice, a sort of "Hidden Mickey" type of merchandise. We suggest that you not miss this place.
- The Gourmet Pantry offers a combination of beautiful cookware and accessories as well as gourmet foods and wines. It also has a wonderful little bakery and deli, as well as a large selection of coffee, wines, candy, and condiments. There is even a small grocery section. This is just the place to go for in-room snacks or breakfasts.
- Team Mickey's Athletic Club features everything from Mouse-logo golf shirts to tennis shoes.
- The Christmas Chalet has an outstanding selection of Christmas decorations year-round. Pick-up a little something special for your tree. This is very nice stuff.

- Discover has "nature" as its theme, and here you will find an assortment of clothing and ecological artifacts. This is an interesting store.
- The Art of Disney is a great place simply to browse. Here you'll find original and limited-edition animation cels as well as other Disney art.

Besides these few shops, a number of men's and women's clothing stores offer some very nice things. There is also a jewelry store, a glass shop, a photo store, and a book store. There's even a Guest Services.

Bargain Hunting for Character Merchandise

If you have access to a car, you might be interested in the Character Warehouse. This large store is located in Belz Outlet Center in Orlando and sells last year's Disney character merchandise at bargain prices. Items that sold last year for $36 might be found here for $15. You never know what you'll find, but at these prices you're certain to see something.

To get there, take I-4 East (to Orlando) to International Drive. Take a left at the light and follow International Drive to the end. Look for Mall #2, with two towers. The Character Warehouse is inside.

PART 3

The Ultimate Romance at Walt Disney World

$\mathcal{D}$isney Fairy Tale Weddings

We must confess, when we first heard that Disney was doing weddings, even we were a bit skeptical. "Why," we wondered, "would anybody want to get married at Disney World?"

A wedding, we reflected, was something between a celebration and a theatrical performance, with the ceremony, reception, rehearsal dinner, and lots of organization and transportation. There would also be accommodations, catering, and entertainment. Who better to create such an event than the imaginative and resourceful people at Walt Disney World? And in what more enchanting a place could one imagine a wedding so rich with possibilities?

On we went, realizing that the choice of locations, accommodations, cuisines, and entertainment was not only superb but virtually limitless. Have the ceremony at the Wedding Gazebo on the garden lawn of the Yacht Club or in the Magic Kingdom after closing. Or be married in the new Disney Wedding Pavilion, on its own tropical isle on the Seven Seas Lagoon. Guests could stay in any of the wonderful Walt Disney World resorts. How about, we wondered, a rehearsal beach-party dinner, calypso-style? Or a South Seas Banquet at 'Ohana at the Polynesian? Or have Mickey and Minnie drop by for the reception at the California Grill, high atop the Contemporary?

That a Disney wedding could be an extraordinary and memorable affair was beginning to make sense to us. A lot of sense. But who could possibly afford such an extravagant event besides the rich and famous? And so we began our exploration of Disney's Fairy Tale Weddings. Our interest had been piqued, and we did not cease until we had discovered that, from the intimate to the magnificent, there is a Fairy Tale Wedding to suit any taste and virtually any pocketbook.

You may not feel that a Disney wedding is right for the two of you. Take a careful look at what Disney Fairy Tale Weddings has to offer, and then make up your minds. Remember, your wedding will only happen once. At Walt Disney World, you can make it a once-in-a-lifetime experience as well.

Types of Fairy Tale Weddings

There are two basic varieties of Disney Fairy Tale Weddings: Intimate Weddings and Destination Weddings. Intimate Weddings are small. With a maximum of eight guests, these lovely affairs are beautiful and private. Larger weddings fall into the next category. Facilities, reception, and accommodations all become factors in an affair that includes more people and more planning. Of course, the bigger and grander the wedding, the greater the cost. Destination Weddings can be either Traditional, Themed, or Theme Park Weddings. This last category takes considerations into yet another arena: private, after-hours use of one of the Walt Disney World theme parks, which means significantly greater expenses.

With the Intimate Wedding costing around $2,500, fabulous honeymoon included, we hope that you are beginning to see the possibilities in a new light. If price is no object, then you may be viewing all of this with great interest. The potential for your Disney wedding and honeymoon will be without limit.

Most weddings do have a budget, though, and reality will very likely demand something more down-to-earth than a Cinderella fantasy in the Magic Kingdom. Between the intimate and the extravagant lies a great deal of territory. Somewhere in this area lies the special Disney wedding for you.

Disney Intimate Weddings

If the two of you are planning a small wedding, the Intimate Wedding may be perfect. Each of these weddings is really a package. For one price, you get a lovely ceremony at one of a variety of beautiful and romantic Disney locations and an unforgettable Disney honeymoon with your choice of luxurious Disney resort accommodations. The Intimate Wedding ceremony includes an official to perform the service, a bouquet for the bride and a boutonniere for the groom, a wedding cake and champagne toast, a solo musician during the ceremony, and a special wedding gift for the bride and groom. You even get your own wedding consultant, who not only will help you make the decisions but will also make all of the arrangements.

And, with the two of you already at Walt Disney World, your honeymoon will begin at once. You'll both be the pampered guests of either the Yacht or the Beach Clubs, the BoardWalk, the Polynesian, the Wilderness Lodge, or the Grand Floridian. Any one of these luxurious resorts is guaranteed to provide an exciting and unforgettably romantic atmosphere. You'll also have, for the length of your stay, unlimited admission to all of the Disney attractions. You'll even have the use of bicycles, canoes, sailboats, and pedal boats at your resort. Also included in this package is a dinner for two at your choice of select Disney restaurants or one Disney character breakfast. You will even receive a specially delivered Romance Basket filled with special treats such as bubble bath, chocolates, wine, and souvenir wine glasses. The World will be yours.

Limited to eight guests, the locations for these Intimate Weddings are varied. The Wedding Gazebo at the Yacht Club is one. Set in a lovely rose garden, it has been designed especially for Disney Fairy Tale Weddings. The stately elegance of this setting provides more than just a touch of romance.

You will approach along a cobbled path that leads through the garden gate and up to the Victorian gazebo. With its carved wooden hearts and Cupid weather vane, this beautiful creation is the quintessential setting for love. Wedding planners have been hard at work before you arrive, and champagne and wedding cake await. This is a white-glove affair. Guests are seated in the rose garden, and the violinist begins to play. After the ceremony, everyone enjoys a champagne toast, all set to the music that you have selected. The cake is cut, the magic begins.

Variations of this theme are what Disney Fairy Tale Wedding specialists do best. We stayed at the Yacht Club and watched as several of these memorable events unfolded. Believe us when we tell you that, time after time, we were moved. These charming affairs are most definitely not performed on an assembly line. Each reflected careful planning as well as the personal touches of both bride and groom. In two days, we witnessed five of these touching ceremonies. Each was unique. All were enchanting.

One ceremony was in the morning, three were in the afternoon, and another was late in the day, near sunset. One couple arrived by horse-drawn coach, another in Disney's vintage white Cadillac motor-car. Others simply arrived on foot. One wedding had a handful of guests, three others had eight, and one simply involved the bride and groom, an officiant, and several attendants.

Music at one wedding featured a singer; at the others, a violinist performed. Tunes varied from "Wish upon a Star" to the more traditional. Mickey, in top hat and tails, and Minnie, in a sparkling evening gown, appeared at several ceremonies. Some were videotaped, and each was well-photographed. The guests were thrilled at the perfection of the event, and so were we.

Each of these wedding ceremonies was definitely traditional. Dress ranged from formal to casually elegant. Even the presence of Disney characters during the champagne toast and cake cutting brought only a touch of Disney to the affairs.

There are other beautiful locations available for Intimate Weddings, and each offers a special and romantic vista of Walt Disney World. Among them are Sunset Point at the Polynesian, the fourth floor overlook at the Wilderness Lodge, and Picture Point at the Disney Wedding Pavilion. Packages for an Intimate Wedding begin around $2,400, with a minimum honeymoon of four nights at the Wilderness Lodge. Choosing one of the other resorts will add to the cost of your package. The Intimate Wedding Package is very attractive, even in its most basic form. "No frills" at Disney still means outstanding. We are confident that your Intimate Wedding will exceed your expectations.

Value-wise, the Intimate Wedding seems equally attractive. Disney figures that the ceremony itself accounts for about $500 of the package, which is exceptional, considering that it includes wedding officiant, location, flowers, musician, cake, champagne, and more. Special resort rates at a wide variety of Disney resorts are even available for your wedding party.

While Intimate Wedding packages do not include a reception, your wedding specialist will be happy to help you arrange something. Or you can simply make your own arrangements for a dinner party at one of the many fine Disney restaurants.

Packages can be elaborated upon to nearly any degree. Additional resort nights may simply be added on. Stepping up to an even more lovely and expensive resort will, of course, cost more. For a four-night stay at the Polynesian, add about $380. Add an additional $530 to the basic package for a stay at the Grand Floridian. Use of the magnificent Wedding Pavilion will cost an additional $400.

The Food 'n Fun Plan can be added to the Intimate Wedding Package. For about $400 for a four-night stay, this plan provides a daily food allowance at most Disney restaurants and select recreation at Disney resorts. For more details, see the section on adding Food 'n Fun in Chapter 1.

There are other Intimate Wedding options too. Choices for music are either a vocalist, violinist, or guitarist. Any other type of performer or additional musicians will be extra. Adding Disney characters to your Intimate Wedding can get expensive. For both Mickey and Minnie, expect to pay $650.

Your Intimate Wedding coordinator will be happy to work out all of the plans with you. Pricing for transportation, Disney characters, entertainment, and other extras are the same as those for Destination Weddings, and we'll give you some of these figures later. Remember, though, that a Disney Fairy Tale Intimate Wedding is limited to ten people, including the bride and groom. If you simply cannot keep your numbers down to this figure, you'll have to step up to the next level.

Planning Your Intimate Wedding

Your Intimate Wedding will begin with a phone call: Walt Disney Fairy Tale Weddings at (407) 828-3400.

If you are calling to reserve your ceremony, a wedding coordinator will return your call within 48 hours. Remember, Disney Fairy Tale Intimate Weddings require a minimum 10-day notice. If you are not in a hurry, a wedding representative will get back to you within a few days. This person will have all of the latest information and, if you two have already made the big decisions, you'll find that everything else will go smoothly. Once your plans are finalized and details are worked out, you will be expected to make a deposit equal to the first night's lodging at the resort of your choice. After that, you simply have to show up.

Destination Weddings

One of the most important things to know when it comes to a Destination Wedding is that it is not a product. You will not be shown Package A, Package B, and Package C. Far from it. Disney Fairy Tale Weddings is a service, one that has been created to help you design your very own and very special wedding.

Since a Destination Wedding involves more people, there will be many more elements to consider. Even a modest wedding will entail such considerations as catering, guest accommodations, floral arrangements, and dozens of other important details. Overseeing, organizing, and orchestrating your entire Disney wedding will be your very own wedding specialist. Throughout the entire process, this specialist will be there to answer your questions, to find solutions to your problems, and to make your every dream come true.

While each Fairy Tale Wedding is a unique interpretation of your wishes, there are three general styles: Traditional, Themed, and Theme Park. You can decide whether to have your traditional ceremony with Walt Disney World as the backdrop or to make your wedding a celebration complete with Disney characters and themed decorations. The choice will also be yours whether to have your wedding at the beautiful Disney Wedding Pavilion or in one of the many other unforgettable Disney locations. Choose the romantic and Victorian elegance of the Grand Floridian, or enjoy the casual, seaside splendor of the Beach Club. Whatever location you select, you will be free to make your wedding as "Disney" as you want it to be.

The use of characters is only one way to make your wedding a themed affair. Props, scenery, landscaping, and special effects can also be used to fashion the ultimate fantasy for any or all of your wedding plans. Such motifs as Beauty and the Beast, Cinderella's Ball, and Aladdin are but a few of the hundreds of themes that can be created. Have a Wild West Wedding at Fort Wilderness, a moonlight wedding cruise on the *Kingdom Queen* stern-wheeler, or let Disney create a storybook Alice in Wonderland setting. There are no limits to the magic at hand.

Of the Destination Weddings, Theme Park Weddings are the grandest of all. Each of these is staged after-hours at either Epcot, Disney–MGM Studios, or the Magic Kingdom. These weddings tend towards the spectacular, with prices to match.

A fantasy wedding at Disney–MGM Studios might be the perfect marriage for two film buffs. It begins with the bride's arrival by motorcade down Hollywood Boulevard. Vintage vehicles, fireworks, and cheering crowds set the scene. The wedding ceremony takes place in the courtyard of the Chinese Theater, finalized with the traditional Hollywood handprint in cement. The wedding party then boards the Great Movie Ride for a trip through the most memorable cinematic scenes of all time. The ride ends as the wedding party arrives in the soundstage, where a glittering and lavish sit-down dinner and dance await. Potted palms, sparkling lights, and a champagne toast begin the evening's festivities. The movie screen backdrop of silent film clips and a small orchestra craft the magical atmosphere for this unforgettable event.

This is but one of countless such scenarios. Have an Under the Sea Wedding at the Living Seas Lounge in Epcot or enjoy something more traditional in the formal English garden of the United Kingdom Pavilion. For something a bit offbeat, there's always the unusual atmosphere of the Twilight Zone Tower of Terror courtyard. The possibilities for Theme Park Weddings are limited only by your imagination.

Planning Your Destination Wedding

Having compared Disney weddings to those that can be arranged outside of Walt Disney World, we must tell you that these weddings are, indeed, expensive. We are talking Disney World here, and, for such a setting and such quality, you must expect to pay more. Exactly how much more will depend on your choices and just how large a wedding you are planning. We suggest that you shop around wherever you live in order to give yourselves an idea of just how much a wedding will cost in your home town. Take into consideration the difference between having your reception at a local restaurant or country club and having it in the Grand Floridian Ballroom.

The Guidelines

Because Disney Fairy Tale Weddings does not charge for the use of private banquet rooms, a $12,500 minimum expenditure applies to all wedding groups that exceed 10 persons. This minimum applies only to what is spent on the actual day of your wedding. It includes food and beverages, entertainment, flowers, transportation, and, if you wish to use it, the cost of the Wedding Pavilion. It does not include guest accommodations or anything that occurs on previous days, such as the rehearsal dinner. It also does not include extras such as the officiant and photographic services.

Minimum food and beverage expenditures are $75 per person for functions held before 2 P.M. and $100 per person for luncheons and dinners held later. All include service staff in tuxedo attire with white glove service, head table, white linen, elegant place settings, tables for gifts, cake and guest book, and, of course, all include the traditional cake and champagne toast. Sales tax, 19% service charge, and alcoholic beverages are additional.

Of course, the menu will be of your choosing. A typical wedding dinner would include a seven-course banquet created by Disney's award-winning culinary staff. Your wedding cake will be a custom-designed, multitiered masterpiece.

Are you still with us? There is more. Both you and your guests will be expected to stay in Disney resorts. A minimum number of resort nights must be guaranteed based upon the size of your wedding party. It is a simple formula, one that you should have no difficulty satisfying. Know too that rooms are available for all wedding parties, with prices beginning at $79 per night. Having your entire wedding group along with you at Disney will enhance the affair, making it even more memorable for everyone. Transportation for your guests will be simpler, and they will be having their own Disney vacations.

A Sample Destination Wedding for Fifty People

Set at the enchanting Wedding Pavilion, this unforgettable ceremony begins with the bride's arrival in the glittering, horse-drawn Cinderella's glass coach. Floral decorations, two bridesmaids, maid of honor, organist, and a full wedding ensemble make this both a charming and a traditional affair. The bride and groom take their vows before the backdrop of Cinderella Castle. Following the ceremony, doves are released and the now-married couple depart for the reception in the glass coach.

The reception takes place at the Grand Floridian Ballroom, where a musical trio furnishes the atmosphere for this white-glove affair. The dazzling menu features platters of fresh fruits and assortments of cheese, and hot and cold hors d'oeuvres. A champagne toast and open bar begin the festive occasion.

Following this, an elegant and formal dinner is prepared by the master chefs of Disney. Table settings feature chair covers with bows, floral centerpieces, crisp linens, and crystal glassware. The menu includes poached filet of salmon pasta, Whitehall salad, roasted potatoes, seasonal vegetables, a choice of entree (beef or chicken), and for dessert a banana and white chocolate pate laced with dark chocolate and Frangelica sauce. Afterwards, everyone enjoys the wedding cake, a champagne toast to bride and groom, and a memorable evening of dancing and cocktails in the lovely ballroom. Special guests, Mickey and Minnie, drop by to wish the newlyweds happiness.

Such a lavish wedding would cost about $14,300, including tax and gratuities. This includes limousine transportation for the wedding party, floral arrangements for the ceremony and reception, a four-hour open bar, three hours of entertainment with a musical trio or disc jockey, and a complimentary wedding night at the Grand Floridian for bride and groom. Not included are photography, wedding invitations, and favors. Considering that the average wedding in the U.S. costs $18,000, this affair, modest by Disney standards, seems reasonable. Keep in mind that the average Disney Fairy Tale Wedding costs $19,000 for 100 guests.

If these figures seems out of reach and your heart is set on a Disney Fairy Tale Wedding, we suggest that you inquire about a ceremony that might better suit your needs. Sometimes, special arrangements can be made for dates and times that are not so busy.

Destination Theme Park Weddings

A Magic Kingdom wedding could take place in the lovely rose garden at the Swan Boat Landing near Cinderella Castle. Guests arrive by horse-drawn trolleys down Main Street. The bride arrives in Cinderella's glass carriage, drawn by six white ponies and driven by two costumed footmen. Following the ceremony is a fantasy reception in the castle courtyard, after which guests ride on Cinderella's Golden Carousel. The new husband and wife appear on the castle parapet, heralded by costumed trumpeters, and guests enter King Stefan's Banquet Hall for a specially prepared meal and a magical evening of dancing.

This storybook wedding includes round-trip transportation for all guests to the Magic Kingdom entrance and private use of the theme park for the duration of the wedding. All setup services for landscaping, dance, reception, and ceremony would be included, as would the sound system, lighting, and a special bridal dressing area.

The food and beverage package would include a one-hour reception with a variety of hors d'oeuvres and a four-hour unlimited open bar. Dinner would feature a seven-course meal, the menu to be arranged with Disney catering services. Cake and a champagne toast cap off the dinner. Floral arrangements, photography, wedding officiant, invitations, and wedding favors are not included. The total cost for this would be about $45,000. For a wedding at Epcot, expect to pay at least $16,000 and for Disney–MGM Studios no less than $20,000.

The Destination or Theme Park Wedding Process

A Destination Wedding or a Destination Theme Park Wedding takes a great deal of planning. On average, couples make their initial contact with Disney about one year before the anticipated day. Tentative reservations may be made one year in advance and plans may be finalized up to eight months in advance. Again, the process begins with a phone call to Disney Fairy Tale Weddings. Request a full information kit and look it over carefully.

Once you have decided upon a date, you are ready to make your second call to Disney Fairy Tale Weddings. A sales manager will happily provide you with any information that you might wish. This person will be knowledgeable in helping you to sort out the many possibilities and to limit the selections to something that reflects your own unique personalities and expectations.

When the magical date arrives to make your reservations, you will both be prepared. This will be the real beginning of your Disney wedding adventure. You will receive a letter of agreement and be asked to make a deposit to secure your banquet hall and special hotel rates. This deposit will apply to your minimum expenditures. At this time, you will also meet your wedding event manager. This knowledgeable and dedicated specialist will be with you throughout the entire process of your Fairy Tale Wedding. Once you have locked in your locations and date, you will be asked to make an on-site inspection to ensure that everything meets your expectations. If you are unable to do this, your wedding event manager will see that you receive the proper information and photographs.

Now that the basics are out of the way, the real fun begins. You will need to make a lot of important decisions, and your wedding event manager will know the ins and outs of the entire process. Your specialist will work within the parameters of your budget to orchestrate every element of your wedding. Invitations, menus, china and place settings, floral designs, entertainment, photographic services, and guest accommodations are just a few of the considerations. Simply looking over locations, inspecting fabric swatches, and tasting sample menus will be a pleasure. Disney's famous and meticulous attention to detail will focus on every phase of your storybook wedding. Due to the numerous wedding events each weekend, planning sessions can only be accommodated Monday through Friday.

Once you have made the decisions, you will be free to enjoy yourselves right up until the traditional preceremonial jitters. All of the work and worry, all of the organization and implementation, will have been done by your wedding event manager and a team of dedicated experts. Disney Fairy Tales Weddings is dedicated to making the reality of your wedding *exceed* your expectations.

The Particulars

You have many options when it comes to Disney Fairy Tale Weddings. The following sections cover this information. Remember, though, that prices are subject to change and can only be guaranteed six months ahead of your wedding date.

The Walt Disney World Wedding Pavilion

Built on its own special island in the Seven Seas Lagoon, this marvelous creation's only purpose is to be the perfect location for your storybook wedding. Like a Victorian summer house, the charming glass-enclosed building sets the perfect stage. Gabled roofs and sloped turrets, intricate gingerbread of carved hearts and cupids, and arched windows and panoramic vistas of the lagoon create an atmosphere that is enchanting and unforgettable.

The location, the elegant pavilion itself, and Disney's unfaltering sense of landscaping come together in an island masterpiece. Quaint yet lavish, the Wedding Pavilion is yet another success for the Disney imagineers.

The spacious chapel is large enough to accommodate 250 guests. Attention has been focused on every detail, from the vaulted ceilings to state-of-the-art sound and video systems. Nothing has been overlooked. Behind the alter, a stained-glass window perfectly frames Cinderella Castle. Sound, lighting, and every possible camera angle have been calculated into this formula for the perfect wedding.

The Pavilion's on-site florist ensures the freshest of wedding flowers. Outside, Picture Point has been placed to provide a picturesque backdrop both for the wedding and for the bridal portraits. Picture

Point's ornate trellis is set amidst a formal rose garden, overlooking the Seven Seas Lagoon and Cinderella Castle.

The Wedding Pavilion also features Franck's Wedding Salon, borrowed from the Disney film *Father of the Bride*. It is in this elegant French Provincial setting that the two of you will meet with your wedding specialist to make your plans. Besides its ideal location and captivating charm, Disney's Wedding Pavilion offers every conceivable amenity for a memorable celebration.

The fee for use of the Wedding Pavilion is $1,500 for 11 to 250 guests and includes an organist. For intimate weddings, Monday through Thursday, cost for the pavilion alone is $500.

Invitations and Bridal Organizer

Fairy Tale Weddings offers a selection of specialty invitations with themes such as Cinderella and Snow White. Available too is a stylish leather accordion file, embossed with a Cupid Mickey Mouse, for collecting wedding mementos such as notes, photographs, and fabric swatches.

Beverage Options

For a four-hour, hosted open bar, expect to spend about $34 per person. For beer and wine, four hours per person costs about $22. Other options are host-sponsored per drink or cash.

Special Transportation

Whether you are arriving in Cinderella's glass coach or departing in a vintage white automobile, Disney offers an assortment of memorable transportation. A horse and carriage costs around $750, and the charming glass coach, complete with four horses and three costumed footmen is $2,200. The chauffeured classic car costs $350 and a Flote boat, with driver, only $85.

Entertainment

Single performers such as harpist, vocalist, or violinist are available from $250. For a duo, prices begin at $450 and for a trio of musicians, such as a jazz or calypso group, from $600. Rock bands, orchestras, and country and western bands all cost around $2,000. A disc jockey is from $700. All prices are based on three-hour minimums.

Disney Character Entertainers

For one Disney character, the cost is $450. For two, $650; for three, $850. A herald trumpeter in full regalia is $300, and the Dapper Dans barbershop quartet is $875.

THEME PARK WEDDING ADD-ONS

* Merlin the Magician and the Sorcery and the Stone show in Fantasyland: $600
* Magic Kingdom attractions: from $1,000
* Fantasy in the Sky fireworks show: $15,000

The Rehearsal Dinner

While it is not mandatory to have a rehearsal dinner, it is common. There is nothing common, however, about the possibilities of a rehearsal dinner at Walt Disney World. From a dinner in the library of the Adventurer's Club at Pleasure Island to a sumptuous meal in your own private room at the California Grill, the options are many. Have a cookout on the beach with a calypso band or a nostalgic seaside dinner at BoardWalk's "Attic." You can choose from any of the fine dining places, the clubs at Pleasure Island, or have a catered rehearsal dinner at nearly any Disney location.

A Fort Wilderness cookout with all the fixings would cost around $20 per person. Something a bit more upscale but still casual, such as a Grand Floridian Summerhouse cookout with grilled chicken and a more gourmet selection of accompaniments, would cost a bit more than $30 per person. Pull out all the stops at the California Grill for a truly sumptuous dinner, and the cost would be about $43 per person.

Other Weddings at Disney World

There are a few options to a Disney Fairy Tale Wedding, but of course none of them are able to offer anything like that of Disney. Arrangements can be made for weddings at the following places: the Lake Buena Vista Resort and Spa, both the Swan and the Dolphin, Shades of Green, the Hotel Royal Plaza, and Fulton's Crab House. For more information, contact any of these facilities.

CHAPTER 9

Honeymoon Packages

Honeymooning used to mean a trip to Niagara Falls. Then a cruise to the Caribbean became the rage. Nowadays, newlyweds are looking for a honeymoon adventure, and Walt Disney World has become one of the leading vacation places for newly married couples. Disney World combines nearly every element desired for a honeymoon: warm weather, luxurious and romantic resorts, great nightlife, and first-class dining. In a single visit, a couple can boat, swim, golf, play tennis, dance, go horseback riding, enjoy gourmet dining, and go out at night, *and* they can also enjoy the Disney attractions. It is easy to see why Walt Disney World has become the number one honeymoon destination in the U.S.

Newlyweds are also eager for all-inclusive packages. These package vacations include everything from resort accommodations and recreation to meals. With all the money paid up front, a packaged honeymoon allows the bride and groom to enjoy their time together without worrying about overspending. With an all-inclusive package, the only worry will be what to do next.

Of course, there is nothing that says you must get an all-inclusive package. If you are careful spenders, we know that you will be able to enjoy your Disney honeymoon with resort reservations and some planning. But you will do this at a cost, and that cost is the carefree and pampered feeling that you get from a package. Without a package, all of the possibilities remain, but you'll have to be careful. We'll give you some ideas later on getting the most out of your own honeymoon "package."

Walt Disney World Honeymoon Packages

Disney currently offers three vacation packages for newlyweds. Each includes resort accommodations and admission to all of the Disney attractions. The Honeymoon Escape is the most basic. The other two, the Honeymoon Enchantment and the Grand Honeymoon, are all-inclusive. Each provides meals and unlimited recreation. The Honeymoon Enchantment is simply lavish. The Grand Honeymoon goes right over the top. Each of the three offer these basic amenities:

- A minimum four-night stay in a choice of Walt Disney World resort accommodations
- Unlimited admission for length of stay to all Disney attractions (includes the Magic Kingdom, Epcot, Disney–MGM Studios, Pleasure Island, Blizzard Beach, Typhoon Lagoon, River Country, and Discovery Island)
- Hourly use of bicycles, canoes, sailboats, and pedal boats, at select Disney resorts
- A Romance Basket filled with special treats such as bubble bath, chocolates, wine, and souvenir wine glasses (contents may vary)
- One dinner, per person, at a variety of Disney dining locations

The Honeymoon Escape

A Honeymoon Escape package for two begins at just over $900 for a minimum of four nights and five days. This package, along with the basic amenities, also includes:

- Your choice of the following resorts:
    The Caribbean Beach
    Port Orleans ♥♥
    Dixie Landings
    The All-Star Resorts
    Coronado Springs
- One breakfast for both of you at your choice of selected Disney dining locations (gratuities included)
- Disney's "Flex Feature," with a choice of one (per person) of the following: a character breakfast, half-hour use of a select motorboat, Planet Hollywood T-shirt, counter-service lunch or dinner, Mickey 'n You photo session, Epcot garden tour, or nine holes at the Oak Trail executive golf course.

The Honeymoon Escape is not an all-inclusive package, because it does not provide meals. What's more, the minimum figure is good only at the All-Star Resorts, which would not be our choice for a honey-

moon destination. You will be able to upgrade to any other Disney re-
sort, but it will cost more. For example, a four-night Honeymoon
Escape at one of the moderate resorts, such as Port Orleans, is about
$1,250, while a four-night Honeymoon Escape at the Wilderness
Lodge is about $1,500.

If four nights doesn't sound like much of a honeymoon to you (it
doesn't to us), then you could easily add more nights to this package. A
seven-night Honeymoon Escape at one of the moderate resorts is
about $1,850.

The Food 'n Fun Plan can be added to any Honeymoon Escape
package for $100 per couple. This provides a daily food allowance of
$110 in most Disney restaurants and use of select recreation, such as
canoes, bicycles, and sailboats. For more details about Food 'n Fun,
see Chapter 1.

The Honeymoon Enchantment

Prices for the Honeymoon Enchantment ♥♥♥ begin at around $2,250
per couple at the All-Star Resorts, for the minimum four nights and five
days. This package includes all of the basic amenities, plus:

* Your choice of any Disney resort
* Unlimited use of all recreational activities, including motorized
  watercraft, golf, tennis, and much more
* Breakfast, lunch, and dinner (gratuities included) in your choice of
  Walt Disney dining locations; does not include Victoria and Albert's
  or room service
* Honeymoon photo session with a keepsake album

The Grand Honeymoon

The Grand Honeymoon ♥♥♥♥ is an exceptionally elegant package. It
is expensive, but it will have you feeling like Cinderella and Prince
Charming. Four-night, five-day minimums begin at around $3,400
per couple. Including the basic amenities, your every wish will be
granted with:

* Your choice of the following resorts:
  The Grand Floridian ♥♥♥♥
  The Yacht or Beach Club ♥♥♥♥
  The BoardWalk Inn ♥♥♥

- Unlimited use of all recreational activities, including motorized watercraft, golf, tennis, and much more
- Breakfast, lunch, and dinner (gratuities included) at your choice of Walt Disney World dining locations, including the unforgettable Victoria and Albert's ♥♥♥♥ and room service
- Private dining ♥♥♥♥ with your personal chef preparing a meal right in your room or wherever you want it (does not include alcoholic beverages, specialty trays, or caviar)
- Private golf and tennis lessons
- Use of health club (does not include massage)
- Special room amenities, including fresh flowers daily, fruit basket, and nightly turndown service
- Use of video camera in theme parks
- Honeymoon photo session with keepsake album

Upgrading to a More Expensive Resort

The prices quoted for these packages are for the least expensive resort listed in the package. Upgrading to a more expensive resort adds to the cost. Here are two examples:

- Four-night Honeymoon Enchantment at the Beach or the Yacht Clubs: about $2,850
- Four-night Grand Honeymoon at the Grand Floridian: about $3,800

Adding Nights

Adding extra nights to these basic four-night packages is easy. For seven nights of bliss and eight days of fun, here are two examples:

- Seven-day Honeymoon Enchantment at the Beach Club: about $4,500
- Seven-day Grand Honeymoon at the Grand Floridian: about $5,400

Upgrading Your Package to a Suite

It is also possible to upgrade any of the honeymoon packages to either a suite or to concierge service. To do this, you'll have to arrange it with the "suite people," who handle all reservations involving suites. For more information, see "Upgrade Your Package to a Suite or Concierge Service" in Chapter 1.

Upgrading to a suite will be an expensive affair. Most suites begin at around $500 per night, and some cost considerably more. We recommend three honeymoon "rooms" that are relatively affordable. Two are at the Grand Floridian and enjoy concierge service: either the honeymoon room on the private Clarendon level or the Turret room, each cost about $530 nightly. The other honeymoon room is at the Wilderness Lodge and costs about $230 per night. (For more information about these rooms, see Chapter 2.) Here are examples of honeymoon package upgrades to these rooms:

- Seven-night Grand Honeymoon at the Grand Floridian, in either of the honeymoon rooms: about $7,500
- Seven-night Honeymoon Enchantment in one of the four honeymoon rooms at the Wilderness Lodge: about $4,500

Some Other Honeymoon Offerings

Disney's Vero Beach Resort's Seaside Romance Package provides the perfect way to end your honeymoon. For $259, relax for another day in a luxurious Vacation Villa overlooking the ocean. Enjoy your own whirlpool tub, breakfast at Shutter's Restaurant, and a special wedding celebration gift. Additional days may be added.

The Disney Cruise Line adds yet another possibility for honeymooning. Sailing in spring of 1998, the *Disney Magic* will feature seven-day land and sea adventures. Combine the Magic of Disney World with the *Disney Magic* of the seas. For more details, see Appendix B.

Honeymoon Versus Non-Honeymoon Packages

Each of the three honeymoon packages resembles one of Disney's regular vacation packages. The Classic, Deluxe, and Grand Plan packages include features similar to the Honeymoon Escape, Honeymoon Enchantment, and Grand Honeymoon packages.

Comparisons will show that the honeymoon packages cost about $350 more than their similar counterparts. With the Honeymoon Enchantment and Grand Honeymoon packages, you get both the

Romance Basket and the photo session with the keepsake album. Is it worth the difference? We'd have to say yes.

While the Romance Basket is merely a nice touch, the photo session is something truly special. You get a two- to three-hour session with a photographer, who will follow you around the parks to your choice of locations. The result is a beautiful and personalized leather keepsake album filled with photographs of the two of you enjoying your honeymoon at your most memorable Disney places. Yes, this makes the package worth it. What better picture memories could you possibly get than this? And how difficult is it to get even a few good pictures of the two of you together?

Compared to the non-honeymoon Classic Plan, the Honeymoon Escape offers the Romance Basket and dinner for two for the additional $150. We'd recommend it over the Classic Plan but wish there were a way to add the photo session.

Creating Your Own Honeymoon "Package"

Not all couples can afford an all-inclusive package. You can easily arrange your own honeymoon and still have a marvelous and carefree time. Here are some tips for getting the most out of your own honeymoon package:

- Make full use of all resort discounts: Magic Kingdom Club, Florida Resident Specials, Annual or Florida Resident's Seasonal Passport, AAA, or whatever you are able to get. Check out all of the sources for the best resort deal.
- Take advantage of value season. You'll save money, and you'll find that the World is a more pleasant and romantic place without mobs of people.
- When you make your reservation, be sure to have them note that it is your honeymoon. Each of the Disney resorts offers a gift to newlyweds. Most will deliver a small gift to your room. Free upgrades to nicer rooms are not unheard of, especially during value season, when those rooms may be vacant.
- The Length of Stay Pass is a good deal and will give you the freedom to hop parks and see whatever you'd like, whenever you want to see it.

- Have your own Romance Basket delivered right to your room. Call Walt Disney World Florists at (407) 827-3505 to make arrangements.
- Some reasonably priced and romantic rooms:
    A Honeymoon room at the Wilderness Lodge, about $230 per night ♥♥♥
    King bed with courtyard view at Port Orleans or the Caribbean Beach, about $139 per night ♥
    One-bedroom Villa at the BoardWalk, about $315 nightly ♥♥♥
- Concierge rooms are expensive, but they still cost less than the all-inclusive packages. They include upgraded room amenities, continental breakfasts, day-long snacking, and afternoon-to-evening wines and cordials. This is a level of pampering that you will truly appreciate. Disney World concierge services are offered at the following resorts:
    The Polynesian concierge, from $325 nightly
    The Yacht Club concierge, from $399 nightly
    The Grand Floridian concierge, from $495 nightly
    The BoardWalk Inn, Innkeepers Club, from $410 nightly

ᕙUR HONEYMOON RECOMMENDATIONS

- If you can afford either the Honeymoon Enchantment or the Grand Honeymoon, go for it. Either will make a special and romantic experience that you will remember always. Honeymoon packages are expensive, but remember this is your honeymoon. If you can't spoil yourselves now, when can you?
- For honeymoon package reservations, call (407) 828-3400 or the Walt Disney World Travel Company at (800) 828-0228.
- Most of the prices we have quoted are for standard-view rooms. Since this is your honeymoon, we urge you to get the best view that you can. The truth is that standard-view rooms just don't provide the magic of looking out on Cinderella Castle or even onto a beautiful garden. There is a time for a standard room, and there is a time for something special.
- Prices quoted here are regular-season prices. Value-season discounts apply to these packages.

- Don't forget to request a king-size bed when you make your reservations.
- For honeymooners, we especially recommend these romantic resorts:
  The Grand Floridian
  The Yacht and the Beach Clubs
  Port Orleans
  The Polynesian
  The Wilderness Lodge
  Disney's BoardWalk Inn
- Here are some of our favorite romantic resort rooms:
  Lagoon-view rooms at the Grand Floridian or the Polynesian
  Any concierge service room
  One of the four honeymoon rooms at the Wilderness Lodge
  Either of the two types of honeymoon rooms at the Grand Floridian
  The Premier King View room at the Dolphin
  Upper-floor Epcot-view room at the Beach Club
  One-bedroom Villa at the BoardWalk Villas or Old Key West
  The suite at Shades of Green
  A Rose Garden Suite at the BoardWalk Inn
- If money is no object, the following are absolutely lavish suites:
  The Yellowstone, Wilderness Lodge
  The Commodore, the Yacht Club
  Garden King suite, Bali Hai, the Polynesian
  The Steeplechase at the BoardWalk

Appendices

Romantic Adventures

Here are a few romantic things that you'll find waiting for you at Walt Disney World, although we're sure you won't have much trouble coming up with some of your own ideas.

- A private IllumiNations cruise for two on *Breathless,* the Yacht Club's vintage 1934 speedboat: ♥♥♥♥
- High Tea at the Garden View Lounge of the Grand Floridian: ♥♥
- A "Wine Flight" at the Beach Club's romantic lounge, Martha's Vineyard: ♥♥♥
- A picnic lunch from a favorite restaurant to Discovery Island after a relaxing morning: ♥♥
- His and hers in-room massages: ♥♥♥
- The free Sassagoula River launch up to Port Orleans and dinner at Bonfamille's Cafe: ♥♥
- A special and unforgettable dinner at Victoria and Albert's: ♥♥♥♥
- Quiet, romantic moments for just the two of you: ♥♥♥
- Fantasy in the Sky or the Electric Water Pageant from the beach swings at the Polynesian resort: ♥♥♥♥
- Breakfast in bed: ♥♥♥♥
- Private dining in your room or on your balcony: ♥♥♥
- A torchlit stroll on the Polynesian grounds: ♥♥
- A sketch of yourselves at Epcot's France: ♥♥
- An espresso and a dessert in the evening at Au Petit Cafe: ♥♥
- The view from the fifteenth-floor observation deck at the Contemporary, or a nightcap at the California Grill Bar: ♥♥

- Send someone you love a rose (Disney Florist, 827-3505): ♥♥♥
- A light dinner at the Pleasure Island Jazz Club while you enjoy the music: ♥♥
- One of the Magic Kingdom fireworks cruises from the Grand Floridian, the Polynesian, or the Contemporary: ♥♥♥
- Drinks and hors d'oeuvres during IllumiNations at Japan's Matsu No Ma Lounge at Epcot: ♥♥♥
- A late-night hot tub: ♥♥♥
- Sushi at the California Grill lounge at night overlooking the Magic Kingdom ♥♥♥
- A night of slow dancing at the Atlantic Dance ♥♥♥
- Stroll the beach behind the Contemporary's north Garden Wing at night and watch the Electric Water Pageant ♥♥♥♥
- Massages for two in the Grand Floridian Spa Couple's Room ♥♥
- Moonlight stroll on the Seven Seas Lagoon's Walk Around the World ♥♥
- The Rolling Basket Tour at the BoardWalk ♥♥
- IllumiNations from the second floor outside balcony at the Atlantic Dance ♥♥
- A Grand Plan vacation ♥♥♥♥
- Late night at Hemingway Cove at the Grand Floridian ♥♥♥
- A hammock-for-two under the stars at Caribbean Beach or the Swan ♥♥♥
- A romantic vacation in the Grand Floridian's Turret Honeymoon Suite ♥♥♥♥
- Wine tasting at the California Grill lounge, Fridays 6 P.M. ♥
- Rent a surrey for two at the BoardWalk and ride around the lake ♥♥♥

The Disney Cruise Line

With the creation of Disneyland in 1955, The Walt Disney Company reinvented the theme park. Next year, it's going to do the same thing to cruise lines. With the maiden voyage of the *Disney Magic,* there will be a new cruise experience afloat and it will be sporting a mouse on its smoke stack. Designed and built especially for the Disney Cruise Line, this vessel will be one of the most modern afloat and will feature all of the details that people have come to expect of Disney. Forget about cabins. The 875 *staterooms* will offer unparalleled comfort and be more than 25% larger than the current cruise line average. Of these, 73% will be outside staterooms and 44% will offer private verandas. And there's more.

The Disney Cruise Line's seven days of magic will begin with a three- or four-day visit to Walt Disney World (see the rest of this book for all that is available there!). The remainder of the week will be a three- or four-day Disney adventure afloat. Passengers will be transported to the Cruise Line's terminal at Port Canaveral, where they will board ship. Once underway, the magic will begin.

Passengers dine nightly in a different, themed restaurant. Enjoy the elegance of Lumiere's, the island excitement of Parrot Cay, and the incredible Animator's Palette. One of the most unique restaurants anywhere, during dinner the Palette will slowly change from a black-and-white "sketch" to full-color animation.

Designed for three distinct audiences, the *Disney Magic* will feature themed areas for children, families, and adults. Almost an entire deck will be dedicated to children's space (10 times the cruise industry average), and with 30 to 40 professional counselors, youngsters will be guaranteed an unforgettable cruise adventure. Age-specific activities will include the Oceaneer's Club, the Oceaneer's Lab (a video and computer workshop), and Studio Sea, a family lounge featuring cabaret acts, games shows, and multimedia entertainment.

With kids taken care of, adults are free to relax and enjoy the cruise. The ship will feature an adults-only pool area and a full-service spa. For adult excitement, there will be Beat Street, an evening entertainment district, with three themed nightclubs. Dance away the night, enjoy an evening of comedy, or relax to some quiet jazz. The ship will also feature an adult-only dining experience, the intimate and stylish Palo. Or you can dine on your own private veranda, overlooking the sea. With intimate lounges, a gourmet coffee bar, and an ESPN Club, you'll have a boatload of things to do.

Of course, Disney means entertainment, and there will be plenty of that aboard, too. The Walt Disney Theater will feature original, Broadway-quality productions in a state-of-the-art, 1,000-seat theater. For cinema lovers, there will be the Buena Vista Theater. But the real pot of gold at the end of this rainbow will be Castaway Cay, Disney's own tropical island paradise. Frolic along a half-mile-long beach in the turquoise waters of the Bahamas or retreat to the adults-only, idyllic beach. Lay in the sun, take a swim, go snorkeling, or enjoy an open-air massage. It's your very own island escape.

The *Disney Magic* will even pay a visit to Nassau, the bustling capital of this island archipelago. This cruise will be an enchanting voyage upon magical waters. With exquisite staterooms and the impeccable Disney service, this cruise line may likely leave all the others sitting at the dock wondering what happened. Three- and four-day cruises and early booking discounts are available. The seven-day land and sea adventures for two begin around $2,600. For arrangements, see your travel agent or call (407) 566-7000.

$\mathcal{T}$he Disney Tours

Disney offers a small assortment of programs and tours designed to give participants a behind-the-scenes look into the workings of Walt Disney World. To make arrangements for them, call (407) 939-8687. There are discounts to each tour for American Express cardholders.

- The Backstage Magic Tour will take you behind the scenes in the theme parks. It includes the Utilidor tunnel under the Magic Kingdom and several attraction operation centers. The tour lasts eight hours and costs $150. Minimum age is 16. It is offered only on Monday and Wednesday.
- The Gardens of the World Program is a three-hour tour of the landscapes of Epcot and is conducted by Disney horticulturists. Offered Monday, Tuesday, and Thursday, this program costs $35. Participants must be at least 16 years old.
- The Hidden Treasure Tour is a three-hour adventure that will give you a look into the architecture, design, history, and costuming of the countries of Epcot. Offered on Sunday, Wednesday, Friday, and Saturday, this program costs $35 for persons 16 years and older.
- The Keys to the Kingdom Tour is designed to give participants both a backstage and an on-stage Disney experience. It includes the Utilidor tunnel and the Disney Production Center and runs only during off season. It begins at 10 A.M. and ends at 2 P.M. You can sign up for it at City Hall in the Magic Kingdom.
- The Inside the Animation Tour will take you right into the working studios to give you a look at how animation is created. You'll even get a chance to make your own cel. The two-hour tour costs $45, and participants must be at least 16 years old.

The Disney Phone Directory

Automotive Service

Disney Car Care Center: (407) 824-4813

Barber and Beauty Shops

Contemporary Hair Styling Salon: (407) 824-3411
Ivy Trellis Barber and Beauty Shop, the Grand Floridian: (407) 824-3000,
   ext. 2581
Niki Bryan Hair Salon, the Dolphin: (407) 934-4250
Periwigs Hair Salon, the Yacht and the Beach Clubs: (407) 934-3260

Birthday Parties

Cub's Den, the Wilderness Lodge: (407) 824-1083
Lil' Toots Harbor Club, the BoardWalk: (407) 939-6301
Theme park: (407) 934-6411

Child Care

Cub's Den, the Wilderness Lodge: (407) 824-1083
KinderCare: (407) 827-5444
Lil' Toots Harbor Club, the BoardWalk: (407) 939-6301
Mouseketeer Clubhouse, the Contemporary: (407) 824-3038
Mouseketeer Clubhouse, the Grand Floridian: (407) 824-3000
Neverland Club, the Polynesian: (407) 824-2000 ext. 2170
Sandcastle Club, the Yacht and the Beach Clubs: (407) 934-3750

Dining

Disney Dinning Experience: (407) 828-5792
Reservations, Buena Vista Palace, Arthur's 27: (407) 827-3450
Reservations, the Dolphin restaurants: (407) 934-4025
Reservations, the Swan restaurants: (407) 934-3000 ext. 2181
Reservations, theme park and Disney resort restaurants, dinner shows, and
    special request meals: (407) WDW-DINE (939-3463)

Florist

Gooding's Florist: (407) 827-1206
Walt Disney World Florist: (407) 827-3505

Foreign Language Services

Foreign Language Center (407) 824-7900

Health Clubs

Body by Jake, the Dolphin: (407) 934-4264
Grand Floridian Spa and Health Club: (407) 824-2332
Muscles and Bustles, the BoardWalk: (407) 939-2370
Olympiad Health Club, the Contemporary: (407) 824-3410
Ship Shape Health Club, the Yacht and the Beach Clubs: (407) 934-3256
Swan Health Club: (407) 934-1360

Information

Disney's Walk Around the World: (407) 272-6201
General WDW Information: (407) 824-4321
Guided Tour Information: (407) 824-4321
Hearing-Impaired Guest Information: (407) 827-5141
Magic Kingdom Club: (407) 824-2600
Magic Kingdom Club Gold Card: (800) 466-5365
NUT4DISNEY newsletter: (888) 376-9688

Kennel (Overnight)

Fort Wilderness Kennel: (407) 824-2735

Lost and Found

Same Day: Magic Kingdom: (407) 824-4521
      Epcot: (407) 560-6105
      MGM: (407) 560-4668
Central Lost and Found, TTC: (407) 824-4245

Medical Facilities

Buena Vista Medical Center Pharmacy: (407) 828-8125 (free delivery for
   WDW resort guests)
Buena Vista Walk-in Medical Center: (407) 828-3434
First Aid and Emergency Dental Referral: (407) 648-9234 or 846-2093
Gooding's Pharmacy: (407) 827-1207
HouseMed/Mediclinic: (407) 396-1195
Sand Lake Hospital: (407) 351-8500

Recreation

Fishing, Bay Lake, Wilderness Marina: (407) 824-2621
Fishing, Bayside Marina, the Yacht and the Beach Clubs: (407) 934-3256
Fishing, The BoardWalk: (407) 939-6486
Fishing, Dixie Landings: (407) 934-5409
Fishing, Lake Buena Vista, Village Marketplace: (407) 828-2204
Golf studio, Advance Tee Times: (407) 939-4653
Parasailing: (407) 824-2621
Tennis reservations, the Contemporary: (407) 824-3578
Tennis reservations, the Grand Floridian: (407) 824-2433
Tennis reservations, the Institute: (407) 827-4455
Tennis reservations, the Swan and the Dolphin: (407) 934-4396
Trail ride, Fort Wilderness: (407) 824-2621
Waterskiing: (407) 824-2621

Resort Reservations

Buena Vista Palace Resort and Spa: (800) 327-2990
Central Reservations Office (CRO): (407) W-DISNEY (934-7639)
Courtyard Marriot, WDW Village: (800) 223-9930
Disney Institute: (800) 4-WONDER (496-6337)
DoubleTree Guest Suites: (800) 222-TREE (222-8733)
The Grosvenor: (800) 624-4109
The Hilton: (800) 782-4414

Hotel Royal Plaza: (800) 248-7890
Magic Kingdom Club: (407) 824-2600
Shades of Green: (407) 827-3600
Travelodge: (800) 578-7878
WDW Travel Company: (407) 828-0228

Resorts, Hotel Plaza

Buena Vista Palace: (407) 827-2727
Courtyard Marriot, WDW Village: (407) 828-8888
DoubleTree Guest Suites: (407) 934-1000
The Grosvenor: (407) 828-4444
The Hilton: (407) 827-4000
Hotel Royal Plaza: (407) 828-2828
Travelodge: (407) 828-2424

Theaters

AMC, Pleasure Island: (407) 827-1300, 837-1303

Transportation

Florida Town Cars: (800) 525-7246, (407) 277-5466
Mears: (800) 759-5219, (407) 423-5566
Taxi services at WDW: (407) 824-3360

Travel Services

AAA Disney Travel Center in Orlando: (407) 854-0770
American Express Office, Epcot: (407) 827-7500
Delta Travel, the Contemporary: (800) 221-1212, (407) 849-6400

Weddings

Disney Fairy Tale Weddings: (407) 828-3400

Index

The Perlmutters arrived at travel writing via a number of other careers. Both have educational backgrounds in writing, Gayle in English and Rick in journalism, and both have worked as registered nurses, Gayle in neonatal ICU and Rick in the operating room. Rick has also been a chef, pastry chef, and baker, and has taught gourmet cooking at a Florida community college (very helpful experience when it comes to restaurant reviews).

Walt Disney World for Couples is the product of the authors' love of travel and adventure, as well as their continuing quest for great Florida romantic getaways. Having lived for nearly 20 years aboard their sailboat, *Big Otter,* the Perlmutters have traveled extensively in the U.S. and abroad. Other interests include boating, diving, biking, cooking, and wines. The Perlmutters retreat regularly to their lakeside camp in Maine to enjoy hiking, exploring, and "life as it ought to be."

The authors have three grown children. Brian owns and operates a chimney sweep business, and Jennifer is a registered nurse. Both live in North Carolina. Tyra lives in California and does costume work in the movies. The Perlmutters particularly enjoy taking their two grandchildren, Guin and Ben, to Walt Disney World.

Caribbean for Lovers

Paris Permenter
John Bigley

U.S. $15.00
Can. $19.95
ISBN: 0-7615-0627-6

Sparkling, azure waters, white, sandy beaches, and warm hospitality. Prepare your way for touring the romantic Caribbean—the islands in love with love. Whatever your destination—Antigua, Aruba, Jamaica, the Virgin Islands—this book by and for lovers covers it all: when to go, what to bring, how to get there, where to stay, and where to dine. Discover the local culture, volcanoes, botanical gardens, rain forests, hiking, snorkeling, and more. *Caribbean for Lovers* even covers the available locations and legal requirements for the perfect wedding on the islands.

Hawai'i, The Big Island
5th Edition

John Penisten

U.S. $15.00
Can. $19.95
ISBN: 0-7615-0656-X

This is *the* must-have guide for every family traveling to Hawai'i. In this fifth edition of his popular book, author John Penisten—one of the best-known and most respected travel writers in the business—highlights the best hotels and restaurants for families as well as the best beaches and day-trip destinations. Fully updated with the most current information, this is the book that makes your trip to Hawai'i truly a trip to paradise.

Maui and Lana'i, 7th Edition

Dona Early and Christie Stilson

U.S. $15.00/Can. $19.95
ISBN: 0-7615-0655-1

In the seventh edition of this comprehensive
guide to the islands of Maui and Lana'i, authors
Christie Stilson and Dona Early give you and
your family the detailed information you need to
make the most of your next Hawaiian vacation.
As long-time visitors and part-time residents of
the islands, Stilson and Early offer up-to-date
listings of the restaurants your children will love,
the hotels that let kids stay free, and other tips
that help your family make the most of your
travel dollars.

Kaua'i, 4th Edition

Dona Early and Christie Stilson

U.S. $14.95/Can. $19.95
ISBN: 0-7615-0187-8

Here is your complete reference and guide to the
tropical paradise of Kaua'i, with up-to-date,
comprehensive information about
accommodations, scenery, roads, and more. With
an emphasis on family travel (and an eye on the
family budget!), this book provides you with all
you need to best experience this beautiful sun-
drenched getaway—including details and
recommendations on more than 125 restaurants,
accommodations for all budgets, Hawaiian
language and history, and recreational
opportunities.

To Order Books

Please send me the following items:

Quantity	Title	Unit Price	Total
_____	_____	$ _____	$ _____
_____	_____	$ _____	$ _____
_____	_____	$ _____	$ _____
_____	_____	$ _____	$ _____
_____	_____	$ _____	$ _____

Shipping and Handling depend on Subtotal.

Subtotal	Shipping/Handling
$0.00–$14.99	$3.00
$15.00–$29.99	$4.00
$30.00–$49.99	$6.00
$50.00–$99.99	$10.00
$100.00–$199.99	$13.50
$200.00+	Call for Quote

Foreign and all Priority Request orders:
Call Order Entry department
for price quote at 916/632-4400

This chart represents the total retail price of books only (before applicable discounts are taken).

Subtotal	$ _____
Deduct 10% when ordering 3-5 books	$ _____
7.25% Sales Tax (CA only)	$ _____
8.25% Sales Tax (TN only)	$ _____
5.0% Sales Tax (MD and IN only)	$ _____
Shipping and Handling*	$ _____
Total Order	$ _____

By Telephone: With MC or Visa, call 800-632-8676 or 916-632-4400.
Mon–Fri, 8:30-4:30.

WWW: http://www.primapublishing.com

By Internet E-mail: sales@primapub.com

By Mail: Just fill out the information below and send with your remittance to:

Prima Publishing
P.O. Box 1260BK
Rocklin, CA 95677

My name is _____

I live at _____

City _____ State _____ ZIP _____

MC/Visa# _____ Exp. _____

Check/money order enclosed for $ _____ Payable to Prima Publishing

Daytime telephone _____

Signature _____